Praise for *The Painful Truth*

Dr. Lynn Webster's compassion for people in pain and for pain care makes *The Painful Truth* a groundbreaking and remarkable book. This book is a first of its kind and needed in the pain awareness movement. Dr. Webster uses true stories and his vast background and experience to remind us why pain is a reality that cannot be ignored. The Painful Truth will change the way this country thinks about pain, pain management, and those who struggle with pain every day.

> —Paul Gileno, founder and president, U.S. Pain Foundation

The Painful Truth is a unique and important book. Through a series of poignant vignettes, Webster brings into stark relief the modern-day plague of chronic pain—one that kills insidiously and slowly, if not always literally, then most certainly socially, emotionally, and spiritually. This book is a treasure. Everyone should read it.

> —Perry Fine, professor of anesthesiology and pain medicine, University of Utah; past president, American Academy of Pain Medicine

With this book, Webster has drawn back the curtain on the disease of chronic pain that so many Americans suffer with daily while they struggle with a medical system that generally lacks understanding or education to help them. *The Painful Truth* is an important read for pain patients, family members of those patients, and perhaps most importantly, the providers who care for pain patients.

> —Chester "Trip" Buckenmaier III, MD, Col (ret), MC, USA; Editor-in-Chief, *U.S. Medicine*

As someone who works on behalf of people in pain and who also knows what it's like to experience chronic pain, I highly recommend this book. One of the most hope-filled, helpful books on pain I've ever read.

> —Janet Favero Chambers, president, National Fibromyalgia & Chronic Pain Association

[*The Painful Truth*] has the potential to be a "game changer." The stories are very powerful.
—Myra J. Christopher, Kathleen M. Foley Chair in Pain
and Palliative Care, Center for Practical Bioethics

This book gives voice to real people who suffer with chronic pain and to their caregivers. With the wisdom and compassion of a seasoned practitioner, he tells their stories. Some are inspirational stories of healing and hope; others depict the disenfranchisement experienced by so many forced to live with chronic pain; other stories are tragic. We would all do well to heed the call of those forced to live with chronic pain. This excellent book is a very good place to start.
—The Rev. George Anthony Hoeltzel,
Episcopal priest, Yonkers, New York

It is not often that you come across a book written by a physician that is filled with more than good advice; it is filled with compassion and understanding for people with pain. From his early childhood, Lynn Webster understood the torment of pain and the importance of just being there and accepting the person in spite of his or her pain. His accounts of his patients are heartfelt, and anyone with pain can relate to the struggles he so perceptively tells. Dr. Webster also looks at the real issues we all face when it comes to access to care for the person with pain as well as the struggles the provider faces in whether or not to treat people with pain in today's climate of opioid prescribing.
—Penney Cowan, founder and executive director,
American Chronic Pain Association

The Painful Truth is an asset for people who deal with pain on a personal level or on a larger scale: people suffering; their loved ones and caregivers; and practitioners of counseling, physical therapy, pharmacy, elder care, and other related professions. Webster avoids jargon in all medical descriptions so that everyday people can understand. And while every thought is given the level of development it requires, the book is not dense; it's an easy-to-read, smooth mix of story and information.... *The Painful Truth* is an invaluable, hope-filled resource for individuals—and societies—consumed by pain.

—*Foreword Reviews*

An intelligent, provocative, and inspiring call to arms for those who simply want relief and a return to normalcy.

—*Kirkus Reviews*

From reading this book one can very well see how compassionate Dr. Webster is in caring for his patients during their most difficult moments. This is quite noticeable in his conversations and treatments with his patients where he tries to balance realism and their need for hope.... This is an intelligent wake-up call in acknowledging that we are not doing nearly our best to get them the treatment they need and often look at them askance when they try to do their best for themselves within the system as it exists today.

—*Bookpleasures*

Powerful, engrossing, and clear-eyed, this is a critical book for everyone—those dealing with chronic pain, medical professionals, caregivers, and anyone tempted to turn a blind eye to a problem that affects 111 million people in the United States alone.

—*BlueInk Review*

The book tackles all different avenues of support—family, friends, medical, spiritual—and tries to offer something for anyone reading it. If you have CPS [chronic pain syndrome], it offers the knowledge that you are not alone, some new ideas and thoughts, and a sense that you are not stumbling around in the dark with something no one can understand. If you know someone who has CPS it can offer you a better understanding of what they're going through and what they might need to support them through it. And if you have never encountered CPS then it helps to shine a light onto a criminally overlooked problem that so many people dismiss as nothing.

—*The Review Diaries*

The Painful Truth

The Painful Truth

*What Chronic Pain Is Really Like
and Why It Matters to Each of Us*

Lynn R. Webster, M.D.

Webster Media, LLC

The Painful Truth
Webster Media LLC
P.O. Box 581113
Salt Lake City, UT 84158

Prepared in association with Edit Resource, LLC (editresource.com)

Details in some anecdotes and stories have been changed to protect
the identities of the persons involved.

ISBN 978-0-9861407-0-9 (Hardcover)
ISBN 978-0-9861407-1-6 (Paperback)
ISBN 978-0-9861407-2-3 (Ebook)

All the author's profits from sales of this book will go toward helping
to bring a voice to people in pain.

Cover and text design by Bookwrights (bookwrights.com)
Printed in the United States of America
First Printing, 2015

To all people in pain who want someone to listen to them

You may not be able to control events that happen, but you can decide not to be reduced by them.

—Maya Angelou

Contents

Introduction

PAIN IS AN UNBIDDEN guest, humanity's shadow companion down through the ages. It is an interloper, a despoiler of dreams, a thief.

Pain can affect anyone, young or old, male or female, rich or poor. No one is immune. Pain can start suddenly, whether from trauma or an operation or from aging, disease, or some unknown cause, and it can stay with us until death. The severity and frequency of pain tend to rise with age, so even those of us who aren't enduring pain now are almost certainly going to have to deal with it in some degree eventually.

At any given time, in the United States, about one third of all people are in pain. Half of all people aged sixty-five and older have chronic pain.[1] Untold numbers, both professionals and loved ones, are caring for those who are in pain.

Literally no one can escape pain's effects.

There is no problem, medical or nonmedical, that is more intimate, that is more personal, and that has more of an impact on more lives than pain.

Everyone is familiar with pain following an acute injury or trauma. This type of pain tells the body that it needs a rest to heal. It also protects us by teaching us what to avoid. (Thanks to pain, we learn at an early age not to touch a hot stove.) People who have the disease called *congenital insensitivity to pain* often chew off their tongues, break their bones, fail to notice infections, and die prematurely—all because they can't feel any pain to tell them there is a problem. This disorder has taught us that without pain we can die. But when pain is greater than is needed to alert us to a problem, or when it goes on past the time when the problem that triggered it has subsided, then the pain itself becomes a medical problem—a chronic disease.

Sometimes people will tell an individual who is in pain, "It's all in your head." The comment is dismissive, as though what the pain sufferer is going through isn't real. I reject this attitude absolutely. The pain *is* real. Yet, in a sense, pain is also in a person's head. Pain is a cerebral experience that integrates attitudes, expectations, emotions, and stimuli. It is invisible. It is metaphysical more than physical. From this perspective, we can say that pain exists in the mind of the one experiencing it. So pain can be cerebral, experienced in the mind, but *not* be imaginary.

Throughout most of the medical profession's history, my tribe has attempted to combat the mysterious condition known as pain with whatever resources we have had available, even if it just meant doling out the juice of the poppy. Yet physicians have often not been as understanding about pain as they could have been. In 1972, John Bonica came near to giving up on his dream of creating a multi-disciplinary approach to pain treatment. As he put it, whenever he brought up the topic, other doctors would say, "Pain is a symptom of disease, and that's it."[2] Thankfully, though, since then attitudes among physicians have begun to change. As I and my fellow pain specialists now assert, pain is not always just a symptom; pain, when it produces persistent changes to the brain and spinal cord, can itself become a disease, a disorder of the body that we should be treating directly.[3] As I often say, the science of pain medicine is still in its infancy, if indeed it's that far along. But at least many of us are now trying in a more concerted fashion to control human pain.

On one hand, modern pain medicine is just another specialty within the larger profession. On the other, it represents a renewal of the crusade against the human race's primal enemy: pain.

Here is where I tilt my lance.

Since 1990, I have been specializing in the treatment of pain, starting out as an anesthesiologist addressing post-operative and cancer pain at Holy Cross Hospital in Salt Lake City, then moving on to open Lifetree Clinic to treat people with chronic pain. Witness to the suffering of so many over so many years, I have been inspired to advance the frontier of what is possible in treating pain by heading up research programs for promising therapies, both medications and procedures. Most recently, I have focused on research combined with education and advocacy for people who are in pain or who have developed an opioid (popularly called "narcotic") addiction due to their treatment for pain. Throughout the years, I have seen many areas of progress in understanding and alleviating pain. I have also seen some backward steps. Although I remain optimistic about the human race's ability to eventually defeat its enemy pain, I am disappointed that we aren't further along by now.

Let me tell you how, as a young physician-in-the making, I first felt the frustration of not being able to do enough to help pain.

The Man in the VA Hospital

In 1976, when I was twenty-six years old and beginning my medical internship at the University of Utah, my rotations took me to the nearby Veteran Affairs medical center. That's how I came to meet a patient whose case would plant a disquiet in my soul that I am still working out to this day.

He was a World War I veteran in his nineties, tall and gaunt, bald headed and age spotted. He had been admitted to the medical center for dehydration and malnutrition, but he had other problems as well, including arthritic joints that made a grinding noise whenever he bent his limbs. Lying in his bed, he was in excruciating pain that no analgesic could touch and that refused to leave him alone day or night, preventing him from getting more than snatches of sleep or enjoying anything at all that life could offer to him at his age.

This man, who in his youth had taken up arms to defend our country, was now barely able to walk, half blind, more than half deaf, and tormented with bowel and bladder problems. He hurt all over and had no family to comfort him in his distress. He was isolated and without hope. He suffered physically and emotionally as much as anyone can suffer, with no prospect for improvement. His only desire was to escape.

Whenever I passed by, he would grab at me and tearfully beg, "Help me die. You're a doctor—you can do it. I'd rather be dead than keep living with the pain. Put me out of this misery. Please, ple-e-e-ease!"

I was startled, even afraid of the man. I felt impotent: I could do nothing for him. I was forced to observe him being tortured by his own existence. It left me with feelings of emptiness and anxiety.

As quickly as I could, I would disentangle my hand from his and speed from his bedside. But then I would stand outside his room, next to the nursing station, frozen, listening to his cries. I wanted to find some other duty that needed attending to, but I was unable to move, as if I were being held by a power greater than myself to imprint his cries and prayers in my soul. *Why can't we help this suffering?* I would ask myself repeatedly.

I left that poor old man, but he never left me. I'd internalized his pain. At night I had nightmares of hearing him scream. In the daytime his situation, or rather my helplessness before it, created a disturbing sense of conflict within me. Here was a man who needed me more than any of my other patients, but what could I do for him? Less than I could for any of the others. And what about his plea that I end his life? I knew I couldn't do that—the very thought nauseated me. Yet I knew that patients like him cannot be ignored, left in their beds of suffering all alone.

This was the 1970s. American medical practice was at the height of its hubris. The attitude of medical practitioners plainly stated, "We can do anything. We're well on our way to creating procedures, interventions, and treatments that will beat back every sort of assault upon human health. Whatever it is, we can fix it. We can cure it." It was heady stuff, intoxicating. And for people like the man at the VA medical center, curing was just what I wanted to do. It was only a matter of time (and perhaps not much time), I concluded, before we would be able to deal with runaway pain like that experienced by the unfortunate World War I veteran. Or anyway, that's how I comforted myself.

I was wrong.

Today, far too many are still in pain. More than that, societal attitudes toward those in pain have not improved much. In some ways, changes that are taking place in society right now (such as changes in health insurance that limit access to pain therapists) may even put people at greater risk than used to be the case. We truly have a problem with pain in our nation. *Crisis* is not too strong a word to put on it.

This is the painful truth we face. What are we to do with it?

The answer is *not* to ignore it. Yet, for the most part, that is exactly what American society is now doing.

As the most common medical problem in America today, chronic pain is more prevalent than cancer, heart disease, stroke, diabetes, and many other health problems that all of us are familiar with. Around 100 to 111 million people in America have chronic pain. The national economic cost associated with chronic pain is estimated to be well north of half a trillion dollars per year.[4] Yet in a poll, only 18 percent of respondents said they believe that chronic pain is a major health problem.[5] Tens of millions of people have untreated or undertreated pain because they can't find, or can't afford, quality medical treatment by a professional who understands pain. The federal budget for research into new medical treatments for pain is a tiny fraction of that for many diseases that affect far fewer individuals. All because we aren't taking pain seriously enough.

To create change, we must squarely face the reality of pain in our society, including both the helpful treatments and services that are currently available for people in pain and the ways that we, as a society, are falling short of giving people the help for their pain that they need. This is why in *The Painful Truth* I want to call forth the emotions of both hope and unrest—hope because there is much that people in pain can do right now to feel better, unrest because we can't settle for the status quo.

Let me introduce a distinction that I believe will help us clarify our goals. There's a difference between healing and curing.

Healing and Curing

It was the refrain of my years as a pain doctor, the plea I heard innumerable times when interviewing new patients:

"Doc, all I want is my life back."

The teenage girl who couldn't concentrate at school because of her blinding migraines.... The father who wasn't able to play catch with his son due to disc degeneration in his spine.... The newlywed whose pelvic pain prevented her from consummating her marriage.... The wife who was unable to participate in dinner parties with her husband whenever she had a fibromyalgia flare-up.... The ex-executive whose retirement was spoiled by the aches and pains of old age.... All of these and many others looked to me to restore their old life as it was before pain. Who can blame them?

"Doc, all I want is my life back."

I wanted to give them their lives back. And of course, in those rare cases when some sort of medical intervention was able to eliminate someone's chronic pain, obviously that was wonderful. But what I learned quickly in my practice was that, for now, a *cure* in many cases is not a possibility. I do, however, believe that *healing* is possible for most people who have pain. When I refer to healing, I mean that people with chronic pain can have an improvement—often a dramatic improvement—in their pain condition and overall satisfaction with life, even if the pain never entirely goes away.

With my patients, I've seen that, as we try a range of medical and nonmedical therapies, their pain generally comes down to a bearable level and their function improves. This allows other interests, duties, and pleasures to resurface in their lives. They engage with friends, lovers, children, neighbors, and coworkers again. They make plans and go after them. And though a person's life is rarely what it was like before pain intruded, it is often a good life in its own way.

Healing—that is what Part 1 of this book is all about. Using stories of real-life people in pain, Part 1 provides helpful information that people can use right now to understand the pain experience better and to seek healing.

Ultimately, of course, when it comes to pain, we still want a cure and not just healing. I believe the day will yet come when many types of pain can be cured. But to get to that point, or even get to the point where everyone in pain can have access to the care that's currently available, we need societal changes that will expand and improve medical treatment. So in Part 2 I'll be addressing the problems and limitations in current-day pain treatment as well as the kind of cultural transformation we need to see if we're ever going to take away people's pain. This transformation is something that each of us can have a part in promoting, leading to an acceptance of effective pain treatment as a human right.

So here's what to expect:

- If you have pain…this book will reassure you that you are not alone, offer validation of what you are feeling, and help you to seek and find the kinds of help you need. It may even turn you into an activist who tries to promote changes in society that will prevent others from having to go through what you are going through.
- If you don't have pain yourself but you care about someone who does…the book will help you understand better what your loved one is going through and learn how you can help. It will also make you better prepared for a time when you may be in pain yourself.
- Even if you don't currently have pain or know anyone close to you who does…this book is still for you. It will open your mind and heart to the number-one public health problem in America. It will make you better able to respond to others' pain or your own when that time comes—and it will.

I have spent most of my medical career trying to help people in pain. I have seen the reality of pain on the individual level, and I have been involved in evaluating pain treatment from professional, research, and governmental perspectives. As my career draws nearer to a conclusion, I am more convinced than ever that pain is misunderstood in our society. It's so much more complicated and multi-layered than many people are willing to accept. And therefore a mere how-to approach to the subject, I fear, would be simplistic and reductionistic. We need realism *and* hope, medicine *and* relationship.

So this is not a self-help book. But it is a helpful book. I have written it to share with you the humanity involved with people in pain that is too often absent in our cultural understanding of pain. It is intended to show how suddenly one's life can change—forever— and what it's like to be treated as if one is a burden to society. The book will leave you with a plan and a rationale for a society-wide shift in attitudes. I hope it will inspire you to be a part of the change that our world needs in its approach to pain.

This book will focus on chronic pain in the United States and issues facing U.S. society regarding pain. But pain is a worldwide phenomenon, and many other countries are dealing with the same issues about misunderstanding pain, stigmatizing pain, and failing to provide adequate relief for pain.[6] People in other nations should be able to translate the truths of *The Painful Truth* into their own cultural contexts with relative ease.

We'll start with what individuals who have pain are going through and how they can promote their own healing. I've discovered that the key to healing is to approach chronic pain, not just as a disease of an organ, but as a potentially devastating condition that affects the whole person—medically, socially, emotionally, and existentially.

PART 1

Hope for Healing

CHAPTER 1

It's Personal

More than just a medical condition, chronic pain affects everything in a person's life.

ONE OF THE CLEAREST memories I retain from my childhood is of my Grandma Al (short for Alfreda) sitting in her wheelchair in the living room of the farmhouse she and Grandfather shared with my family in Nebraska. Encased in her chair made of metal tubing and vinyl, she was able to talk, able to pat our dog Ring, but hardly able to shuffle her legs more than an inch at a time. Frail and thin in a cheap print dress, she spent most of her days looking out the window at we able-bodied members of the family doing our chores or at the occasional car sending up a cloud of dust along our dirt road. She had advanced multiple sclerosis. She was always in pain.

Sometimes her legs would jerk uncontrollably—the longer it lasted, the more painful it became for her. The doctor I am today understands that her disease had demyelinated the nerves in her spinal cord and brain responsible for movement, leading to a loss of voluntary motor control and causing her legs to act as if they were having a seizure.[1] But as a young boy in the 1950s, all I understood was what I could see: my grandma grimacing, shifting her weight in her seat to try to ease the discomfort, breathing heavily in her exhaustion, often crying, sometimes screaming in pain.

"Dear God," she'd pray out loud, "make this jerking stop. Make it stop now! Oh, please, God." But it seemed God did not hear.

Many times I would stand by her chair. Using my nickname, she'd say, "Butchy, hold my feet down."

I would take hold of her feet in their white socks and moccasins and press them with all of my young might into the pillows my grandfather had placed on the floor for her. Sometimes this was all that seemed to give her any relief. I would hold her feet still for ten minutes, fifteen, twenty, until she was better. Then I could stand up and see the relaxation appear on her face and feel her hand weakly gripping mine, the spasm having receded like a summer storm on the Plains. We both knew it wouldn't be long before another rose on the horizon.

Partly because of my experience with Grandma Al, I would eventually leave the farm and study to become a doctor at the universities of Nebraska and Utah. Working in a Salt Lake City hospital, I developed an acute pain service to ease the recovery for patients and later went on to open a clinic to help people with chronic pain.[2] I was never able to treat my grandmother's multiple sclerosis—she died from complications of her disease in 1970 while I was in college. Yet, many years after she was gone, I felt a great sense of satisfaction when the first patient into whom I implanted a device to treat pain was a woman with multiple sclerosis.

Looking back today, I wonder if I may have been more help to Grandma Al when I was a child than I had thought. It wasn't just the way I pressed her feet into the pillows that brought her relief. With me by her side, she knew she wasn't alone in her suffering. She had someone who would keep her company and talk with her, someone who loved her. Of course I was not the only one who provided this kind of help. My grandfather, especially, was an unfailing and uncomplaining servant to his wife as her condition worsened. But still I believe that, in my own way, even as a young child, I was able to contribute to her comfort.

What if a little help from others was all it would take to feel better?

Therapies of the Heart

The disease of pain affects the mind, changing pathways in the brain and altering moods. The mind, in turn, can affect pain, with experts in the field of neuroplasticity revealing ways that some people can use their thoughts to control their pain. But the experience of pain goes even further than that. It also has a lesser or greater impact on all of a person's relationships, influencing social interactions with spouse, parents, children, coworkers, and others. And finally pain, for many, is a spiritual experience, with religious beliefs and practices impacting their pain and their pain causing their faith to evolve.

Pain, in short, is a bio-psycho-social-spiritual condition. It affects the whole person.

Because pain is such a broad-based experience, it requires a broad-based approach to bring healing. This is what physician John Bonica was trying to promote back in the 1970s. The multidisciplinary approach (sometimes called the multimodal approach) is still the gold standard for chronic pain care. If there is no cure available, then healing is most likely to occur through trying to beat back the advances of pain across a broad front. This means using any of the tools in a pain physician's toolbox that might help in a given case, whether interventions (such as implants and bioelectric devices) or drugs (analgesics, muscle relaxants, and more). The multidisciplinary approach also means using nonmedical approaches, at times including cognitive behavioral therapy or other forms of psychological counseling, physical therapy, exercise, improved nutrition, meditation, yoga, massage, acupuncture, biofeedback, hypnotherapy, and other options.

And then there are the intangible things that help, things that aren't considered medical therapies as such but that are crucial to healing from pain: Acceptance. Love. Compassion. Listening. Respect. Encouragement. Trust. Kindness. Patience. Presence.

You might call these offerings "therapies of the heart." They are so simple yet so vital to a truly broad-based approach to healing the whole person. You don't have to be a medical professional to offer these gifts to someone in pain. Or if you're in pain yourself, you don't need a health insurance plan to seek them out in others. Anyone can provide these "therapies of the heart," just as I did to my Grandma Al when I was a young boy.

People in pain need to be both *treated by medical professionals* and *supported by all the important people in their lives*. So a key to healing a loved one in pain is simply...being there.

Trust me, it's powerful.

"I Believe You"

Shortly after I opened my pain clinic in 1990, I saw a patient I'll never forget. She was a middle-aged woman with an unsmiling expression and shoulders that sagged as she sat on the end of the examining table. When I asked, "What can I do to help you?" a light of hope that hadn't been there before suddenly flickered in her eyes. I wasn't rejecting her or putting her off. Maybe someone was there for her after all!

She proceeded to tell me a long tale that would soon grow familiar to me in its outline—of developing severe chronic pain, of being passed around by doctors, of being ignored or misunderstood by her so-called friends. And still the pain went on.

At the end of her narration of suffering, which seemed worn from repeated use, I simply told her, "I believe you." I wasn't necessarily expecting her to react to my comment. Or perhaps I thought she might say, "Thank you." But that's not what happened.

She burst into tears.

This surprised and disconcerted me. I didn't know how to react. So instead of delving into why she was crying, I handed her a box of tissues and waited for her sobs to subside, then gently restarted a conversation about her medical treatment options.

Later that evening, at home, I had the leisure to think over what had gone on in the exam room. I knew that, when it comes to pain complaints, many people find that their friends and even their physicians doubt them. It's all in their head, people conclude. They're exaggerating. They're seeking attention. They're seeking drugs. Maybe it's depression. Can't they just get over it? So for me to say "I believe you" signaled to this woman that someone was taking her and her pain seriously. I could understand why that would be welcome to her.

But still, that outburst of sobbing—why such a strong emotional reaction? My overture of trust and cooperation clearly meant something significant to her.

Then a memory drifted into my mind.

I must have been about six years old. I was sick and lying down on the sofa in the living room of our house, wishing that I could be outside helping my father with the farm work. Just then he walked in, a broad man wearing denim overalls, brow coated with sweat and hands hardened from manual labor. "Son, how are you feeling?" he asked me.

I complained about the cold or stomach virus or whatever it was that had me down.

At that, he placed his hand on my head and left it there for a few moments before saying, "You'll be better soon, son."

Inside, I was flooded with comfort and joy. I felt the strength of my father. I knew I was going to be better soon. In fact, I was already better, just because my father listened and cared and was there with me, encouraging me.

Remembering that experience, I understood better how the woman in my office had felt. Having someone listen to and validate her was what she needed most just then and wasn't getting anywhere else. I believed her and I was ready to work with her. She felt a sense of caring. She wasn't alone. There was hope for relief.

If I could build on what we had established, I decided, it might be the beginning of a relationship between us that could enable us to work together on a plan to relieve her suffering. And that is how it turned out—for her and for many other suffering people who would follow her.

For some of the men and women of my profession, it comes naturally to offer a comforting and accepting presence. For most of us, though, we've got to work at it. I've spent decades improving my bedside manner, and I know that I'm still far from perfect at it. Most important, I've learned that my caring has to be more than a "manner"; it has to be something I truly mean. A person in pain needs a doctor who genuinely cares, who sees a person and not just a patient, a cause and not just a case. *Then* a relationship—one that's professional and yet profoundly human—may be established to bring about improvement in the patient's well-being.

But the truth is, *anyone* who knows and cares about someone in pain can be the person to minister an inner sense of healing, merely by trying to understand what's happening and being there with compassion and reassurance. Furthermore, anyone who is in pain should look for, and I would say expect, this kind of care and connectedness from those closest to him or her.

Humankind is a social species. We live and thrive in community. When ill, we look to our community for physical and emotional restitution. Religious communities have served this role for millennia, and so have families, friends, and other groups. My father offered it to a sick and lonely six-year-old. So while pain is a primal enemy, the support of loved ones and professionals is a primal ally in our battle, perhaps one we've forgotten as we've looked to the marvels of medical science to solve our problems.

What can I do to help you? I believe you. Pure magic.

Now I want to tell you a story about a young woman I met who learned firsthand the destructive effects of rejection and the reconstructive influence of compassion.

A Journey Taken in Company

Jessy was a sweet-tempered, soft-voiced Navajo girl of twelve living in Page, Arizona, when she began to experience pain in her pelvic area. She was going through puberty at the time and thought she was just having cramps. But the pain kept going and even got worse. By the next year, in the eighth grade, friends had to carry her school-books and open the heavy doors at school for her because any stress on her body would worsen the pain. Sitting for hours on the hard seats in the classrooms of her junior high school was a misery.

Vickie Klain, Jessy's mom, became the girl's chief locus of emotional support and her best advocate. Vickie always believed Jessy, never stopped encouraging her. She began taking Jessy to see doctors, starting with her pediatrician and then branching out to specialists, including an obstetrician-gynecologist, neurologist, gastroenterologist, and urologist. This presented a serious financial hardship for her family, which included the single mother and Jessy's three older brothers. Vickie even resorted to holding garage sales and bake sales to raise money for doctor visits. She was determined to get help for her daughter.

If only she had met with greater receptiveness. Often the doctors would say to Jessy, "Has someone been abusing you?" "Are you sure it's not just menstrual cramps?" "Are you having an argument with a friend?" No, no, no. The doctors hypothesized appendicitis, endometriosis, and other conditions, only to rule out each in turn. (The actual cause of Jessy's pain was probably pudendal nerve damage when she fell astraddle a ladder as a child, the nerve damage worsening when she went through puberty.) Some of the doctors prescribed pain medications that partially relieved Jessy's discomfort, but this benefit came at the cost of mental confusion and personality changes in Jessy.

Her life had gone off in an unwanted direction almost before it had fairly begun.

Even with her closest friends, Jessy did not feel like opening up about her pain problem because of its peculiarly private nature. But that didn't stop people in the community from indulging in lurid speculations. Jessy, they whispered, had been sexually abused by one or more of her older brothers. Or Jessy had undergone an abortion. Or Jessy had given birth and put the baby up for adoption. All wrong.

As the rumors worked their way back to Jessy, they brought her to tears. Emotional pain overlaid her physical pain because her friends and neighbors believed such things could be true even when she denied them. At age fifteen, because of both the physical and the emotional pain, she left her public school to be homeschooled by her mother. Her world was retracting.

She was more desperate than ever to find relief for her pain. So was her mother.

Vickie Klain had grown up in a traditional Navajo family on the reservation in northern Arizona but had converted to Mormonism as a youth and had moved to Page after graduating from high school. But Vickie's mother-in-law was still living on the reservation and was a medicine woman practicing traditional healing rituals. So, with some misgivings, Vickie took Jessy for treatment by the grandmother.

The medicine woman on many occasions prayed and sang for her granddaughter in Navajo, holding items handed down through generations, including rocks, feathers, and corn pollen. Jessy held arrowheads and feathers while her grandmother massaged her body. Yet the pain persisted.

Unfortunately, Western medicine didn't seem to be helping Jessy any more than did its traditional counterpart. She shuttled from doctor to doctor looking for a treatment plan that would make a real difference but not getting it. Then came the day when the last doctor Vickie knew to take Jessy to told them, "I'm sorry, there's nothing more I can do for you." His words seemed to suck the last reserve of hope out of young Jessy's heart. When the doctor left the room, Jessy remained behind, weeping and talking in despairing tones with her mom about their lack of other options.

A nurse happened to walk by and overheard some of the conversation. She stepped into the room and told them, "I shouldn't be saying this, but I have a brother who works at a cancer facility in Salt Lake City. Upstairs from it is a pain clinic." She was referring to Lifetree, the clinic I had founded. "Why don't you give them a try?"

That's how Jessy first came to see me. She and her mother had to travel several hours to reach my clinic. Jessy would lie down in the car as they traveled to and from Salt Lake City because it was too painful for her to sit for the full duration. But a stubborn determination was goading them both.

In our early visits together, we talked and got to know each other. I learned a bit about the Klains' culture, and they learned something about me as a person. The truth is, I felt close to Jessy and her mother because of my upbringing. I had lived in as rural an area as they did. I had been poor like they were. Like theirs, my relatives believed in the strength of family and friends to feel better and to get through difficult times.

Over a period of time, we tried a number of treatments for Jessy. One was a spinal cord stimulator—a battery-operated device implanted under the skin of the lower abdomen to deliver a small amount of electricity through a wire to the spinal cord, interrupting the flow of pain messages. The device worked wonderfully for Jessy. She reported that her pain dropped 75 percent when she used the stimulator. It's not the same as an elimination of her pain, but with monitoring of her condition and the occasional use of over-the-counter pain medications, she's able to get by very well, avoiding the opioids she never liked taking.

Jessy has earned her GED, received a driver's license, and resumed her favorite pastime of hiking in the Arizona desert where her ancestors lived. Eventually she wants to become a wife and have a family. Before that happens, though, she plans to study to become a radiology technician—she has a dream of giving back to other hurting people.

"If it weren't for the stimulator, I don't know where I would be," she said to me one time. "Thank you for listening to me and working with me till we found something that made a difference."

Then she went on. "I don't know where I'd be without my mom either. She's been there with me through everything. Her comfort helped me keep going. This victory is hers as much as mine."

There it is: the combination of medical treatment and emotional support producing an improved state of well-being and hope for a brighter future. This is healing. In fact, I would go so far as to say that Vickie was as much her daughter's healer as I ever was. Together, a mother's love and a doctor's involvement have brought Jessy to a point where her life is in forward motion again.

As for those "friends" who circulated rumors about her? They're out of her life now. She's got a new set of friends who can better accept what she's been through, and she says that finding them may have been worth it all. I feel privileged to call myself one of her friends.

The kinds of healing relationships Jessy has had in her life are the kinds I'd like for everyone in pain to have with their physicians, friends, and family.

My Prescription

Like Jessy Klain, other people who have chronic pain are in the process of dealing with the changes that have been thrust upon them and are building a new life the best way they know how. From the bedside or in the examination room, I've been privileged to hear about the profound changes, for both good and bad, going on in thousands of people's lives. Yet few who haven't gone through such a situation themselves, and few who are just beginning the journey of living with pain, have much comprehension of what it is like.

This is where Part 1 of *The Painful Truth* makes its contribution. The following eight chapters, rather than describing pain clinically, tell the stories of people in pain empathetically. Pain isn't just biological. It's also psychological, social, and spiritual. It's *personal*. So my prescription for the lack of understanding and the underwhelming level of compassion about pain in our society is this: story.

I've already told you briefly about my Grandma Al, the middle-aged woman who burst into tears in my examination room, and Jessy Klain. In the chapters ahead, I'll be profiling several other people who have had pain. All of them are connected with Lifetree Clinic in Salt Lake City, because that's where until recently I practiced pain medicine. These people represent their numerous counterparts all over America and around the world, with the same needs and implications for healing. Through their portraits, you will see what a pain experience is really like and what works and what doesn't in bringing the best of our humanity to people in pain.

The stories ahead will illustrate answers to the following questions:

- What kinds of misconceptions do people in pain run up against?
- How does chronic pain affect family and other relationships?
- What are the kinds of losses that come with pain?
- How great is the risk that certain pain treatments will lead to addiction? And what works to wean a person off an addicting medication while still managing pain?
- How is a family member impacted by assuming the role of caregiver to a person in pain?
- How can a person in pain be proactive in getting the best possible help?
- What kinds of unsought rewards can a battle against pain give back?

While you're working your way through this book, you may wish to go to ThePainfulTruthBook.com, where you can find further inspiration, practical resources, and videos of many of the people featured in this book.

In the next chapter we'll be meeting Carolyn Tuft, a woman whose story powerfully illustrates the truth that pain can come to a person suddenly—and that no matter how bad the pain is, there's hope.

_____ ⋎⋏⋎ _____

CHAPTER 2

More than a Survivor

Even in the worst pain situations, it's possible to pursue a fulfilling life.

PERHAPS THE MOST BEAUTIFUL and peaceful place I have ever been in my life was a guest house in Provence called Le Levandin. My wife, Holly, and I spent a week there in June 2009.

One morning we sat at a large dining room table in the guest house for breakfast. We were soon joined by some other guests: three women friends and a married couple. Naturally, we all went around the table introducing ourselves. The three friends, it turned out, were from Utah. They gave their names and identified themselves as a nurse, a teacher, and an artist. I noticed that the artist, Carolyn, a woman with mid-length blonde hair, leaned stiffly in her chair and appeared somewhat fragile. The married couple were from California. My wife explained that she was a pediatric intensive care nurse practitioner from Salt Lake City, and last I described myself as an anesthesiologist who specialized in pain medicine.

Upon my introduction, the three women from Utah all seemed excited. The real estate agent said to the artist, "Carolyn, tell him your story. Go on."

Carolyn hesitated for a moment, then sat straighter and began to tell her story in a subdued voice.

There could be no more jarring contrast between the story she told us and the tranquil setting we were in. Even though my wife and I were used to stories of injury and suffering, this story sickened us as soon as we heard the words "Trolley Square Mall" and realized where the narration was heading. I remember that the California pair got appalled expressions on their faces as they listened to the story and eventually excused themselves from the table before the discussion among the rest of us had ended.

Yet if they had stayed they would have realized that the story was one of hope as well as tragedy. Carolyn had in abundance the quality that people who are seeking improvement in their pain need most of all—a belief that a good life is possible and a determination to go after it. Her story illustrates many of the challenges that people in pain face, and yet, extreme as it is, it also reveals the possibility of sucking the honey out of life despite pain.

For anyone, pain can come on suddenly and unexpectedly. It can be excruciating. Yet there is always hope.

Trolley Square Mall

At a quarter to seven on a Monday evening, February 12, 2007, Carolyn Tuft parked her car outside the Trolley Square Mall in Salt Lake City. Then she and her fifteen-year-old daughter, Kirsten Hinckley, headed into the mall to shop for Valentine's Day cards.

Carolyn at that time was a divorced, forty-four-year-old mother of four. She had, and still has, a fun-loving nature, and she enjoyed a good relationship with all her children. She was known for celebrating life—participating in vigorous sports, taking adventurous trips despite her limited income as a housecleaner, and staging fun parties for her kids and friends.

Her youngest child, Kirsten, closely resembled her, with a slim figure and long blonde hair. On this particular Monday, Kirsten had taken part in a drama presentation at school, so she was dressed up and had done her hair in curls. When Carolyn came to pick the sophomore up outside her high school, the mother paused for a moment to appreciate how beautiful she looked with the sunlight streaming through her hair. Carolyn wished that Kirsten would have the courage to talk to the cute boys standing nearby, but though Kirsten was eyeing them, she was too shy to respond to their flirting.

Carolyn had driven to the school with her older daughter, Kaitlin. When they all went back to the car, Kirsten called out, "Shotgun!"—the customary way in their family of claiming the front seat. But Kaitlin jumped in the front seat anyway, setting off a brief argument between the two girls. Carolyn didn't think much about this exchange at the time, but afterward it would seem to her to have a kind of prescient horror to it. Today she hates the word *shotgun*. Kirsten sat in the back, sulking, until Carolyn dropped the older sister off at her workplace on the way to the mall.

When Kirsten and her mother at last entered Trolley Square Mall, Carolyn noticed how empty the place seemed. It gave her an eerie feeling, but her only conscious concern about it was that her favorite shopping center might be losing so much business that it would close. The plastic heel of Kirsten's shoe had come apart earlier that day, and she had fixed it with tape. Now Carolyn could distinctly hear the *click, click* from the damaged heel as they walked down the hallway to Cabin Fever, a store offering eclectic gifts and cards.

Moments after they stepped into the store, mother and daughter heard a loud *pop!* They stopped to listen. Carolyn wondered if a gang member might be firing a gun in the street. But she felt safe where she was, in such an ordinary store, in an ordinary mall, on an ordinary Monday evening.

Kirsten had just started drawing her mother's attention to a gag gift on a rack when they heard another *pop!* Actually, more like a blast—closer this time. Carolyn took a few steps toward the window facing the hallway to see if she could tell what was going on, but because of glare on the glass, she couldn't see who was on the other side.

Unfortunately he could see her.

He was Sulejman Talović, an eighteen-year-old immigrant from Bosnia and Herzegovina. A high school dropout and loner, he spent a lot of time hanging around this mall. No one would ever know for sure why he showed up on this particular evening armed with a shotgun and a revolver and intent on killing. One person on the scene would later report hearing the young man call out, "Allahu Akbar!" He was wearing a tan trench coat.

Though Carolyn could not see him, he could see her plainly. He fired the shotgun in her direction.

Carolyn saw a bright flash at the window. Then she noticed that tiny shards of glass were sticking to the sleeve of her sweater. She started to pluck them out with her fingers. It occurred to her that she was in a store that sold gag gifts; could she have been the victim of some kind of trick?

"This is not funny," she said to Kirsten. "What's going on?"

Just then, the window that Talović had fired through started splitting and falling to the floor in a noisy waterfall of glass fragments.

"Get down, Mom," said Kirsten as she followed a couple other store patrons who were running toward a wall to hide. Kirsten lay down facing the wall, next to some card racks. Carolyn crouched not far from her.

The next thing Carolyn knew, someone was standing two or three feet away from her. Glancing over her shoulder, she saw a young man in a trench coat. He looked her in the eyes. He raised his shotgun. He fired.

This time he couldn't miss. The shot took off the back of her right shoulder and sent pellets deep into her chest, piercing her right lung and shearing the brachial nerves that extend from the neck to the arm. The force of the shot threw her forward onto her face. She tried to get up but didn't have the strength for it. She was spewing blood from her mouth, more blood bubbling from her nose, and she was struggling for every breath. Stunned, she looked over at her daughter, a few feet away.

The shooter pivoted and fired at Kirsten, shooting her in the back as she lay facing the wall. The blast blew pieces of major organs out of the hole it left in Kirsten's belly. The injury was unsurvivable.

But for the moment she was still alive. Kirsten rolled over on her back, and Carolyn could see the girl's face. She was wincing and crying in pain.

Carolyn looked around at the happy pink walls of the mall card store and thought, *Oh, Kirsten.* And then, *I cannot believe we are going to die on the floor of Trolley Square.* It seemed surreal.

Talović stepped into the hallway.

Carolyn started lurching across the floor toward her daughter, using her uninjured left arm and knees to propel herself. She managed to get to a point where her head was just a foot away from Kirsten's. Then she felt the muzzle of a gun pressing hard against her back. Talović had returned. To Carolyn, the pressure of the gun was a clear message from him: "You're not going anywhere."

This shot entered her lower left back, next to her spine, scattering shotgun pellets inside her pelvis and abdomen and blowing away her hipbone. Her head slammed into the cement floor and her ears started ringing. More and more unreal.

Later Carolyn would feel guilt over having crawled toward her daughter, because maybe, she thought, her action drew the gunman's attention to Kirsten. Talović put his gun muzzle next to Kirsten's lovely blonde hair and, as her mother looked on, fired.

For a moment Carolyn wasn't sure what she was looking at. Her daughter's head was an unfamiliar shape and she saw some kind of gray substance. Then she realized she was looking inside her daughter's skull, through the huge hole that the blast had caused, and seeing Kirsten's pulped brain. This could not be happening, could never happen, yet there it was in front of her eyes.

Carolyn knew Kirsten was gone. Feeling sickened and helpless, she whispered, "I love you." Then she reached out and gripped Kirsten's hand tightly with her own, as if she would never let go.

In the minutes that followed, Talović shot the two people Kirsten was lying next to, had a brief argument with and then shot another man in the store, raced across the hallway to Pottery Barn, where he was cornered by a couple of quick-acting police officers, and finally was taken down by SWAT team members who rushed to the scene. He'd killed five people, including Kirsten. He'd injured four others, including Carolyn.

Throughout the climax of the violence, Carolyn was lying in a spreading pool of blood next to the body of her dead daughter. To all appearances, she herself was dead. But as the final shootout was going on down the hallway, a brave eighteen-year-old named Rachel Bass rushed into the store. She had been hiding elsewhere in the mall while the gunman had been on his rampage, and now she was hoping to find someone she could help. A scrub tech at LDS Hospital who had put in some time in the emergency room, Rachel realized what it meant that Carolyn's body was still pulsating blood from her shoulder. She quickly put pressure on Carolyn's wounds and slowed the bleeding until paramedics arrived to take over.

A police officer on the scene would later say that the hardest thing he ever had to do in his job was to pry Carolyn's hand from her dead daughter's hand so that the paramedics could take her to the ambulance.

A Life with Pain

Kirsten's sufferings were at an end. Carolyn's had only begun. Her heart stopped as she was on the way to the hospital, and paramedics frantically worked to restart it. She spent three weeks in intensive care at LDS Hospital and underwent seven surgeries. The pain from her devastating wounds was so intense for the first few weeks that she begged the doctors to put her into a coma so she could escape it. Her skin grafts were so sensitive that the nurses created a tent over her so that nothing would touch her, not even a blanket.

As the physical pain finally receded a bit, the emotional pain over losing her daughter rose to the surface. There were three days when she never spoke a word—she had retreated inside her own mind. For some time, whenever she closed her eyes, she would dream of the shooting, of watching Kirsten take her last breath, seeing blood, blood everywhere. Even when she woke up in a white room with snow falling outside, it still seemed as if everything before her eyes were blood red.

As time passed, though, her dreams about Kirsten changed. Now she would see Kirsten at age two or three, and she would be lifting the child out of bathwater, or playing with her in the backyard, or wrapping her in a blanket. She wouldn't dream of her anymore as a fifteen-year-old but only as a toddler, a child young enough for her to protect.

Carolyn's surviving children, the daughter and two sons, delayed Kirsten's funeral for a month, until Carolyn could attend. The family made it an event to celebrate Kirsten's love of living. Carolyn and her children all concluded from the tragedy that they, too, had to live every day to the fullest. Because now they knew how quickly mortal life can come to an end.

Carolyn also had learned how quickly and unexpectedly—and ineradicably—physical pain can come into anyone's life. The damage to her nerves had been so severe that pain became her constant companion. She was not just going to have to deal with acute pain—the temporary hurt any of us could go through after an injury or operation. She had joined the ranks of those in chronic pain—the pain that just keeps going and becomes a condition that has to be treated and accommodated like any other chronic disease. And sadly, Carolyn's pain was among the most severe anyone might have to endure. Even with medication, her pain level ranged between a 5 and an 8 on the 0-to-10 pain rating scale.

She sought treatment at a Salt Lake City clinic connected with a teaching hospital, meaning that she saw a different doctor every time she went in. She had to tell her story all over again each time, and this in itself made her pain worse. In addition, the doctors were reluctant to prescribe opioid pain medications to her. "It was angering," she told me later. "It made me feel terrible that I had to beg for the narcotics when I was in that much pain." She felt as if she were being treated like a druggie coming in off the street looking to score a high.

There was more than one reason why Carolyn's doctors had the attitude toward her that they did.

Although they certainly recognized the legitimacy of her pain complaint (who wouldn't?), the clinic doctors probably were reluctant to prescribe opioids because they were concerned about exposing Carolyn to the risk of addiction. If she became addicted, not only would it be dangerous for her, including the possibility of overdose and unintentional death, but also it could become dangerous to the doctors themselves. The looming presence over the shoulder of any doctor who prescribes controlled substances is the Drug Enforcement Administration, which has the power to criminally prosecute any doctor it deems as misusing the script pad.

In addition to these risks that accompany opioids, there was another reason why the clinic doctors were reluctant to prescribe to her. Carolyn had no health insurance and little savings, and so she might never be able to pay off her mounting medical bills. Carolyn could have benefited from an aggressive, coordinated treatment plan for her pain. Such a plan might have included cognitive behavior therapy, physical therapy, and perhaps a multidisciplinary team approach in which she would have been taught how to maximize the activities of her daily life by being active, getting more sleep, and so on. But because of her lack of insurance, she was only receiving pain pill prescriptions, and those grudgingly.

With some aggrieved determination on Carolyn's part, she was able to get a fairly regular supply of opioids from the clinic. OxyContin, in particular, helped her noticeably. Nothing eliminated the pain, but Carolyn was at least getting by.

Then another problem arose. Carolyn was taking her OxyContin pills responsibly, but one of her sons—a young man who has a form of autism called Asperger's and who was himself dealing with depression because of what had happened to his mother and sister—began stealing the pills for his own use. Here was another unintended consequence of pain treatment that is so common it causes doctors to think twice about prescribing opioids. As the number of opioid prescriptions has gone up, so has the number of people reaching into medicine cabinets and taking out pill bottles that don't belong to them. This can easily lead to overdose. In the case of Carolyn's son, thankfully he received treatment that enabled him to put his drug abuse behind him.

At about this time, Carolyn's doctors rotated her to a small dose of morphine to reduce costs. But while cheaper, this medication failed to provide any relief for Carolyn's pain. She was back to suffering as much as she ever had since coming home from the hospital.

That's where the situation stood in the summer of 2009, when she scraped together the last of the money she had received from the sale of some property and decided to spend it on a trip to France.

New Reality

During her trip, Carolyn had told her friends that she really needed to find a pain specialist, because the clinic doctors she had been seeing were no longer doing her any good. And there at the same breakfast table in France was a specialist with a practice two blocks from her home!

At the end of the horrific story of the Trolley Square shooting and its aftermath, I assured Carolyn that I would be glad to see her when she got back to Utah. And three months later she appeared in my examination room. Carolyn had taken a mid-afternoon appointment slot because her pain situation made it hard for her to get up and get moving in the morning. I walked into the exam room with her chart that fall afternoon and greeted her as if we were old friends. It was apparent that the introduction in Provence had fended off some of the formality that is normally associated with a new patient visit. After all, she had already told me the most terrifying experience of her life. At one level we were already acquainted.

On another level, I still felt somewhat in the dark about her condition and wasn't sure whether I would be able to offer anything new that would help. Of course I had looked at her x-rays, and there I had seen the dozens of pellets still lodged in her abdomen and other evidences of a what a shotgun had done to her body. I had also read the reports from her previous doctors. They had done a credible job, it seemed to me, though they had not gotten around to trying some of the available treatments.

So, as always with a new patient, I needed to hear from Carolyn's own lips what her medical situation was like. What, specifically, did her pain feel like? How well had the treatments she had tried worked for her, and why had some never been tried? What was her daily living experience like? What was she looking for from me? Without saying so, I wanted to pick up on her attitude, gauge her spirit.

Carolyn told me, in the same quiet voice I had heard in France, that her arm felt as if it had a severe sunburn but also felt frozen, like when you leave your hand in ice too long. Her shoulder always hurt, especially when she moved it. The pain from her back was deep and severe and traveled down her legs. This was the reality of pain she was trying to accommodate to. It had changed her life drastically.

Unable to maintain the housecleaning business she'd had before the shooting, Carolyn hadn't been able to keep up with the rent on the condo she'd shared with her kids. She had received $10,000 from a donation fund set up for Trolley Square victims, but that money was long since gone. So she had moved into her parents' home, and when the parents soon died within weeks of each other, Carolyn's siblings had agreed that she should stay in the home they had jointly inherited. She had recently taken a part-time job at a home décor company, but her income remained small and she wasn't covered by insurance. She had applied for Social Security disability benefits but had been turned down because pain is not one of the qualifying conditions. Carolyn was sitting on a slowly sinking financial iceberg.

The trip to France had used up nearly the last of Carolyn's cash savings. The decision to go on that trip, though, was vintage Carolyn Tuft: If she was down to her last couple thousand dollars anyway, she thought, why should she fritter it away on gas and groceries? Why not blow it on a trip she would love and would remember for the rest of her life? She would have to economize, sharing a room with her friends, and she wouldn't be able to get around and do all the touristy things, but vacations had always been restorative for her and perhaps this one would be healing in some way. So she talked her two friends into going to France with her, sharing the expenses, and helping her get from place to place.

Under severe constraints, she was doing the best she could to get help for her pain problem and to live a normal and worthwhile life.

Although Carolyn didn't put it to me in quite these terms, it was apparent that, along with mourning the loss of her daughter Kirsten, she was also grieving the loss of her former self. She had once been an accomplished artist, creating stunning sketches and watercolors. Now she couldn't hold a pencil well enough to draw. Previously, she had been a professional housecleaner who had bustled around her clients' homes, sweeping and polishing. Now her own home was messy because the effort it took her to clean the dirty dishes in the sink or pick up dropped items from the floor was sometimes more than it was worth. Formerly, she was a high-energy person who loved hiking and rock climbing and considered a day wasted if she hadn't biked fifty miles in the clear Utah air. Now she found it hard to pedal even short distances.

Sketch pencils lying unused in a case. A mountain bike leaning with soft tires against a wall. These were some of the symbols of what she had left behind.

Pill bottles: signs of her new life.

Pain had brought on many losses for Carolyn. I pondered how I could help her get to a better place in life. Unfortunately, the options were few. Although Carolyn now had a job and was getting some income, she was still without health insurance. Quality pain treatment can be expensive. And even if cost were not a consideration, Carolyn's situation was a challenging one because most of her pain came from nerve damage.

One thing we could start with was methadone. I chose this option, not just because it was a less costly treatment than some other medications and procedures, but also because methadone is one of the few opioids that tends to work well with nerve-related pain. Most procedures and medications to reduce pain that I would otherwise consider for Carolyn had been tried and were not helpful or had even worsened her pain. This one might make a real difference. I wrote a prescription and gave a clear warning about the drug's respiratory depressant effects.

At a second visit, Carolyn told me that her pain was more manageable, though she didn't like the way the methadone made her so sleepy. I intended to monitor her progress with methadone and hoped to add some other therapies later, if she ever acquired health insurance.

But then she stopped coming to my office. Although I didn't know it at the time, she had decided that she was unwilling to accumulate more debt from medical expenses and would wait before seeing me again. She discontinued the methadone and went back to morphine.

For about a year, I lost sight of my new friend from Le Levandin.

"I Want to Play"

After the year's absence from Lifetree Clinic, in 2010, Carolyn Tuft made another appointment to see me. She had been raised to full-time status with the home décor company where she worked, and she felt more able to afford medical services. I began treating her again, even getting her into a research program that would cover her drug costs. Since retiring the following year, I have kept in touch with my friend, and so I have continued to observe her journey with pain—the good and the bad of it.

She still faces serious challenges. Among other things, she is suffering from lead poisoning due to the shotgun pellets her surgeon was not able to remove from her body. She had been told that she would likely begin seeing early signs of dementia as a result of the poisoning, and in fact, in recent years, she has begun experiencing bouts of muddled thinking and forgetfulness. This could be due to brain changes from chronic pain as well as to lead poisoning.

In addition, because of the lack of physical therapy and other treatments she couldn't afford, and because of a slow build-up of scar tissue, her pain has begun growing worse again.

Morning had been a bad time of day for her ever since she had come home from the hospital; now it is worse. She doesn't need an alarm clock to wake up, because her pain rouses her early in the morning. The first thing she does is take a pain pill, then she lies back down in bed and waits for the medication to dull the pain. Once she gets up, she might stand in the shower until it runs out of hot water, just so she can ease the stiffness and ache in her muscles. It can take hours for her to get dressed, as she will take frequent breaks to rest. Sometimes her daughter checks on her over lunch break and finds that Carolyn still isn't out of her pajamas.

Everything she does during the day—making food, crossing a room, answering the doorbell or not—requires a conscious decision. Something like leaving the house to see a doctor or go shopping is a significant event that requires planning and an investment of energy. A trip like the time she spoke at a gun control event in Washington, D.C., requires a monumental commitment from her.

Many don't understand what it is like for her. Carolyn tells me, "I finally get my makeup on and get out and they're like, 'You look great. Are you feeling better?' I'm like, 'No,' because I'm in so much pain when I wake up that I have a hard time just pushing myself to a sitting position from the bed and then to a standing position and getting my medication." As usual, pain does its work on the inside, invisibly. In doing her best to have as normal a life as possible, Carolyn cultivates an appearance that belies her true experience.[1]

Meanwhile, Carolyn's financial straits grew narrower again after she lost her job at the home décor company. The manager who hired her was willing to let Carolyn come to work late because it took so much time for her to get going in the morning and because she had no car. But then a new manager took over who was less sympathetic, and soon Carolyn was out of a job.

Today, virtually Carolyn's only income comes from occasionally preparing wedding flowers or doing other décor jobs as a freelancer. "I don't even like to open my mail anymore," she says, "because all it is, is a stack of bills, and I can't pay them. It's really depressing." At one point she bought a junker of a car for $500, and it actually caught fire on the freeway before she could get it home! She eventually acquired a better vehicle. She lives in fear that someone will knock on her door and say, "We're going to take your car, since that's the only asset you have."

Carolyn continues to be poor in health and poor in finances, but she is rich in relationships and hope. The same woman who refused to die on the floor of Trolley Square also refuses to let pain prevent her from living her life as well as she can. This isn't about medical treatment. It's about the other things in her life that keep her going.

The American Chronic Pain Association describes the journey for people in pain with an analogy to a car with four flat tires.[2] Pain medications may be able to inflate one tire, but to resume life's journey requires more than medication or surgical interventions. This "more" might be many things, differing somewhat from situation to situation. (We'll look at many of these helpful options in the rest of Part 1.) For almost everyone, though, inflating the other three tires requires emotional support. In Carolyn's case, she has lots of caring friends as well as her three beloved children: Scott, a Hollywood film producer; Parker, an art student; and Kaitlin, a pastry chef.

Her children, in particular, are always keeping in touch with her and helping when they can. They encourage her and give her practical help, such as driving her to appointments. Perhaps more important, simply by being around her and bringing their friends to visit, they bring life and laughter into her existence and remind her of the good things in life she can still enjoy. "My kids are my reason to be positive," Carolyn once told me. "They are my life."

With relationships like these, as well as her interests in life, such as taking short trips and planning creative parties, she has solid reasons to look forward to the future.

"I don't want to just live," she once told me. "I want to play." I loved it when I heard that! This told me that she wants not just to survive but to make the most of survival.

"So many people don't get it," she went on. "They don't have any joy in their life. They just grumble. I don't want to live that way."

Carolyn, her pain derived from a tragedy as horrific as I have ever personally come into contact with, is also one of the most outstanding examples I know of someone who wants to be responsible for maximizing her life despite pain. As with most people in pain, she does not want to be defined by her pain. Despite all the losses that pain has caused—and there have been many—she is replete with purpose and love.

Carolyn doesn't waste her time hating Sulejman Talović. She doesn't complain about a broken healthcare delivery system or dwell on her victim status. She believes she has opportunities and a future. She spends more energy than most of us to just get moving in the morning, but she never complains about it. She is a determined person with a spiritual core that gives her hope and a sense of contentment that there is a reason for her condition and that, with enough effort, life will get better. A key to Carolyn's peace is her acceptance of what she feels God has given her. Her ability to get by without large amounts of medications illustrates that the center of control is within Carolyn and not with me or other caregivers. Carolyn exemplifies the truth that it's possible to have a meaningful existence even in the face of disabling pain.

A couple of years ago, Carolyn's daughter Kaitlin was married. On the wedding day, Carolyn was there, doing everything the mother of the bride is supposed to do—just slower. But all in the wedding party acutely felt the absence of Kirsten, who should have been the maid of honor. To symbolically make up for the loss, Kaitlin placed a photograph of Kirsten on a table in the reception area and laid beside it the bouquet of flowers Kirsten would have carried down the aisle behind her sister. Looking at this display, Kaitlin and Carolyn hugged for a moment and cried a little...and then proceeded with their wedding preparations. They were going on with life. Kirsten would have understood.

Pain can intrude on any life at any time, with long-lasting repercussions that extend to all those who are close by. But even with terrible physical pain that's connected to terrible emotional suffering, like Carolyn's, it is possible to have a survivor spirit that insists on creating a good life anyway. A life in which it's even possible to play.

CHAPTER 3

Caught in a Web

Pain influences, and is influenced by, everything else going on in a person's life.

CHRONIC PAIN IS NEVER an isolated piece of a person's life. It affects such things as income earning, mood, recreation, the desire and ability to make love, and creativity. Pain, in turn, is affected by such things as conflict in relationships, job stress, laws, social support systems, even the weather! The pain experience is complex and multifaceted.

It's important for us to get beyond narrow-mindedness about pain because this attitude is responsible for much of the misunderstanding and unintentional hurtfulness many people in pain feel from those of us who surround them. If we remind ourselves about the complex interactions of pain with the rest of a person's life, we won't be so likely to think or to say, "Oh, not this again" or "Just get over it" or "Why aren't you the person I remember?" If we want to be helpful, we need to recognize how a person's pain changes what he or she can do or cannot do as well as to recognize what's helping the pain and what's making it worse.

Rachel Hutchins's story vividly portrays the way flawed relationships and vulnerabilities beyond one's control can worsen pain and hinder healing. It also shows how putting together a healing plan that involves smart medical treatment and lots of personal care can reverse the progress of the disease of chronic pain.

Best Intentions

Rachel was in the third grade in 1989 when her infant sister, Veronica, died of leukemia.[1] When Rachel arrived at St. Catherine of Siena Catholic Church in Salt Lake City for the funeral, she saw a white box resting on a pedestal up front in the sanctuary and asked her parents, "What's in that box?" No one had thought to prepare the eight-year-old for the sight of a casket with her little sister's body inside. She, like all her family, was mired in grief and confusion.

What impressed her at the time, and what she still recalls the most from that period, was that the parochial school she attended had shut down for the day and that all the teachers were present at the funeral and all the students had written cards of sympathy. Her faith community gathered around the family for support when they needed it. Rachel's favorite teacher, the elderly and kindly Sister Margaret, squeezed the shoulder of the slender girl with long dark hair. Rachel told me much later that it felt like having an angel looking after her.

That kind of support was rare in Rachel's young life.

Her parents came together temporarily to support one another and their surviving children amid their shared loss. But not long after Veronica's death, the long-standing dysfunctions within the family began to reassert themselves. The parents, both business managers with high-stress jobs, argued a lot and traded accusations of infidelity. Rachel's mother was often absent. Her father was around more but was neglectful of Rachel. Worse, he physically abused Rachel's older brother, Paul ("Paulie"). Rachel can remember watching her father pick up Veronica's unused high chair and hit Paulie with it. Another time he sent Paulie through a plate glass window.

Her parents divorced when Rachel was ten. She and her brother and mother went to live for a while with her widowed grandmother, Grandma Ann. Like Sister Margaret, Grandma Ann was a figure of care and acceptance in Rachel's life. Even when Rachel's mother bought a house down the street and moved there with Paulie and Rachel, Grandma Ann continued to be a presence in the children's lives. She would pick them up from school every day while Rachel's mother worked.

Sometimes Rachel would miss Grandma Ann while at school and would pretend to be sick. From the school office, she would call her grandmother, who would pretend to believe Rachel was sick and would take her to Eat-a-Burger for lunch. They would talk and laugh together like girlfriends, then go shopping. These occasions were a kind of therapy for both of them.

Rachel's mother eventually remarried but continued to be away from home during her long workdays. The stepfather, a well-meaning but aloof man, didn't know much about befriending children. Rachel felt lonely at home.

During this period, she desperately wanted to be Daddy's little girl. She spent as much time as she could with her biological father, who on the right occasion could be just as charming as he could be violent. He owned a bar as a sideline, and that's where she would often go to visit him. She gratefully accepted whatever scraps of affection he gave her in their times together, trying to impress him with her tales of success on the soccer field or volleyball court at school. Gradually, though, she came to realize that he drank too much and was using illegal drugs. The substance abuse was hurting his relationships as well as his performance at his corporate day job. Rachel grew to be disillusioned about her daddy and no longer asked to see him so often.

Her older brother, meanwhile, reacted to his difficult upbringing by turning to drugs while still a teenager. Paulie climbed quickly up the ladder of illegal drugs and was a heroin addict before he graduated from high school. Very likely, he had inherited his father's genetic vulnerability to addiction. The emotional trauma in his life caused this disease to express itself when he was exposed to addictive substances through friends at school. By taking drugs, Paulie was trying to feel normal. It was his way of numbing emotional pain and receiving the love chemical, dopamine, from his drugs, since he wasn't getting love the normal way within his family.

But the drugs took more than they gave. After school one day, Rachel discovered her brother slumped over and unconscious in his room, his skin puffy and his lips blue. He had overdosed. Horrified, she called an ambulance. Paulie recovered, but he quickly went back to taking drugs. He barely managed to graduate from high school and never went to college. He went from job to job, from rehab to rehab, growing sickly and aged before his time. His reputation as a user and a loser solidified about him.

Seeing what substance abuse was doing to her father and especially her brother, Rachel developed an early determination to avoid mood-altering substances. Even when she began having headaches as a young teenager, she refused the "migraine cocktail" (opioid plus anti-nausea medicine) that her doctors offered her. "I didn't want to feel out of control," Rachel explained to me later. "It seemed better to just deal with the pain on my own and move on."

Rachel's early experiences with pain seemed manageable to her. But having grown up with poor models, examples of secretiveness, and a shredded support system, she would be vulnerable when tougher experiences came along. However sincere her resolution to avoid drugs may have been, her genetic heritage put her at great risk of becoming enmeshed in the same kind of addictive behaviors her father and brother had manifested.

This young woman wasn't prepared for the complications that pain—and pain treatment gone awry—would present in her life anymore than, as an eight-year-old, she had been prepared for the sight of a small white casket.

From Use to Misuse

One evening, when Rachel was a junior in high school, she was at a party with friends when pain erupted in her lower abdomen. At first she tried to ignore it and acted like she was still having a good time. But when the pain became unbearable, she called her stepfather to pick her up. Rachel threw up in the car, and her stepfather drove her straight to Primary Children's Medical Center. Before she was wheeled into the OR to have her appendix removed, a nurse gave her a shot of morphine. This was her first experience with opioids. As she watched the lights spin in front of her eyes while she was taken down the corridor on a gurney, she was scared by the effect.

When Rachel was still experiencing pain weeks after the appendectomy, a doctor investigated and discovered that she had an ovarian cyst—a painful and long-lasting, though not necessarily dangerous, condition. So her doctor began to prescribe Lortab for her whenever she requested it. And once she had accepted opioids for this condition, it became easier to agree to opioids for her migraines as well. Both conditions would continue to be sources of pain for her for a long time, the headaches more severe than the pelvic pain, and both would give her reasons for taking opioids. In this way a girl who had wanted to stay off drugs because of what they had done to her brother found herself taking opioids regularly.

A few years passed. Rachel worked as a waitress and took classes at Salt Lake Community College. She moved in with a boyfriend named Billy who had a wild streak, partying hard and sometimes abusing her when he was drunk. Rachel became pregnant and gave birth prematurely to a son who died. Quickly—without having time to fully grieve her loss—she became pregnant again. This time she gave birth to a healthy daughter, Amy, in 2006. Almost simultaneously, Billy was hauled off to jail for a six-month sentence on drug charges.

Rachel found herself at home alone with her baby daughter a lot during this time. She loved Amy but didn't enjoy the constant childcare. She was bored and tired and felt cooped up. She missed her boyfriend and wondered if their relationship had a future. She wanted to get back to school, back to work, back to seeing her friends. Then her mother informed her that Grandma Ann was sick; would Rachel take care of her?

Over the years, Grandma Ann had continued to be Rachel's closest confidante. Rachel was also still close with her brother, Paulie, but Grandma Ann was Rachel's best friend. So it was especially painful for Rachel to see her grandmother declining in health. The end would not come for a while, but it was now in sight. Rachel stepped in to take Grandma Ann to doctors' appointments and would stop by her home to make sure she was taking her medicines and eating well. Although Rachel was glad to be able to help, being the caregiver for an elderly person at the same time she was raising a baby elevated her stress. The worst were the days when she had debilitating headaches, which seemed to be coming on more frequently at this time.

This was the tipping point in her relationship to prescription pain medications.

Whenever she ran out of the Lortab prescribed by her gynecologist or her headache specialist, she began to feel sick. Her body had become physically dependent on the medication, and when she began going off it, she experienced early withdrawal symptoms. This was not indicative of addiction at this time but rather was a normal sign that her body had come to expect the medication. Stopping her Lortab could have been handled medically without her experiencing withdrawal, if Rachel had sought the help of a doctor experienced in this area—but she didn't. She kept the problem to herself and was trapped in her physical dependence on opioids.

In Rachel's case, because she had migraine headaches, the withdrawal situation was even more complicated than usual. Migraines cause pain, nausea, and vomiting. Withdrawal also causes pain, nausea, and vomiting. She could not always tell if she was experiencing symptoms from her migraines or if they were due to low blood levels of Lortab. Drug withdrawal could even induce a migraine. So she was doubly motivated to keep taking opioids. When the pain resurged and the withdrawal symptoms came on, Rachel became almost frantic to avoid the sick feeling.

This common reaction is often confused with addiction. It is not addiction. It is physical dependence. She was not craving a high or the rewarding properties of the opioid, at least not yet. Nevertheless, the cycle of withdrawal and nonwithdrawal she was experiencing was contributing to her behaviors that would eventually lead to harm.

But there was another reason why Rachel wanted to increase her intake of the opioids. Never having had an easy life, now she was going through an especially tough time with her emotions, feeling depressed, bored, anxious, aimless, resentful, and sad. She discovered that when she was on the opioids, these negative feelings lifted. The conclusion was easy, not even requiring conscious thought: keep taking the opioids. It was not so much that she was trying to feel euphoric; she was just trying to not feel miserable about the problems in her life. And for a while it worked. The drugs suppressed emotional distress at the same time they erased withdrawal symptoms, seemingly cutting the knot of what bound her. Every time she was feeling extra stress, she relied on the painkiller.

It is not uncommon for people in pain to take the step from using their opioid medications for the pain to using these medications for emotional distress. Pain causes stress; stress enhances pain—it's a vicious cycle from which there is no easy exit. Consequently, many people make the transition from using opioids for a legitimate medical purpose to relying on them for an emotional escape. According to some estimates, this happens in 20 to 30 percent of people prescribed an opioid.[2] Some of these individuals will progress to the disease of addiction.

Rachel was among those people who learned that opioids can be destructive and may prevent them from having the life they want. Like her father and brother, she had a genetic predisposition to addiction. Rachel's stress (caused by two types of physical pain as well as many other problems in her life), combined with exposure to the opioids prescribed to her, was more than enough to put her in the drugs' bondage. What had seemed like a solution actually secured her more firmly in a web of suffering than before. She was no longer just physically dependent; the compulsive use despite harm tipped her into addiction.

I find that there is widespread and woeful ignorance about addiction in our society. Becoming addicted is not a willful error committed by "losers." Medical science is clearly showing that addiction is a disease, one that some people are vulnerable to with the very first exposure of a substance. It is not a character defect. It is about our biology as humans. Some people develop diabetes and others develop depression; still others develop addiction. It is not a sin to develop a disease, any disease—even addiction. And addiction doesn't come in one size or color. The disease has a spectrum of severity, though all of its degrees are destructive.

No one is destined to be addicted, although a small percent are highly vulnerable. Some people, in fact, are lucky enough to be spared the addiction genes. But most of us, given a stressful or painful situation, could find ourselves looking to medications for relief. This is especially true if we don't have a caring, loving community around us.

Rachel didn't have that support at the critical point when she was slipping into addiction. Mom too busy, dad intoxicated, boyfriend incarcerated, grandmother dying—no one stepped in to help. But when the stress built up in her life, the opioids were there. She began to rely upon them more and more.

One occasion that inspired stress-induced drug taking was her wedding in 2008. By that time, Billy was out of jail and clean, their relationship was looking up, they were parenting a child together, and they had decided to get married. Like any bride, Rachel wanted her wedding day to be special. But her family's dysfunction continued to haunt her. Some family members weren't getting along with each other, and Rachel was trying to act as a mediator. Stronger-willed persons in the family were trying to press their ideas about the wedding on the compliant Rachel. She felt pulled in many directions. With all the tension, she was worried that she wouldn't get through the wedding without some chemical assistance.

So, in the midst of the wedding prep chaos, Rachel made a decision. She told me later, "I called my gynecologist and told her I had bad cramps and asked for a prescription. But it was a lie. I wanted to have them for the wedding. I wanted relief from all the stress." She got the prescription. This was another step toward danger: it was the first time she told a complete falsehood to get drugs.

Then the day of the wedding came, and it was worse than Rachel had even imagined.

To begin with, it was one of the hottest days of the year, and the air conditioner at the chapel broke. The guests sweated in their suits and dresses as the temperature inside rose to one hundred degrees.

Later, at the reception, one of the guests became drunk and began conveying some highly inappropriate sexual information to young children, enraging the parents when they found out. This same guest also started breaking things in the hotel and taking off his clothes. Rachel herself, still wearing her wedding gown, lost her temper and kicked him down the hallway for ruining her special day. A shouting match broke out. Another wedding party stared at the scene in horror. The police arrived and cuffed the drunken man. They nearly took Billy in for public intoxication as well, but let him off with a warning when they learned he was the groom.

Rachel had been hoping for one day in her life to be perfect. It was anything but. She went to her room and popped another pill.

The pattern was firmly established now.

And it would get worse before it got better.

Buyer

Some weeks after her wedding, Rachel maneuvered her maroon Civic into a parking place at Coachmans Pancake House on State Street. In the back, strapped into a car seat, was two-year-old Amy. Next to Rachel in the front was her brother, Paulie. Rachel was nervous.

She had been out at a party the night before and had realized that being on her pain medication was making the party more fun for her. She also knew that she was about to run out of the pills and that her next doctor's appointment was days away. In the meantime she couldn't use the cramps excuse again. She was worried about how she would feel, physically and emotionally, if she had to go off the pills for a while. Her brother, when she told him all this, had said, "Don't worry. I know somebody you can get those from."

So now they were parked a few spaces from a gray car where a large woman sat in the driver's seat. "What if somebody sees us?" Rachel asked her brother. She had never felt more like a criminal.

"Don't worry," Paulie told her. "Nobody's watching us. Relax, all right?"

With a guilty glance at her daughter, Rachel handed over some money, and Paulie took it to the gray sedan where the woman waited.

This woman's name was Maureen. Rachel didn't meet her that day in the pancake house parking lot, but she would get to know Maureen well in the months and years ahead as she continued to illegally buy drugs from her. Since Rachel's doctors would not prescribe Lortab in the amounts Rachel wanted, she would get extra supplies from Maureen for $8 or $10 a pill. For months, Paulie made the buys for Rachel and for himself, using money Rachel provided. Then, when Paulie began a stint in jail, Rachel started buying the drugs directly from Maureen at Maureen's home.

Rachel never knew exactly how Maureen came into possession of so much Lortab. Maureen was sick—Rachel could tell that just by looking at her. She apparently went to more than one doctor to get pain prescriptions, which she would then fill at more than one pharmacy. Whatever she didn't use herself, she would sell to others. It was a side business for her. She was a travel agent by profession, at least until her health deteriorated and she lost her job. She was supporting herself through being the kind of drug diverter whom doctors do their best to look out for but aren't always able to spot. Today, drug monitoring programs help to identify doctor shoppers like Maureen, making it harder to obtain prescriptions from physicians, but at that time Maureen was able to manipulate the system to her advantage.

Maureen didn't look anything like what Rachel thought a drug dealer would look like. She was in her late fifties, overweight, with thinning hair. Above her lip was a prominent mole with hair protruding from its center. She lived in a tiny, filthy apartment that she shared with her daughter, her daughter's boyfriend, and several cats. She smoked incessantly. Even when she got to the point where she had to wear an oxygen mask at home, she would slide the mask out of the way to take a drag from her cigarette.

This unlikely drug dealer would sit on the edge of an unmade bed and count Rachel's money. Rachel would watch, fascinated by Maureen's yellow fingernails and the tremendous extension of ash that somehow never fell from the tip of her cigarette.

Sometimes, while waiting, Rachel would examine the photos on the apartment wall showing Maureen as she had been as a young woman. Maureen, it turned out to Rachel's surprise, had once been a beauty. Back then, she had a slim waist, no mole, and an abundance of allure. In one picture, she was a beauty pageant winner wearing a bathing suit and crown.

From this beginning, the Maureen of the illegal pill trade had somehow emerged in the decades gone by.

With Maureen's help, Rachel was now taking fifteen Lortabs per day on average. This was a quantity much higher than she needed to control her migraine and pelvic pain. It was, in fact, a dangerous amount. Since Lortab contains acetaminophen, she was fortunate that she didn't suffer acute liver failure. But even if she had fully understood the risks she was taking, I don't know that it would have stopped her. She was desperate to hold off the distress of her life's disappointments and to keep the withdrawal sickness to a minimum.

She had a nagging sense of shame and guilt for what she was doing, and she also feared that the pills would make her a bad mom, but repeatedly she shoved all that away from her consciousness. She would deal with that later, she thought. For now, the drugs seemed to offer an answer.

I believe Rachel would never have arrived at this place if she had been receiving the personal and professional support she needed. Her community had shrunk. She was afraid to admit to the people closest to her—her husband, mother, father, grandmother, and friends—what was going on in her life. Would they understand? Would they judge her and reject her? She also feared going for help to the medical community. Her doctors were, in part, her drug suppliers; what if they cut off the flow? What if they reported her to the authorities and she went to jail, leaving her young daughter in the care of a father who had no desire to be a full-time dad?

Incredibly, the only person in her life who knew she was addicted to pills and buying them illegally was her brother. She hid the pills and took them in private. If her husband or parents asked her to account for an absence, she would say she'd been at a counseling appointment. They believed her, or pretended to—it was easier that way.

Rachel was secretive for many reasons, not least because she didn't want to hurt others. She had seen how Paulie's never-ending drug travails had cost everyone in the family. She didn't want to do the same to her loved ones.

One time Rachel was sick when the pills ran out. She was pale and sweating and kept running to the bathroom to throw up. "Can I help you?" asked her mom, concerned.

To her mother, Rachel blamed her doctor for prescribing too many pills and said she was trying to get off them. She thought for a moment of confessing to her mom about the extra supplies she was getting from Maureen, but she quickly decided against it. She later told me about the event, "I think deep down Mom knew what was going on. But she didn't want to know, not really. And I didn't want to dirty the waters of our relationship."

Sadly, I have seen the same mistake repeated many times. Silence worsens a drug use problem when families communicate poorly.

So the family entered into a compact of willful ignorance. It left Rachel alone and without support. Who knows how much more quickly she might have obtained professional help if she'd sought and received the encouragement and advice she needed?

The fear of admitting a problem, particularly a drug problem, has major social and personal implications. And the causes of this fear need to be owned by the whole community, not just the person who abuses drugs. I am certainly not condoning Rachel's drug abuse. On the contrary. She made choices, and they led to the illness of addiction, which was harmful to her and to her family. But how a community responds to this type of illness is critical to the outcome. Our response can be punitive or supportive. Supportiveness is necessary for healing.

Light of Hope

Rachel was all alone, caught in the web that pain and her own poor choices had woven. But then, in the month of June 2011, two epiphanies appeared in her life that caused her to take positive action to extricate herself.

Early that month, she dropped her then-five-year-old daughter off at a day camp. Amy had begged and cried to be able to stay with Mommy that day, and Rachel wished she could spend the day with Amy too, but she had run out of pills once again and knew she faced a day of dealing with withdrawal sickness and trying to get hold of Maureen for another supply. She couldn't manage a five-year-old on this particular day.

After dropping Amy off with the camp leaders, Rachel got back into her car at the edge of the parking lot. Instead of turning on the ignition and heading for home, she just sat there for a while and stared at the slatted wooden fence in front of her. Although Rachel was feeling anything but beautiful inside, the weather on this summer day *was* beautiful, with the early light streaming through the gaps between the fence boards. As if mesmerized, Rachel stared at the streamers of golden light and told herself gloomily, *This summer will never come again. Every day I don't spend with Amy is a day I'll never get back. I'm wasting my life because of the damned pills.*

Then, like a flywheel, the determined core within her spirit began to spin, throwing off more-hopeful thoughts. *No, I'm going to get control of this, and soon,* she told herself. *Next summer, Amy and I will have fun together. I won't be sick anymore. We'll go to the swimming pool and play together all day. I'll be a good mom and a good wife.* There was light, and a better life, on the other side of her present circumstances.

But despite her brave promises to herself, she mistrusted whether she would actually fulfill them.

The second epiphany was heralded a few days later when the phone rang. It was Grandma Ann.

This beloved grandmother was quite old by this point and living in a rehab center because she was suffering from a chronic infection that would clear up whenever the doctors put her on antibiotics and then return whenever she got to the end of the course of treatment. She was in a lot of pain. When Rachel had visited her recently, Grandma Ann had been bedridden. But on the phone Grandma Ann's voice was bright and she said, "Rachel, I have a surprise for you! Come over and see me."

Rachel went to the rehab center and found her grandmother in the physical therapy room. She was amazed to see her grandmother wearing a dress colored bright pink, bright green, and bright purple. Rachel had seen this dress in her grandmother's closet, but she had never seen Grandma Ann wear it, or anything like it, before. Even more amazing was that Grandma Ann, who had not walked in two weeks, was on her feet.

"Watch this!" the grandmother said with pride in her voice. She started walking on her own steam, a therapist at her elbow.

Grandma Ann looked up and counted ceiling tiles to measure her progress across the floor. One ceiling tile, two tiles, three... She was grimacing as she went, but she kept going. "Eighteen tiles!" she said at last. "I wanted you to be the first one to see, Rachel."

She went on: "I'm going to get better and get out of here. You'll see. It's going to be a good summer for both of us."

Rachel had tears in her eyes. She was thinking, *Here's Grandma Ann. She's ninety and she's been through so much in her life. But she's making herself walk even though she's in a massive amount of pain. And me? I'm about to turn thirty, and all I'm doing is trying to numb my pain. What is the rest of my life going to be like?*

A feeling like a wave of hot air ran through her. She was not a particularly religious young woman, but she remembered the feeling of community surrounding her that she'd had from her Catholic congregation when she was a child and her sister, Veronica, had died. Now her grandmother was there for her one last time when she really needed it. In some way, this was a sacred moment.

The memory of the glow around Sister Margaret's face so many years ago.

The vision of sunshine streaming through the fence slats at the day camp.

Now Grandma Ann's brightly colored dress and lit-up face.

It all was part of one thing: a promise, a call, a light of hope.

People with addiction often have a turnaround point in their lives when addiction's downward spiral ends and the healing begins. It looks different from person to person. They may call it "hitting rock bottom," "getting a wake-up call," or something else. For Rachel, it came as a combination of events that convinced her there must be *some* way to get out of her self-destructive behaviors and manage her pain in a healthy way.

Despite Grandma Ann's brief moment of progress, she deteriorated over the next week and died. Rachel, though, remained determined to turn her life around. She was ready to extricate herself from the web that bound her.

"We All Need Somebody"

Rachel wondered how to get off the prescription pill merry-go-round.

Her first information about how to get treatment for her addiction, oddly, came from the same person who got her started buying drugs illegally—her substance-addicted brother, Paulie. She told him about her desire to get clean, and he told her about methadone. "It's this stuff that people take if they don't have their drugs," he said. He stole some methadone pills from a friend's supply and gave them to Rachel to try. When she took them, she was thrilled to find that she was able to function normally without the other medications she had been abusing. But then Paulie's friend's refill prescription for methadone ran out temporarily, and Rachel didn't know what to do. She started alternating hydrocodone that she obtained from Maureen with methadone when Paulie could get it from his friend's medicine cabinet.

This was not the best or safest way to get off drugs, and Rachel knew it. On her lunch hours, she would go to a sandwich shop, open up her laptop, and eat lunch while watching YouTube videos about how to wean yourself off pain medicine. She considered selling her possessions to come up with the $6,000 that one advertisement said it would cost to go to Las Vegas and undergo a rapid detox. Wisely, she decided against that. But then she did try a program that sold dietary supplements touted to relieve drug addiction naturally. She found that the supplements did her no good.

Finally Rachel enrolled at an outpatient drug rehab center that her brother told her about. The program helped her in some ways. But it was expensive. And it was inconvenient, with counseling appointments scheduled for 5:00 a.m. Most significantly, she perceived that the staff were critical and judgmental of her. She still wasn't getting the support she needed to make the big change in her life that she craved. She had no community.

So she went back to the Internet, and this time, instead of learning about rapid detox or home remedies, she discovered me. I was listed on the Substance Abuse & Mental Health Service Administration website as a physician certified for buprenorphine treatment of addiction. She made an appointment to come in to Lifetree Clinic in late 2011.

That's when I first met Rachel. I began prescribing a form of buprenorphine called Suboxone, a synthetic opioid used to back people down from their opioid addiction. Rachel also began meeting with Debra Hobbins, a nurse practitioner at my clinic. Debra offered a powerful sense of caring, connection, and listening for Rachel. Debra knew what Rachel needed to begin healing because she had lost her son to heroin overdose many years earlier. With understanding and compassion, Debra gave her what Sister Margaret did and what Grandma Ann did—nonjudgmental, unconditional love.

"Something happened in the universe when I met Debra," Rachel told me. "My reaction was, 'Oh! I feel like this is the first person in a long time who really accepted me.' I felt like we could work on this problem together."

The first pieces of a support system for Rachel had finally come together, and she instinctively felt that this was a major turning point in her healing. The Suboxone, combined with the care and love she was feeling from Debra, meant that Rachel could finally stop taking the other opioids, legally or illegally procured. She said goodbye to Maureen for the last time.

But of course the problem that had started it all was still there: her pain. Her pelvic pain had at last gone away, but she was still having headaches, and she knew she should expect to have them for the rest of her life. So she still needed to figure out how to deal with the pain. She was like many people in pain who have developed an addiction—she didn't want to live with the pain, but opioids were too risky as a therapy for her. It was a precarious spot.

I have retired, so am no longer serving as Rachel's physician, but I know what her current medical team is thinking. It's not a simple decision to taper Rachel off the Suboxone until she's entirely opioid free. That may be possible or it may not be. For one thing, when new stressors crop up in her life, then in the absence of Suboxone, she might develop a craving for drugs again and suffer an addiction relapse. In addition, the Suboxone is helping to manage her pain. She might always need it for that reason.

Many people with significant pain feel they need to be on an analgesic for the rest of their lives. They may not always need something as strong as an opioid, but then again, there aren't always effective alternatives. Some people are on opioids for decades after developing severe chronic pain. This is most likely to occur in middle-aged or elderly people who can't tolerate other medications or who have pain so severe that nothing but opioids seem to help. Someday, I believe, effective non-habit-forming treatments will be developed for pain. For now, however, some people still express a need for analgesics as strong as an opioid. It is important that we treat the pain but also prevent addiction, if possible, by understanding the vulnerabilities and mitigating them, while always seeking alternative methods to treat pain.

Meanwhile, a strong support system can positively impact the pain and the social stressors that play on one another. Rachel's ongoing relationship with Debra, the nurse practitioner, has been a part of this system for her. But Rachel also needs to develop more supportive relationships in her personal life. She is beginning to see the truth of this.

"When I grew up, I thought I was different from others," Rachel said, "because I watched my little sister die, and my parents got divorced, and there was the fighting and my brother's heroin. I always hated the kind of attention I got. But I've learned everybody goes through pain and everybody has their struggles. We all need somebody to hug us and bring us closer when we are in trouble. We all need somebody—somebody like a grandmother."

Another Kind of Web

Rachel's experience illustrates something I've learned in my years as a pain doctor. Pain experience is more than the physiology of pain; it is the sum of life's experience plus the physiology. Rachel is an example of a person whose totality of pain was both physical and emotional. Sometimes she couldn't tell which type she was more interested in medicating. Because of her genetic vulnerability (established by the history of drug and alcohol abuse in her family), she treated both kinds of pain with the cocktails of drugs she was able to lay her hands on. As her life slowly became incarcerated by addiction, these drugs were her warden.

If we want pain treatments to help and not hurt someone who is suffering, then we've got to look at the pain situation in relation to everything going on in that person's life: genetic vulnerabilities to addiction, family dynamics, and much more. A pain condition affects everything a person is, and everything a person is affects her pain. When we treat pain only as a symptom of a physical insult, our treatments may be ineffective. In fact, failing to address all of the contributions to the expression of pain can unwittingly lead to a downward spiral of a person's physical and emotional health.

People who are in pain often feel themselves caught in a web of pain, stress, grief, loss, depression, loneliness, and possibly addiction. They begin to heal when they can tear apart that web and replace it with another system made up of quality medical treatment, other appropriate therapies, and especially love, acceptance, and encouragement. They can begin to feel, not trapped in a web of suffering, but supported in a new network of caring.

CHAPTER 4

———— ⁄⁄⁄⁄⁄⁄ ————

Friendly Fire

Cultural attitudes toward pain too often make a pain experience worse than it has to be.

WHEN I WAS A boy growing up on our family farm in Nebraska, I would notice how healthy livestock would segregate themselves from the sick ones. Ever since then, I've noticed the similar phenomenon of healthy people distancing themselves from others who appear different, disabled, or diseased. It's happened to people with leprosy. It's happened to people with cancer. It's happened to people with HIV/AIDS. It's happening still to people living with pain.

Sociologist Erving Goffman said that someone who has been stigmatized has been "reduced in our minds from a whole and usual person to a tainted, discounted one."[1] Rejection, suspicion, prejudice, diminishment, doubt, judgment, isolation—these are all reactions that people with pain encounter regularly in others. To pursue healing, they have to learn to deal with the stigma unfairly placed upon them and to hold their heads up high. For those of us who are hoping to help others heal from pain, we need to first root out the vestiges of prejudice against pain that may linger inside us, then go on to counteract society's stigma against pain with the truth about this health condition.

Unfair cultural attitudes toward pain show up in all parts of society. They seem to be especially pronounced in one environment that values proving how tough you are: the military. The story of a young man named Jason Bing shows how biases against admitting pain and seeking certain types of medical care can prolong suffering—and even call into question whether life is worth living.

Learning the Ropes

In the fall of 2001, starting his sophomore year at Brigham Young University, Jason Bing was a medium tall and athletically built young man with black hair, dark eyes, and an intent, self-controlled manner about him.[2] When he watched the 9/11 devastation unfold on a television in his dorm, he was as stunned as everyone else. Fired with patriotic feelings that didn't seem at all out of place in the mood of the time, he was ready to enlist in the U.S. Army the next day. His family, however, persuaded him to finish his year at BYU before signing up. They may have thought this would give him time to change his mind, but if so, they were mistaken. He completed his school year, spent one last carefree summer as a civilian back home in Birmingham, Alabama, and then in early August took a bus ride across the border to Georgia's Fort Benning for basic training.

Jason had been assigned to the combat arm of infantry school— the toughest training the Army dished out. The goal of basic training at Benning was to push the recruits to their limits and teach them unhesitating obedience to their superiors at the same time that it instilled the fundamental skills of foot soldiering in them. But it did more than that—it also introduced them to a military culture that seemed to regard pain as good and complaints about pain as a sign of weakness.

Jason's drill sergeant was harder on recruits even than most drill sergeants are. He wasn't just tough; he was cruel. "I'm going to bring the pain, you bitches," he promised Jason and the other men who fell into his charge that steamy August of 2002. And he proceeded to make good on his promise.

In the second week of training, Jason was in the middle of an obstacle course, pulling himself hand over hand along a rope suspended above the ground, when he lost his grip, fell twenty feet, and landed on his right foot. At the moment of impact he heard a loud pop and felt excruciating pain in his ankle. Rolling on the ground and gritting his teeth, he could feel the ankle swelling up. He reached for his boot to remove it...and then hesitated because he realized that if he took off his boot it would be a long time before he would be able to put it back on.

Just then the drill sergeant came over to him and said, "You've got two options, Private. You can leave your boot on and do what you've got to do. Or you can go to the infirmary. If you do that, you're probably going to be there for several days and you're going to have to start over. You want to go on MPH?"

Drill instructors are required by Army regulations to let injured soldiers receive medical care if they ask for it, so this man was technically doing what he had to do. But having too many of their recruits go to the infirmary looked bad on drill sergeants' evaluations, and therefore many of them used intimidation and embarrassment to discourage recruits from seeking medical help. "MPH"—Fort Benning parlance for a sick call—is short for "My pussy hurts."

During one of the hundred-degree-plus Georgia days Jason had already experienced, he had seen a fellow recruit nearly die from heat stroke when they were ordered to spend hours crawling up a hill with a hundred pounds of gear on their backs and no water to drink, walk back down, then crawl up again. The other recruit had pushed himself until he passed out. That's how much some of the men were willing to put up with to avoid being labeled as an MPH malingerer.

But Jason wasn't so much concerned about looking weak and womanish; what discouraged him from going to the infirmary most was the prospect of being "recycled." Any recruit who missed two days of basic training in a row for any reason would be held over until the next course of training started and would have to go through it all again. For Jason, that would mean waiting around at the base for three months with nothing to do and nowhere to go and would delay his return to school, forcing him to reapply to BYU and face the possibility of losing his scholarship. More than that, he knew that being recycled would be a blemish on his military record that would never go away. If he were ever to be commissioned an officer, as was his dream, that blemish would count against him every time he was up for a good assignment or a promotion. Somebody else who was not a basic training holdover would get advancement ahead of him.

All these calculations ran through Jason's mind in seconds after his drill sergeant laid out the alternatives. Lying there, Jason could not feel his toes. His swollen ankle was pressing painfully against his boot. But he forced himself to stand up and limp back to the start of the obstacle course to begin it all over again.

Once Jason made it through the afternoon's training, he thought the worst was over. It wasn't.

Someone in the company had done something that the sergeant didn't like, and so the drill instructor decided to use a particularly vicious form of punishment for the whole group. That evening he took them to the bay—the big open room where sixty of them slept on bunk beds—and said, "Put on your wet weather gear. We're going to do over-unders."

New to the Army, the recruits didn't yet know what over-unders were. But they sensed it couldn't be good. Quickly, they put on their rain-resisting camo pants and matching jacket with hood, cinching these garments tight against their bodies.

"Gas masks too," the drill sergeant said.

With their gas masks covering their faces, the men were almost completely encased within their gear. It was incredibly stifling. The room had no fans and the thermometer registered over a hundred degrees. Who knows how hot it got inside the wet weather gear?

Then the sergeant gave them their instructions. This particular form of punishment was called over-unders because the recruits had to lie down on the floor and crawl to the nearest bunk with their chest to the ground, then crawl over the bunk and back down to the floor, continuing to the next bunk, crawling under that one instead of over it. The sixty recruits were like a circle of snakes slithering under and over the obstacles in an unending circle. Soon the mattresses all slid to the floor, leaving bare metal bed frames for the men to scrape themselves over. Jason had to do all of this with a severely strained ankle. The punishment went on for three hours, until the sergeant judged that the company had paid for the offender's infraction.

Although the drill sergeants called this maneuver "over-unders," the recruits called it "rain man." When the men in Jason's group were finally allowed to quit the punishment and open their wet weather gear, sweat poured out. The floor of the bay was as wet as if a rain shower had passed through. Jason couldn't see across the room because of the fog that was hanging in the air from the men's perspiration.

The first sergeant came in and bawled Jason's drill sergeant out for doing something so dangerous to the men. But the drill sergeant continued to mistreat the men when he had them away from his superiors' eyes. Jason's ankle—evidently strained but not broken—hurt for another week or so, and during that time he forced himself to run and do everything else asked of him despite the pain.

For Jason, the day of the fall from the rope and the "rain man" punishment set the tone for what dealing with an injury in the military is like. Suck it up. Hide it. Deal with it on your own. It was this attitude that was destined to get him in trouble with pain treatment.

Enter Chronic Pain, Enter Opioids

Three years passed. Jason completed basic training without the disgrace of being recycled, was promoted to private first class and then specialist, went back to BYU and finished his degree, and upon graduation was commissioned as a second lieutenant. It was a proud day for him when he slipped a silver dollar into his pocket so that—according to an obscure Army custom—he could give it to the first soldier who saluted him as lieutenant and then buy the soldier a drink.

Assigned next to the military intelligence branch of the U.S. Army, he reported to Fort Huachuca in Arizona for the Officer Basic Course. That's where, before dawn one day in May of 2005, he was doing grass drills during group physical training. Running in the dark, he failed to notice a hole in the ground where he was running, and the twisting fall that resulted hurt his lower back. He had a knot on his spine and a lumbar disc protrusion. It was very painful, but three years earlier he had learned a lesson in basic training about dealing with pain, so he decided to keep his mouth shut and hope the problem would fix itself.

This time, though, the pain got worse instead of better, and so after a few days Jason reluctantly reported to the base clinic. He was put on bed rest and then given physical therapy to try to relieve the pain. When that wasn't enough, his doctors began prescribing muscle relaxants and a series of opioids, including hydrocodone, oxycodone, and fentanyl.

Up to this point in his life, Jason had scrupulously "just said no" to the kinds of illegal drugs used by other young people and had tried to avoid taking prescription or over-the-counter medicines when he could. By Army standards, he wasn't even much of a drinker. But now he realized that he had to take the medicines for his back pain. He didn't feel quite like himself while taking the opioids, but they did make the pain more manageable, enabling him to get through painful physical therapy exercises and go back to work. Most of all, he didn't want anything standing in the way of his career.

His pain stabilized, Jason was cleared to return to duty. He graduated from his officer course and was promoted to first lieutenant. He was working the way up the ladder of responsibility in the Army, just as he had hoped to. He looked forward to leading his own company.

The next year he was sent on assignment to Iraq.

The TS in PTSD

In Iraq, the newly made first lieutenant commanded a unit in charge of refueling helicopters and other Army vehicles. He was stationed part of the time in Mosul, a city in northern Iraq, and part of the time in Abu Ghraib, the Baghdad suburb made infamous a couple of years earlier by military personnel who abused their prisoners. He continued using lower-dose opioids during his service there, especially when the heavy packs he had to carry made his spinal pain worse, but he took as few pills as he could bear, since he didn't want the drugs impairing his reactions. He needed to be at his best.

The prospect of serving his country in the Middle East was what had motivated Bing to join the Army in the first place, but the reality of the place proved more traumatic than he could ever have anticipated.

The worst were the tense motor convoys between the Baghdad area and other outposts of the U.S. Army. Everyone knew America's opponents in Iraq were using 155mm howitzer shells, improvised explosive devices (IEDs), and rocket-propelled grenades (RPGs) to ambush convoys. Any trip outside the Green Zone was a trip into danger, a trip you might never come back from in one piece. Inside their vehicles, the troops held their weapons at the ready and remained on alert for anything on the road or in the surrounding area that looked suspicious.

Bing was present in one convoy through "RPG Alley"—the most dangerous area south of Baghdad—when the forward Stryker armored vehicle tripped a roadside bomb and was flipped on its side by the explosion, throwing out one of its passengers. From where he crouched inside his Humvee, Bing could not see well...but he could hear and he could smell. The man thrown from the vehicle was on fire and was screaming in agony. "I'm burning! I'm burning! Somebody shoot me!" he shouted to his comrades as the fire ate his flesh. "Kill me! Kill me! Please!" Bing remembers thinking this was nothing like in the movies. It was so much more awful. The worst thing for him was that he could not get out of his Humvee and go to the injured soldier, because, like everyone else in the column, he was pinned down by small arms fire. He was forced to listen to the man's screams and to the crackling of the flames that continued to consume his body after he died.

Jason survived that hellish trip through the "Alley." Afterward, though, he couldn't get the sound of the screaming nor the smell of burning flesh out of his mind. During the day, he could press the memories down so that nobody could tell he was distracted, but at night in his bunk they resurfaced in the form of nightmares.

He decided that he wasn't going to let happen to him what had happened to that man who died alone and in agony by the roadside. He realized that, since he always sat on the passenger side of a Humvee during a convoy, it was likely that an IED explosion would strike him on his right side. So the right-handed lieutenant went to the firing range and practiced firing his pistol with his left hand. He was determined that, if he were badly injured in an ambush, rather than burning in the wreckage of his vehicle or being captured by the enemy, he would shoot himself in the head with his left hand. Others sometimes asked him why he kept flexing his left fingers. He made some excuse to avoid telling them the truth—the truth that he was obsessively rehearsing in his mind the suicide that would let him escape his final pain.

Jason was never personally involved in another ambush and never had to use his left-handed trigger skills. But one other incident, even worse than the IED explosion, would be seared into his memory. It was the incident he had the most trouble recounting to me.

U.S. military convoys in Iraq had orders not to stop for anything until they got to their destination. Any distraction or temptation to halt progress could be a means for the enemy to spring an ambush. One day Jason was in the second vehicle in the file while threading through a narrow street in Mosul. Up ahead he saw a little girl of perhaps five or six walking down the street toward the line of vehicles. She was slight and dark eyed, wearing a green cloak and a lighter hijab veil covering her hair and wrapping around her neck. She seemed to be lost and confused, as if she were looking for somebody. Then she froze when she saw the oncoming vehicles. Jason's mind, meanwhile, started racing: The road was just wide enough so that, if she flattened herself against one wall, she could probably stay safe while the convoy passed. But would she be able to? She was so young and all alone. Maybe the driver up ahead would disobey orders and stop long enough to help the little girl stand aside. But then it was possible that she was, cruelly, being used for that very purpose by men who might be hiding behind walls or on rooftops with rifles and grenade launchers.

The lead vehicle didn't stop or even slow down.

Jason should have turned his eyes aside, but he didn't. He told me later it looked as if the little girl exploded in a mist of red spray.

Home Front

I don't know what emotional repercussions the driver of the vehicle who struck the little girl later had to endure. I do know that following this incident Jason Bing began exhibiting classic symptoms of post-traumatic stress disorder (PTSD). After coming home—first to an army reserve base in Provo, Utah, and then to Fort Carson, near Colorado Springs, Colorado—he suffered raging insomnia, sometimes going days without sleep. When he did get some sleep, his rest would be punctuated with nightmares and he would wake up sweating and feeling as if he had run a marathon in his sleep. He didn't like it whenever someone was standing behind him. He felt claustrophobic whenever he was inside an enclosed space. Sudden noises would startle him. In public places, such as shopping malls, he had panic attacks. He chewed his fingernails until his fingertips were so raw that he couldn't touch anything. He didn't like to be around children, especially little girls of five or six. He was depressed and suicidal, feeling guilty over what he had observed, every morning trying to come up with a reason to keep living.

Jason Bing was a naturally private person. It was the way of the men in his family to keep their troubles to themselves. This tendency had been magnified by his experience with the military, where the stoic survivor is the ideal. So now, even though he went ahead with the planned marriage to his college girlfriend—Amber—after returning from Iraq, he didn't share with her much of what was going on inside him. When he told her that he wanted to sleep in another room from her, he blamed it on being a light sleeper. He didn't want to admit that he was afraid of hurting her in his sleep. Whenever she brought up the possibility of having children, he put her off, no longer sure he wanted to be a father after what he had seen in Iraq. Amber became increasingly curious and concerned about what was going on with this husband of hers.

The truth was, Jason Bing was haunted. Just as chronic pain is pain that goes on long after the injury or disease that caused it has subsided, so PTSD is a "fight or flight" stress response that lingers after a person is removed from danger. Jason had left Iraq, but Iraq hadn't left him.

But he noticed that when he was on opioids for his back pain, the medication held the ghosts at bay. Pop a pill, wait fifteen minutes—torment gone! Easy "solution." And the truth is, at this point he would have done almost anything to keep from hearing a man begging for death or seeing a little girl explode over and over again in his mind. So he took the so easy, so treacherous step of consuming more opioids than he really needed for his back pain. He doctor-shopped by getting pain meds from his base doctors and then going off base to get more from civilian doctors. He tried to always have a large supply on hand. Before one dose wore off, he took another. He felt ashamed of himself for doing this, but the opioids even eased the shame and made him feel good...for a while. When the effect wore off, of course he needed more.

It wasn't long before Jason realized he couldn't stop taking the drugs even if he tried. Back pain, memories of the horrors he had witnessed, and withdrawal symptoms all came roaring back to fill the vacuum left behind whenever he stopped taking the opioids even for a short time. The young man who had once been scrupulous in avoiding drugs now was forced to apply the "A" word—*addict*—to himself. It was a bitter realization. He still had back pain, but the "cure" had become worse than the cause.

When people hear about others who have an addiction to pain medications, they often think that the addict merely wants to get "high." But as we learned with Rachel, in fact there's almost always more to it than that, and the usual process is well illustrated in Jason

Bing's situation. First he incurred debilitating pain that wouldn't go away. Then he encountered opioids, prescribed in reasonable doses as a legitimate treatment for his pain. Next, his pain was compounded by emotional stress—in his case, warrior's post-traumatic stress disorder. And then came overuse of opioids to medicate both the physical pain and the emotional pain. The cycle of more, more, more took off from there.

A Warrior in Transition

Diagnosed with post-traumatic stress disorder, Jason was assigned to a Warrior Transition Unit (WTU) at Fort Carson. The Army's WTUs were designed to provide long-term care to wounded soldiers and those suffering mental health problems. Jason qualified for a WTU because of both his back pain and his PTSD. From the unit's doctors, he received nerve blocks—injections of an anesthetic into the spine—that would relieve the pain for a few weeks at a time. To calm his inner turmoil, he also began receiving counseling paired with prescriptions for benzodiazepines (psychoactive drugs used to ease anxiety and insomnia).

Jason appreciated the help he was getting for his inner and outer pain, but what he wasn't telling his superiors was that he also had another problem: his overuse of prescription pain medications. He knew that, if the Army found out about his addiction and misuse of these medicines, he would very likely be discharged. End of advancement. End of career. Humiliation.

An irony was not lost on him: He had seen firsthand the way that alcohol use was accepted and even promoted in the Army despite the fact that it can lead to fighting and other unbecoming behaviors. And if a service member developed alcoholism, it wasn't hard for him to get help from the Army without much discredit. But drug abuse—that was a different matter entirely. If you became addicted to drugs, you were treated as if you were weak. This didn't seem fair to Jason, but it was the way it was. In his most self-condemning moments, Jason even agreed with the Army's prejudice.

Worried about his problem, he began going off base to participate in a drug addiction support group. He also met with a local doctor who told him about synthetic opioids, such as methadone and Suboxone, that could be used to wean a user off the regular opioids with minimal side effects. This sounded appealing to Jason. He was scheduled to attend a four-month officer leadership course at Fort Sill, Oklahoma, which was basically boot camp for officers. He remembered well how his first boot camp experience with the bring-the-pain-you-bitches drill sergeant had gone; he wasn't sure he could make it through this new boot camp experience while addicted to opioids. But he read that it was possible to function normally while on Suboxone. His doctor gave him a prescription for Suboxone, which Jason quickly found out would cost him around $1,000 per month if he paid for it out of pocket—practically a fortune for a soldier.

Jason wondered if he could get the Army to cover the cost of the drug. To find out, he called the base pharmacy pretending to be the husband of a soldier. He knew that if he were to admit on the phone that he was a soldier himself, he would be required to give his Social Security number and the Army would soon know that he had an addiction problem. This had to be a covert operation.

Getting the base pharmacist on his phone, he said, "Hi, I'm a dependent," he claimed. "I have a question about a medicine."

"Okay, go ahead," said the pharmacist.

"If my wife has a prescription for Suboxone from an outside doctor, can she get it from the base?"

"That medication is illegal in the military."

"It's really expensive to get off base. Even if she has a prescription from a civilian doctor, you're saying the Army won't cover it?"

"If you're in the military, you can't have it, period. You can't have it in your system no matter what."

Jason ended the call.

It was a case of irony upon irony. Not only did the Army excuse excessive alcohol use while disapproving drug use, but it also passed out opioids for pain while refusing the medications that would help those who got caught up in excessive use of opioids. The reason was that pain was a medical condition (even if it was viewed as somehow less than soldierly to admit to it), while addiction was seen as the result of a character flaw. Despite having invested heavily in a soldier's training, the military's solution to the problem of addiction was to show an affected soldier to the exit.

After the phone call, Jason had his answer, and it wasn't a surprise to him. He decided he would have to somehow pay for the Suboxone on his own and keep it secret. He would be aided in the deception by the fact that standard urine drug tests used by the military at that time did not reveal the presence of the active molecule in Suboxone.

Jason was feeling very much alone. The Army would not help, and he didn't want to involve his wife. As it seemed to him, he had only himself to rely upon. He managed to get through his officer course in Oklahoma with the help of Suboxone, but he couldn't keep shelling out the $1,000 per month. He knew it might be just a matter of time before the Army found out about his addiction and the treatment he was receiving. He thought, *Where is this going to end?*

His addiction seemed to have him trapped. But the Army offered one more, very slim hope.

Might as Well Be Dead

Uniform neat and clean, hat under his arm, First Lieutenant Jason Bing stood outside the office belonging to his commanding officer (CO), rapped three times on the door, and waited until a bellow instructed him to enter. Once inside the room, he crisply stepped to within two paces of the lieutenant colonel's desk, halted, saluted, and formally stated, "Sir, Lieutenant Bing reports."

Jason had been dreading making this report to his CO at Fort Carson, but in more ways than one he felt he had no choice. For his new wife as much as for himself, he knew he needed to get control over his misuse of prescription pain medications. So he had inquired about what one had to do to get into the Army Substance Abuse Program (ASAP). He was told that, while enlisted men could seek out help from ASAP whenever they wanted without its becoming a part of their military record, officers like him had to be accompanied by the CO for the initial evaluation.

Could Bing's military career survive a request for treatment from the ASAP? Doubtful, he thought. But maybe, just maybe, if it turned out his commanding officer was understanding and helpful, he would be able to get rid of his addiction while holding on to his career. He still wanted to serve his country as an Army officer, and in fact he had begun the process of evaluation for promotion to captain.

Standing at attention, Bing explained to the lieutenant colonel in a few well-rehearsed words that he had been injured during training and had since developed an addiction to the pain medications he was given by Army doctors. Then he respectfully requested that the colonel accompany him to an appointment with ASAP.

For a few moments, the lieutenant colonel said nothing in reply. He was a stocky Vietnam War vet whose short, graying hair petered out in a bald spot at the back of his head. Bing didn't know him well, but when the lieutenant colonel stood up, Bing remembered that his CO was shorter than the impression left by his dominating presence. Then it began:

"Bing, how could you do this? You are an officer. People below you are looking up to you!"

These opening words were all it took for Bing's slender hope for his career to snap like a reed. If the colonel took such an attitude, then this was the end of his involvement, much less his advancement, in the U.S. military. Ever since his fall from the rope in basic training, he had tried to avoid doing anything that would place a black mark on his military record. Now his leadership potential was fatally besmirched in the eyes of his superiors.

The lieutenant colonel started pacing the room as Bing remained at attention, like a tree trunk unmoving yet defenseless before the wind. "I'll go with you to mental health," the lieutenant colonel said. "Regs say I've got to. But you know what, Lieutenant? Back in my day, you would have had your ass kicked for bullshit like this, and then you would not have had a drug problem anymore."

The harangue continued in the same vein for a while, the lieutenant colonel sometimes getting in Bing's face like his old drill instructor used to do. Throughout the whole embarrassing scene, although standing stiff and straight on the outside, Jason was shrinking on the inside. He told me later, "I never felt lower in my life. I thought, *I should kill myself. Obviously my career is over. That means Amber is going to find out what I've done. My life might as well just be over.*"

As much as neither the lieutenant colonel nor Lieutenant Bing wanted him to, the lieutenant colonel went along to the ASAP intake evaluation. Bing described it as feeling like he was a child again and had a babysitter looking after him. His sense of shame warred the whole time with his inculcated military stoicism. At his side was, not a loving caregiver like I've seen many times with my patients in the exam room, but a shaming, condemning authority figure who thought Bing needed punishment more than treatment.

Afterward, the lieutenant colonel explained the situation to Jason. By admitting to taking Suboxone, Jason was chargeable under the Uniform Code of Military Justice. He would be convicted and, though he would probably not have to do stockade time, he would receive a less than honorable discharge and consequently lose his benefits. But the lieutenant colonel said there was an alternative. Jason was coming up to the end of the contract he had signed when joining the Army. If he didn't re-sign the contract (an action called "extending out" that Jason had intended to do), then the Army would proceed with separating him from the military (called "processing out"). If news of his addiction didn't spread any further, he might receive an honorable discharge and be able to keep his benefits, though the lieutenant colonel couldn't promise it.

It was resign or be prosecuted.

That evening, Jason decided he needed to get drunk. Not wanting his wife to see the spectacle he was about to make of himself, he checked into the base hotel—a utilitarian cinder-block building—carrying a bottle of Wild Turkey Bourbon in a bag. He went to his room, with its dated and worn furniture, turned out the lights, and sat on the bed drinking the whiskey as he stared out the window at a field of dry grass blowing in the wind under the fading light of day.

As he drank, he became more and more emotional, wiping at his damp eyes and not always managing to hold in a sob before it escaped. He hadn't been sleeping well, so he wasn't in a healthy frame of mind even apart from the liquor. Now round and round went the thoughts about his situation.

His career was over unless he wanted to fight it out in military court and risk his much-needed benefits. So after years of dedication to the Army, and being on the brink of promotion to captaincy, he was going to have to give up his dream of a full military career and be processed out. Even then he might lose his benefits. Regardless, everybody who knew him was going to ask why he was leaving the Army, and they would find out about his addiction to prescription pain medicines. He wouldn't be able to hide his shame from them any longer. Worst of all, his wife was going to know. What would she think of him? Maybe she'd leave him. Maybe he would never find a way out of his addiction. Maybe he would wind up on the streets as a homeless vet, stoned out of his mind and mumbling to his demons. Nothing was ever going to change. It was hopeless. He might as well be dead.

He took a swig.

Yes. What if he killed himself this very night? His suffering would be over, and he would spare his wife the shame of being married to an addict. She would receive his life insurance payout and could start a new life without him. The outcome would be better for everybody.

Another swig.

In Iraq, Jason had made plans to shoot himself to escape pain if he were horribly injured. Now he proceeded to use the instruments of his shame—his medications—to escape the emotional pain of his situation. He had a bottle of the sleep aid Ambien and another bottle of the part-opioid painkiller Vicodin with him. He grabbed them. Thirty count of Ambien and twice that number of Vicodin, chased with the remains of the Wild Turkey, went down his throat. Oddly, now that he had taken action, his tears dried up. He became grimly calm. He lay down to lose consciousness and slip out of this life.

A few minutes later, though, he for some reason woke up. He didn't know where he was or what he was doing in the hotel room. Although the lethal amount of Vicodin in his gut hadn't had a chance to kick in yet and take his life, the Ambien had given him temporary amnesia. He stumbled out the door and fell to the hallway floor. A fellow soldier, hearing the clatter, stuck his head out of a door down the hallway and then came running to the rescue. Quick action by base medical personnel saved Lieutenant Bing's life.

Army authorities declared the incident to be an accidental overdose. Jason told his half-horrified, half-relieved wife the same story.

Actually, his overdose had been intentional. It was his survival that was an accident.

Moral Courage

When I asked him to reflect on his near-suicide, Jason had some important things to say. In a surprising way, he was motivated by a high value in the military: honor. Let me repeat his words verbatim:

> When you're in the military and battling pain and drug dependency, the last thing you need is to have to think, *If someone finds out I'm addicted to painkillers, I'm going to lose my job. I'm going to be disgraced. I'm going to get a dishonorable discharge. Ten years I've sweat blood and tears!*
>
> If you're found out, serving goes from something of honor to something of dishonor. That's a heavy thing to place on somebody.
>
> Going through combat and having PTSD and all of the terrible things that you're asked to do to other people, the one thing that I would say separates you from a common murderer in your mind is the fact that you did it with honor. You did it because it was something you were told to do by your commanders. Take that honor away from someone, and what's left? You feel like a murderer. There is no reason to live anymore.

After the overdose, any doubt that Jason would have to leave the Army was swept away. The procedure for Jason getting the second silver bar of a captain was quietly canceled and the Army began processing him out of its ranks. He had two sessions of counseling with ASAP, but because he was leaving the Army in mere weeks, the ASAP team didn't bother with him much. Their mission was to help active-duty soldiers.

Jason Bing received a medical discharge in June 2010. It enabled him to keep his Army benefits and to receive the services of the Veterans Administration system. He moved back to Utah with his wife, Amber, and eventually found a job in a sign-making company. Jason has entered a methadone treatment program for addiction, and today the VA pays for his methadone treatment through a private clinic. The methadone keeps his back pain under control while enabling him to stay away from other opioids. A while back, to make a few extra dollars, he took part in a research program that I was heading up to investigate the interaction between methadone and an experimental drug that was in the pipeline—and that's when I first had the privilege to meet him.

With the help of a psychiatrist, his PTSD symptoms are abating, though he knows they may never entirely go away any more than his back pain will. He and his wife are talking about moving to his home State of Alabama. They've recently had a child—a dark-haired, dark-eyed girl too young to guess at the reason for the troubled expression that sometimes comes over his face when he looks at her.

Jason continued to have lingering shame over his misuse of opioids, but that finally began to change one day in January 2011. He was at his computer, visiting an Army website, when he came across a republished *USA Today* article about Lieutenant General David Fridovich, one of the highest-ranking officers in the U.S. Army. The article revealed that Fridovich had developed a dependency on opioids given to treat his pain. This respected officer addressed the problem in the military of admitting that you have a drug issue. The words that stood out most to Bing were these: "Nobody wants to show weaknesses. You want to be perceived as perfection. But sometimes moral courage kicks in where moral courage is demanded."[3] This reframed Bing's experience for him. It was true that, as an Army officer, he hadn't wanted to show weakness or be perceived as imperfect. But maybe addressing the problem openly was actually an act of courage, an act in the best Army traditions of honor. And maybe the military was beginning to recognize it.

Maybe Jason himself should recognize it.

He had felt small and beaten down ever since the earful he got in his lieutenant colonel's office. Reading this article, he stood up a little straighter. Someone in his community understood his problem.

He started showing the article to anyone he thought would be interested. Talking it over with his wife, he opened up with her more than he ever had before about his drug problem. And he found that she was more understanding and supportive than he had dared to hope. Perhaps, he thought, he should continue to be more open in telling others what he had been through and accept help. Perhaps it would bring the long nightmare to an end.

Jason Bing has paid a high price for serving our country under arms. Due to old prejudices, in fact, he's paid a higher price than he should have. But maybe because of what soldiers like he and General Fridovich have been through, service members in the next war won't have to pay quite so much.

There's a lesson here, not just for the U.S. Army, but for all of us.

Destigmatizing Pain

I do not tell Jason's story to indict the U.S. Army for its treatment of people with pain and addiction problems. In fact, I'm pleased to say that, since Jason was on active duty, the military has developed an exemplary program for treating soldiers in pain. They have psychologists, rehab physicians, and primary care providers working together to provide interdisciplinary care, including acupuncture and other complementary forms of therapy, to the warriors. The military is now providing methadone and Suboxone treatment for its members who have become overly dependent on opioids.

I include Jason's story in this book for illustrative purposes. Both inside the military services and outside them, people with pain tend to be rejected and mistreated by others. Some people act as if pain is such a downer to be around that it spoils their fun, or as if pain is a contagion that can be caught, or as if the problem will go away if they ignore it. Of course there are exceptions to all this—some people are understanding and compassionate. But more commonly, if a family member comes down with fibromyalgia, or an employee needs accommodation for back pain, or a fellow church member admits to overtaking oxycodone, we back away, we judge, we cut them off. Just when others need us most, we make their life harder. We subject them to our own friendly fire.

I know that when people act this way, it may not entirely be their fault. They may not know any better. They may even be reacting to some kind of self-protection instinct. I have long wondered if the livestock on our farm avoided the sick animals in obedience to some evolutionary imperative. Maybe it's the same for humans. But if this sort of behavior is allowed to continue, it means the people who have pain are condemned to loneliness and untreated suffering.

When it comes to our own kind who are hurting, can we not assert the humanity that raises us above the other species and countermand our own survival-of-the-fittest instincts?

Doctors, one would think, should be able to overcome their own prejudices against pain. Yet countless people suffering pain can tell tales of having gone from doctor to doctor, finding that many won't listen, don't believe them, and blame them for being in pain. The evidence on this is not all anecdotal. Research has proved that doctors sometimes look at people with persistent pain complaints as mentally weak and shunt them off to others.[4]

Why do some doctors refuse to treat people for chronic pain? And why do others quit after giving it an initial try? Why do some offer treatment in a less than sympathetic or respectful way?

One reason is that physicians are worried about the repercussions for themselves if something goes wrong for a patient. Although doctors normally have a desire to help, counterbalancing that desire are pressures to comply with federal and state laws, to avoid possibly harmful overtreatment, and to be able to justify treatments if called to account. Similarly, doctors know that health care insurance companies refuse to acknowledge some diagnoses common in pain treatment because of the potential financial liability associated with those diagnoses. It's easier for a doctor not to get into a conflict with the insurance companies. (I will discuss the pressures on physicians more closely in Chapter 10.)

Another reason is that physicians in the West are trained in a mechanistic worldview that largely separates mind and body. This view permits physicians to validate only that which they can see. Only recently have we been able to identify some types of pain through medical scanning, and for the most part still today, physicians must rely on patients' self-reporting about the severity of pain. Some physicians are uncomfortable in treating the invisible complaint of pain. They may even doubt the claims of people coming to them for help.

A third reason is that some physicians have trouble empathizing with people in pain. Perhaps they have never had much pain themselves. Perhaps a cultural, ethnic, or socioeconomic gap lies between them and their patients. Empathic physicians must intuitively, by the nature of their personality, or through learning, be able to listen, validate, and vicariously experience the patients' pain. They must do so while at the same time using their medical training to analyze a complex problem and propose a path forward that is realistic and yet projects hope. Not all physicians are able to accomplish such a daunting task day after day.

A fourth reason is that, like everybody else, physicians seek the inner reward of satisfaction in their work. They like to see a positive result—the quicker and the more complete, the better. Yet the nature of treating chronic pain today is to make gradual progress (if any progress at all) toward what will most likely be only a partial resolution of the problem. Reducing someone's pain from an 8 to a

4 is a victory, but it doesn't always seem like much of a victory to the doctor any more than it does to the patient, because 4 can still be disabling pain. Both may be disappointed in the result, and both may be disappointed in each other. The doctor may get frustrated or lose interest.

Whatever the causes of doctors' prejudice against people who have pain, they may just turn away patients or refer them to some other health care practitioner. They may look upon patients suspiciously as possible addicts and drug seekers. They may think—or even say out loud—that patients are malingering, lazy, helpless, or stupid. There is even a diagnosis called *somatoform disorder* to legitimize the transference of accountability from physician to patient, because it's "all in the patient's mind."

All of these reactions stand in the way of people in pain getting the best treatment that medical science is able to render at this time. More so even than others in our society, doctors need to learn to overcome their biases against people in pain.

I have only two things to say in conclusion in regard to this story's message. My points are simple, but they are immense in their implications. First, people who develop pain need to ready themselves for people abandoning them and to look for those rare ones who will stick by their side. Just as Jason Bing finally found a supportive community, so others who are enduring pain must keep working to find family, friends, colleagues, health care workers, and others who will help to provide a better life for them, not a worse one. Second, we need to flip the attitude in our society toward people who have pain. If the U.S. Army can start approaching pain and pain treatment differently, as appears now to be the case, then surely the same can be true everywhere. It starts with me and you.

CHAPTER 5

_____ ꙮ _____

The New Scarlet Letter

Opioids can become more curse than cure, but it's possible to overcome addiction to these medications.

THE FIRST TIME I met Hal Garner, it was 2006 and he was forty-four years old. He was shuffling into my examination room next to an armed guard, wearing the jumpsuit of a Utah State Prison inmate, with shackles on his ankles and wrists. At six-foot-four and muscular, he was an intimidating presence. When I learned his story, however, I realized that he was really a gentle person. I found out that he had once worn a very different kind of uniform and had led a very different life. What had brought him from the former place to a much worse spot was a declining path of pain and addiction. It has been a privilege for me to be one of many people walking with him on the long climb back to a new life.

As we've already seen in the stories of Rachel Hutchins and Jason Bing, opioid use can eventually cause problems for many who take these drugs for their pain. In fact, in the perception of many people, everyone who is receiving medical treatment for pain is branded with the scarlet letter "A" for *addiction*. This is unfair, since not all people in pain take opioids, and of those who do, the great majority never become addicted or misuse the medications in any way. Yet addiction—and all the other problems that go with it, including drug diversion, overdose, and crime—is a serious problem, one that we must face if we want long-term progress toward healing.

We need to understand addiction better. And we need to understand the available ways to recover from addiction. Hal Garner, perhaps more so than any other person I've met, shows how addiction can come alongside pain as a twin foe—and how it's possible to achieve victory over both pain and addiction. Hal is a fallen and risen hero.

Final Play

On a hot day in early August 1992, the Buffalo Bills, one of the leading NFL teams of that era, were completing five weeks of twice-a-day practices at their training camp on a state university campus an hour's drive from Buffalo. On the last play of the last day of practice, six-season veteran linebacker Hal Garner was in his two-point stance behind the defensive linemen when the ball was snapped on the other side of the line of scrimmage. The quarterback lofted the ball toward a racing receiver. Hal leaped to block it. While he was airborne, an opposing tackle seized him by the legs and flipped him face first to the playing field, simultaneously bending his back farther than it was designed to go. Hal heard a *pop-pop-pop* and in that instant knew his career in football was over.

Hal's body had taken a lot of punishment already in his then-thirty years. When he was eleven, he and some other boys at a friend's house in his hometown of Logan, Utah, were taking turns running from a hallway inside the house to the patio and then cannonballing into the swimming pool. But when it was Hal's turn to make his run, the homeowner, not knowing the game was going on, shut the glass door leading to the patio. Hal ran smack into it, knocking himself out, tearing ligaments in his leg, and receiving lacerations that would require three hundred stitches to close. He was told that he might never be able to run again. But he was determined to recover, and he did. A few years later he was playing football for Logan High School, even helping his team win the state championship in 1978.

On the advice of football legend Merlin Olsen (another Logan native), the prep star chose to stay in his hometown and play for

Utah State, where he earned All-American status on an otherwise lackluster team. The Buffalo Bills noticed his gifts and selected him in the third round of the 1985 NFL draft. As a linebacker in both college and professional football, Hal spent his sports career racing behind kickoffs and punts and colliding into blockers and ball carriers. His back, knees, and shoulders paid the price. He had two knee surgeries while in college and two more while with the Bills. When he suffered the 1992 practice injury to his spine, there was no coming back.

Except that the Bills management made him come back, telling him that he had to suit up for the team's preseason game against the Kansas City Chiefs on August 24 if he wanted a chance to keep his spot on the roster. Hal couldn't believe it. His left leg was virtually useless. He could barely walk, let alone propel his body into a ball defender at high speed. But the team bosses had ordered it, and Hal was struggling emotionally with the prospect of ending his football career, so he did what he'd done many times before: he played injured. He participated in just a few plays before defensive coordinator Walt Corey growled, "Get him out of there." What Hal couldn't understand was why he'd been sent out there in the first place; he surely wasn't in a condition to play that day. Only later did he conclude that the team management wanted to have him on film playing in a game after the injury so that, in the event of his filing a lawsuit, they would be able to say, "See, he was still able to play."

That was the last time Hal wore the red, white, and blue uniform of the Buffalo Bills. Two days after the Kansas City game, the team leaders called him in to an office and told him that they were releasing him. "You're getting too old and you can't compete anymore," they gave as their reason. They denied that it was about his back injury—his back was fine, they said. Hal knew better. In one play, he had gone from being able to play at the pinnacle of the sport he loved to not being able to play it at all.

Hal expressed his reaction to me like this: "To them, you're just like a racehorse. As soon as you break a leg, they put you to sleep."

At the end of the meeting, the team leaders told Hal to go

downstairs to meet with a team doctor and sign a release form saying that he wouldn't sue the team for his injury. They had released
him—now they wanted *him* to release *them*. Hal was naive enough
at this time that he was planning to do what they said. On the way
downstairs to see the doctor, however, his friend Jim Kelly, star
quarterback, pulled him aside. "Don't sign their release form," Jim
told Hal, slipping him the phone number of Buffalo attorney Robert
Villarini.

Minutes later, down in the doctor's office, Hal was shown x-rays
that supposedly proved his back was fine. Actually, x-rays cannot
show disc problems. An MRI scan would have given a much more
accurate view of Hal's spine than x-rays could, but the team hadn't
ordered an MRI.

The doctor said, "The spacings between your vertebrae are fine,
Hal." Although that may have been true, a spinal injury doesn't necessarily affect vertebral spacing.

Armed with Jim Kelly's advice, Hal wouldn't sign the release
form. Instead, he flew home and drove straight to the University of
Utah Medical School for an MRI. The scan revealed the true extent
of his injury, and shortly afterward he underwent a disc fusion operation. Then, once his back had begun to heal, he engaged Villarini to
file the lawsuit that the Bills management had been hoping to avoid,
seeking disability payment for an injury on the job.

The testimony from team personnel in the legal hearings,
claiming that Hal hadn't been badly injured that day in training
camp, enraged the former linebacker. Outside the courtroom, one
team trainer exposed what was really going on when he confided,
"Hal, it's nothing personal. We're just doing our job, trying to save as
much money for the team as possible." It took two years and a lot of
Hal's savings, but in the end he won disability payments, not just on
the career-ending back injury, but on all his injuries acquired while
with the Bills. He was also awarded a 25 percent early payment benefit through the NFL Players Association when he retired.

A lot of my patients face a hard battle in obtaining insurance or
other payments they deserve to cover their injuries and pain, and

few of them are as well connected and well supplied with money as Hal was in those days to be able to hire a great attorney. I find it bemusing that even a multibillion-dollar industry like professional football holds the purse strings tightly when it comes to compensating injured players upon whom teams had once lavished rich contracts. Hal is far from being alone as a professional athlete who left it all on the field for his team but who has been repaid by being cold-shouldered by the team afterward. Professional athletes in many sports deal with brain trauma and other injuries as well as post-traumatic stress disorder and addiction to prescription medications—problems that sometimes don't surface until years after leaving the sport. It seems that, for everyone, persistence and an insistence on one's rights are requirements for receiving due support for painful disabilities. Fortunately, in Hal's case, he eventually received what he deserved: he would be able to get medical care for his injuries in the years to come.

It looked like he could get on with his life now. But what kind of life was it going to be?

Ill Treatment

After being dropped by the Bills, Hal had moved back to Logan, a city of fifty thousand population in the far north of Utah. With him was his wife, Becky, a beauty he'd met in college. They had two children—a son, Zack, born in 1990, and their daughter, Carson, born four years later. The family lived in a big house on a five-acre ranch, from which Hal drove his gleaming pickup truck into town to check on his businesses. He was part owner of two pawnshops and a grocery store, and he also worked as a bail bondsman and bounty hunter. When he was in public places, Hal noticed with a certain pride when others would point out the former NFL player. He wasn't averse to talking over his glory days on the gridiron, especially those two Super Bowls when he'd come this close to earning a winner's ring. From all appearances, it was an enviable life. Here, surely, was a local hero justly basking in the glow of his achievements.

There was just one problem. Like so many retired athletes, Hal Garner was hurting. After the double-disc fusion operation in 1992, he had to have two more operations, one of which involved the installation of two rods and six screws in his spine. The pain never went away, spoiling his enjoyment of the life he'd made for himself. He didn't like the way he would have to shift his weight from one side to the other in his seat while he was driving his truck, just to ease the pain. He didn't like not being able to hoist his kids into his arms while they were still young enough for such an embrace. After so many years as a top-performing athlete, the restrictions on normal, everyday activity that he had to submit to were galling. There could be no more traipsing through the woods with hunting bow in hand, no more horseback riding, no more jogging down country roads as the sun rose.

Then one day he happened to see a sign for a local spine clinic. Without giving it much thought, he set up an appointment with a doctor at the clinic. Thus, so easily began an involvement with pain management that would palliate his pain but eventually led to unintended and disturbing outcomes.

This was the 1990s, and we didn't have a full understanding of the risks inherent in opioids. The best evidence at the time suggested that fewer than 1 percent of patients given an opioid would develop an addiction—a number that would eventually be hotly debated in professional circles and the media. People desperately seeking any type of relief became victimized by the very medications handed out in an earnest attempt to help them. This is what happened to Hal Garner at the spine clinic he went to. The doctors started prescribing pain medications, and over the years he was prescribed increasingly higher doses, ultimately moving on to the strongest medications. Hal went from Lortab to OxyContin to fentanyl and eventually received multiple drugs at the same time.

In 1998 he had a device implanted in his abdominal wall that contained opioid medication. A catheter from this computerized reservoir extended to the intraspinal space where the spinal cord and spinal fluid existed. It was an unusual, but not unheard-of, delivery system for opioids in tough cases of pain.

In prescribing these medications, Hal's physician was doing what physicians were taught back then. At the time, all pain medicine physicians had a belief that no one should have to suffer from pain and that we should give enough medication to "give their lives back to them." As a profession, we did not know, nor did we believe, that we could cause harm by doing this. This wasn't hubris or carelessness; it was simply a lack of knowledge.

The history of medicine is replete with examples of therapies that have led to more harm than good. Once, medical practitioners would drill burr holes into the skulls of people with migraines, seizures, or mental disorders, seeking to release the demons they believed were at work. For decades, women underwent mutilating breast surgeries because in the nineteenth century the father of modern surgery, William S. Halsted, became convinced that cancer was limited to what you could see and therefore could be excised. Today there is still debate about recommending mammograms. Opioid treatment for pain is another instance where unintended consequences showed up after benefits were touted. We're still in the process of establishing a wiser standard of care.

This was the trap Hal Garner unfortunately became caught in. He became "addicted."

A Genetically Influenced Disease

The very word *addiction* can unfavorably brand an individual for life. Employers often choose not to hire individuals with a history of addiction. Addiction can be used against a spouse in divorce proceedings. Many persons have been denied pain treatment because of the stigma associated with addiction. So it's crucially important to understand what addiction really is.

To doctors, addiction is a *brain disease*. It's not a character flaw, some type of willful weakness, as it's popularly thought of. A majority of the population can develop behaviors consistent with addiction in certain environmental conditions when exposed to a rewarding drug like an opioid.

In laboratory experiments, different breeds of rats have been used to test the abuse potential of drugs.[1] One breed—named Fischer 344—is resistant to addiction. Even after a Fischer rat has been repeatedly injected with a highly addictive substance, the rat will refuse to self-administer the drug when given that option. A second breed—Lewis rats—acts in just the opposite way. They are so genetically predisposed to addiction that, even if the drug they have been given is only slightly addictive, they will do anything to access that drug, even walk across a burning-hot plate to get to it. Then there is a third breed, known as Sprague Dawley rats, whose behavior falls between those of the other two breeds. If subjected to stress (exposed to loud music or forced to undergo sleep deprivation in the experiments), the Sprague Dawley rats will act like Lewis rats and seek the rewards of addictive drugs. If not stressed, they will act like Fischer 344 rats, showing no interest in the drugs.

If these laboratory results can be superimposed on the human population, they suggest that some people (for reasons we don't as yet fully understand) are naturally at higher risk of addiction than are others and that outside influences can invite drug use. A small percentage of human beings may be resistant to addiction. They are like Fischer rats. A larger number, but still a minority (probably less than 25 percent), of human beings are genetically vulnerable to addiction. They are like the Lewis rats. They can easily develop a dangerous dependency upon rewarding substances (nicotine, caffeine, alcohol, benzodiazepines, opioids, sleep aids), if exposed to them, and will have a very hard time discontinuing them. Many of these people have mental health disorders, such as anxiety (think of Rachel Hutchins), bipolar disease, post-traumatic stress disorder (think of Jason Bing), and depression, that can contribute to overuse of opioids and benzodiazepines (often prescribed for anxiety and insomnia). Then there's a majority of the human population who are like the Sprague Dawley rats: they will normally not consider using drugs to get high, but under stress they might go against their natural tendency and begin to abuse alcohol or drugs.

A study published in 1975 investigated heroin use by U.S. military personnel, both while they were serving in Vietnam and after they came home.[2] The study showed that about one third of the service members used heroin while overseas. But when they came home, their levels of opioid use returned to prewar levels. In other words, the stress of war was responsible for much of the drug use, and when that stress went away, so did the drug use. That's the Sprague Dawley kind of behavior in action.

What's the lesson here?

Far from being a sign of a character flaw, abuse of drugs and other substances can be traced in large part to external conditions. Therefore, just as anyone can acquire chronic pain through an unexpected injury, so nearly anyone can develop an addiction under the right circumstances. Some people are so genetically vulnerable to addiction that any exposure to rewarding substances can lead to addiction. The rest of us, if under stress (such as pain) and exposed to addictive substances (such as opioids prescribed to treat pain), could also develop an addiction. As long as the stress continues, it will be difficult for us to step back from the addictive behavior.[3]

Hal Garner belongs to the majority group: he normally would not have considered using drugs to get high, but under the stress of constant pain, he found an escape from his pain and stress by overusing the pain medications he was prescribed. Subsequently he needed the drugs to avoid withdrawal. None of this made him an addict by itself, but Hal did develop behaviors that were self-destructive, and that *is* a sign of addiction. He manifested the "three c's" of addiction: *craving* for drugs, impaired *control* over drug use, and *continued* use of drugs despite harm. His was an acquired disease due to environmental exposure, not a genetic propensity, but nevertheless he had an addiction.

In addition to the stress of chronic pain, there was one more factor that may have made it harder for Hal: he no longer was getting the thrills and rewards from sports that he was accustomed to. A self-described "adrenaline junkie," Hal was used to the excitement of playing a football game before a crowd of fans every week during the season. Now all that was gone—the thrill, the glory—and he was going through a kind of adrenaline withdrawal. The drugs he took helped him ease these withdrawal symptoms too. Soon he needed the drugs as much as, if not more than, he had needed the excitement of a football game before.

It was not long after Hal started on the medications prescribed at the spine clinic that he got to the point where he was asking himself, *Which is worse: the pain or the addiction?* For the time being, he was stuck with both.

Alone

Hal's family life survived another five turbulent years after he started excessive prescription drug use. These were years that produced emotional wounds within Hal and those closest to him that are still healing to this day.

The drugs changed Hal's personality. Even before the drugs, Hal could sometimes be too goal focused, but he had essentially been a loving husband and father, son and brother, good friend and hard worker. Now, though, he would argue with his wife over differences large and small. His kids wanted his attention, but he wasn't emotionally available to them. He lost his temper and alienated others. This wasn't the Hal he had once been.

Due to some of the non-opioid medications he was taking, his behavior became increasingly bizarre. He would become confused and not understand what was going on. One time when Hal was trying to get off his drugs cold turkey and had become dehydrated, he first thought people were breaking into his house and then started raving about the Taliban setting off a dirty bomb. These hallucinations cleared up quickly when he went into the hospital and was rehydrated with intravenous fluids, but they left his family disconcerted.

Another time, he showed up at a neighbor's house in the middle of the night and beat on the front door, hollering crazily. When police officers arrived in response to the phone call from the frightened family holed up inside, they found Hal standing in the driveway and staring into the sky.

"Hal, the folks here say you were beating on their door," one officer said. "What were you doing that for?"

"Well, it's a little game me and my daughter play," Hal said nonsensically. "She gets up on the roof and throws the basketball through the hoop so it's like a slam dunk."

Hal had no idea where he was.

Becky did her best to cover up incidents like this and protect Hal's reputation, though rumors were already swirling around Logan as thick as a Utah blizzard. When it came to Becky's own children, though, she wasn't willing to take risks. She tried and often failed to convince Hal not to drive when he was intoxicated with drugs—in the end, that was his risk to take. But she refused to let her kids ride in a car with him when he was in such a state.

Some people tried to help Hal. His old high school coach took him on as assistant football coach at Logan High, and Hal at first performed well in the role. The young players loved his enthusiasm for the game. Soon after, though, when the coach took Hal along with him to a different coaching gig at Sky View High School in nearby Smithfield, things didn't go as well. Hal often showed up high and one day sideswiped some vehicles while driving to the school. That was the end of his coaching career.

By 1999, Hal was spending less time with his family and more time on his own or with friends in town. He rarely participated with his kids in their activities. As a common side effect, the drugs had suppressed his libido, wedging even more space between him and his wife. He wasn't getting along with his business partners and impulsively began the process of selling off his share in the companies. Everyone in his family, including his four brothers and sisters, warned him that he was going downhill, but he kept denying it. In part this was because the medications he was on prevented him from seeing his situation clearly, and in part it was because he was stubborn and wanted to prove others wrong, just as when a boy he had wanted to prove the doctors wrong about being able to run after his leg injury. Communication between Hal and Becky had broken down, so even though he would have liked to have had a heart-to-heart talk with her about his situation, it never happened. Somehow in the midst of all this he doesn't recall anyone ever suggesting to him the possibility of going into a drug detox and rehabilitation program.

Then one weekend when Hal was in better shape than usual, he took his kids on a skiing trip. He couldn't ski because of his bad back and knees, but he knew Zack and Carson liked going down the kids' runs. When they got home, Becky's parents were there and he could tell from the atmosphere in the house that something was going on. After the kids were in bed, Becky came out with it: "It's over, Hal. I want a divorce." She just couldn't handle what drugs had done to their marriage and their family, and what worse things they might yet do.

The Dark Years

The divorce, finalized in 2000, was only a stage in Hal's decline. So many losses. He had already lost his career doing the one thing at which he excelled: football. Now he'd lost his cars and the dream house out on the ranch. He moved into a smaller house and was allowed only periodic visits with his kids. Spending long hours on his own, he grieved the separation from his kids as well as the loss to death of both parents, a beloved aunt, and a close friend, all occurring during this interval. His reputation in town was slipping away rapidly—when people pointed at him now, it wasn't to brag about him. Without his businesses to keep him busy, he spent a lot of time alone. During this period, he actually increased his use of prescription pain medications. Now he wasn't only trying to kill the pain in his body; he was also trying to kill the pain in his heart.

Number 99, who had once swept down the football field in the exhilaration of the game, was now rootless, goal-less, his life unstable, untenable. He became deeply depressed. He felt himself losing his grip on life.

I've seen repeatedly that, when an individual is in severe pain and has an addiction, it takes a community to bring about healing. Perhaps sometimes an individual can do it alone, but it is far more difficult to heal in the absence of people who care. Hal had a few people who stuck by him, but for the most part he was abandoned. He might have had a less traumatic journey if he'd received more support, but at this point in his life, it just wasn't there.

Hal knew the excessive level of drugs he was on was at the core of his problems, and he'd tried stopping the drugs more than once. Then in 2001, when the New York manufacturer of his implanted pump to deliver pain medication to his spine went bankrupt after the 9/11 disaster, Hal decided to take the opportunity to make a supreme effort at getting clean. He shut himself up in his house for a month and went through the "shits, shakes, and shivers" of withdrawal, as he put it. In the end he was so weak and dehydrated that his brother-in-law had to take him to the hospital.

Soon he was going back to his doctor for more pain medication.

If anything, Hal's behavior became even more bizarre. He would wake up in the morning and find his house a wreck and his pain meds spilled about and wonder who had been in the house. Friends came over one night to observe what happened in the nighttime hours, and they told Hal the next morning that he was getting up in the night and taking more drugs. They also said he had been acting just like he was playing with his kids—who weren't there at the time. He didn't remember any of it. Nor did he know what was happening when neighbors found him sleepwalking down a street, pajama clad, in the middle of one January night. A combination of pain, sleep deprivation, and side effects of the medications was causing these bizarre behaviors. Hal was lucky that his temporary amnesia in the night didn't cause him to overdose, as it has done for others.

At around this same time, his serious problems with the law started. He was issued his first citation for driving under the influence of his medication in 2001 and his second the following year. According to Utah law, being convicted of driving under the influence three times within ten years automatically made a person a felon, so when he received his third DUI in 2003, he knew he was in trouble. Possibly, if he'd been able to afford a good attorney, he would have been able to get away without doing jail time, but his money was mostly gone by this time and he couldn't afford good representation.

Hal was hoping that the judge would sentence him to drug rehab. The judge, however, would hear none of it. At the end of the trial, the judge said, "I'm going to make an example of you, Mr. Garner. Look at you! You were a local hero. Now you're an addict."

Hal spent a year at the Cache County Jail in Logan. Being locked up with criminals was humiliating to him. Even more humiliating was being taken into the streets of his hometown in a jail uniform and shackles to visit his local pain doctor. His family, though, were relieved that he was in jail, because they figured he was safer there than on the streets. One good thing that happened during this year in jail was that Hal was weaned off his pain medication. He exercised a lot and was feeling great by the time he got out. It was apparent that exercise was a key therapeutic modality Hal needed—it provided him both physical and mental improvement.

But upon leaving jail, he couldn't find work. He became agoraphobic and spent most of his time at home, with no work or activity. Physical activity is important to minimizing most types of pain, but in particular back pain. Therefore, the lack of physical activity contributed to the recidivism of his pain. Soon he was going back to the same doctor and taking the same pain medications, resulting in the same crazy, risky behavior with hardly any indication he had learned from his previous experiences.

After a fourth DUI in early 2006, Hal woke up in a jail cell and couldn't remember even getting in the car the night before, much less what he'd done to get pulled over. *Oh my God,* he thought, *did I hurt somebody? Did I kill somebody?*

Fortunately nothing as serious as that had happened. The judge at his trial said, "You have a choice. This time you can spend two years in Cache County Jail or you can go to prison. What will it be?"

"If those are my alternatives, I'll take the state prison, Your Honor," he said. Hal knew that the state prison was down in Salt Lake City, where fewer people knew him. It would be less embarrassing to be a prisoner there, he figured.

During the ten months Hal actually stayed at the state prison, he continued to receive high doses of medication to his spinal canal. At the same time, he participated in a drug rehabilitation program called Conquest. And he spent a lot of time reconsidering his life. Mostly he was wondering, *What is my family thinking about me? What are my kids thinking? Are their friends saying, "Oh, your dad was such a big football player. Now he's a drug addict in jail"?* His pride was shattered and the future looked dim. This, however, was the darkest hour before his dawn.

As part of his sentencing arrangement, the judge had said Hal could not go back to the two pain specialists he'd been seeing in the Logan area. That is why he started coming to see me at Lifetree.

Heroism

When Hal came to see me with his prison guard by his side, and I reviewed his record, I could hardly believe the dosage of opioids he was on. By magnitudes, it was higher than anything I'd ever seen before. Hal could easily have been paralyzed from complications with the catheter he still had in his spine if he had continued using the same concentrations of medication. Or he could have joined the ranks of better-known celebrities who ascend into the national consciousness one last ghoulish time when they are found dead after taking too many prescription drugs.

Keri Fakata, a member of my staff, commented to Hal, "This

much medication could kill a horse." This wording may not have been original, but for some reason it got through to Hal more clearly than anything else. Perhaps because he'd been such a magnificent physical specimen at one time, a thoroughbred, and because he had since found out how flawed he could be, the comment made him pause.

After he'd become more comfortable with me, Hal said, "Dr. Webster, I've been wanting to back down on the drugs I've been taking for a long time. But those other docs just kept giving me more narcotics. Can you help me? I'm really ready now."

I believed him. With some people who have serious substance abuse problems or mental health issues, I judge that it's better not to treat them with opioids at all—they might not take medications as prescribed and thus I might wind up doing more harm than good. But I had a sense that I could work with Hal, prison garb and shackles notwithstanding. Questioning about his background revealed that he was basically a responsible person who had become enmeshed in substance abuse through well-meaning but misguided prescribing by doctors. Because Hal was like the Sprague Dawley rats—not naturally of an addictive inclination but rather drawn into overuse of drugs through stress—he was capable of being led away from excessive drug taking. It would be a step-by-step process and not easy, but the destination was worth it.

One of the first things I did was to introduce Hal to Suboxone, hoping it would provide reasonable pain relief and reasonable protection from the effects of withdrawal as he stepped down his opioid intake. This is the same medication that Rachel Hutchins and Jason Bing both used for their own addictions. Hal agreed to try it, and over the course of a year and a half we weaned him off opioids entirely. This wasn't as difficult for him as his self-directed attempts to stop cold turkey had been, but it was still tough on his body, his mind, and his work performance as he gave up the medications that had been his security for seventeen years. He later told me that he considered it the biggest accomplishment of his life—bigger, in other words, than becoming an All-American, winning a spot on a professional football team six times, or going to the Super Bowl twice. This is the kind of struggle some patients face daily.

At the same time that I started Hal on Suboxone, I also tried a supplementary strategy. I wanted to replace his current prescription with something that wasn't opioid based at all. For this, I had an alternative that had been available for prescription only briefly at that time and that came from—of all places—the ocean floor.

Cone snails are a group of mostly tropical sea snails that have colorful cone-shaped shells and that will extend a barbed, harpoon-like "tooth" to paralyze their prey with venom. Biologists at the University of Utah began investigating the uses of the venom, called ziconotide, shortly after I completed my residency there. I became one of the early principal investigators, and by the time the FDA approved it for use under the trade name Prialt in 2004, I had used it on more patients than most other physicians. I'd seen firsthand this drug's potential—it gave some patients amazing relief—and I was glad to be able to prescribe it to people like Hal.

This drug can only be delivered directly to the spine through a catheter, and it can sometimes cause side effects, such as psychotic disorders, so it's not for everyone. Hal, however, was a candidate for the medication. The new drug gave him an alternative that worked without the use of any opioids, which had all but destroyed his life. We put it in his medication pump and began its infusion. It helped him instantly.

With the Suboxone and Prialt treatments, I saw Hal Garner turn into a different man from who he had been when I first met him. While he was still behind bars, he impressed the penitentiary staff with the seriousness of his intentions. After receiving an early release on probation, he left the prison but stayed in the Salt Lake area, away from the bad memories and broken relationships at home in Logan. Gail and Sydney Waite, owners of Salt Lake City manufacturer Roto Aire, bravely gave him a job despite his checkered past. In the early months of his employment, there were days when he came to work "loopy" with the medications or could not come in at all. Over time, though, he persevered and proved to be a determined worker, bringing the same energy and discipline to the job that he'd once shown on the athletic teams he'd played for.

Hal had to fall a long way before he hit rock bottom. Once he'd done that, he could start to climb back up. Just as those who have lost a loved one to death must go through stages of grief before arriving at acceptance of their new reality, so, I believe, chronic pain sufferers must proceed through stages of processing the losses that the pain extracts from them. They might have to go through shock or anger or bargaining with God. They certainly have to give up their denial about what has changed for them and accept that they aren't going to get their life back just as it was before pain, for only then can they go after the new life that could be. This is the point Hal had reached. Chronic pain and addiction, aided oddly enough by divorce, prison, and rejection, had brought him to the point where he was ready to embrace a new life.

In contrast, I have had countless patients tirelessly, and dangerously, try to restore the life they once had with medications. And fail. Some patients may be resistant to opioid abuse and can tolerate large amounts for prolonged periods without difficulty, while others are highly vulnerable and even a small exposure can unmask an addictive demon that can destroy. A changing environment (stressors) will change the thresholds of resistance, so individuals need to be aware of human precariousness and vulnerabilities.

Not all reach the point of acceptance and rebuilding. Hal did.

When he was young, Hal Garner had taken the gifts he'd been born with and worked hard to make the most of them. Daily, he'd run and lift weights and practice on the ball field to become the best football player he could be...right up until his last injury at the Bills training camp. All the hard work had carried him to the peak of his profession with a spot on a Super Bowl–bound NFL team. Now, after being brought down by pain and addiction, he undertook what to my mind was a more noble, if not more difficult, attempt to rise again. He broke his dependency on opioids, obtained and held a job, and began earning back the respect and trust with his loved ones that he had squandered. There were no coaches (unless you count me and Keri), no scouts, no journalists to watch. And that makes his achievements all the more admirable.

If he wasn't a hero before, today he is. He deserves a ring.

And therein lies the lesson for anyone who is in pain...

Building Back Up

Hal Garner lost a level of public glory that most of us never experience. His crashing to earth was an epic fall. The truth is, though, everyone with pain experiences losses and consequently grieves the life they once had. Everyone with pain has to adjust to major changes. They know it and their loved ones know it.

Sometimes the desire to get back to the vanished life can lead people who have pain to make mistakes that actually cause their situation to get worse. In part, that was Hal's problem. He was using opioids, not just to treat his legitimate complaint of physical pain, but also to replace the adrenaline rush he'd known for years as a competitive athlete. Opioids, in their turn, stripped him of everything he had, right down to his civil rights.

A better response would be to get to a place of acceptance that things have irrevocably changed, as Hal finally did in the jumpsuit of a state penitentiary convict. This is the acceptance stage in the five classical stages of grief. I realize that acceptance doesn't come quickly for most people. Those of us who care about people in pain can gently nudge them toward acceptance, but ultimately each one has to work his or her way through the process of disillusionment on an individual schedule in order to find the acceptance that lies on the other side.

The beautiful thing is that, when someone who has chronic pain reaches the point of acceptance, it doesn't merely bring a new sense of peace. Acceptance also creates a floor to build upon. It marks the beginning of an uphill climb, not to the old life, but to a new one that may be just as satisfying.

Hal Garner has been able to build a positive new life for himself. Today he lives in Salt Lake City and goes to work every weekday at

Roto Aire, where he's now in charge of the production of air-purify-ing filters. His management job doesn't require him to put too much stress on his painful back, but it does keep him on his feet all day. It's both physically and mentally challenging, and he likes it that way. His pain score is at a 2 or 3 most days, a constant presence as always, but for the most part not an impediment to living life the way he wants to. He's back to exercising every day, enjoying fishing, hiking, swimming, biking, golfing, and other activities. He believes that eating well and keeping active are important components in managing one's own pain.

For years after his release from the state prison, Hal avoid-ed going back home to Logan, because he knew that if he went into Walmart or some other public place, it would happen again: people would point and whisper. In his head he could imagine what they were saying: *There's that Hal Garner. He used to be a pro football player, but now he's a drug addict. He's been in and out of jail, you know.* Now Hal's courage and self-respect have re-vived to a point where he has decided that he isn't going to hide anymore. He goes back to Logan regularly to visit his daugh-ter or to watch his son's rock band, September Say Goodbye, perform at a local venue. Now, when he thinks of the whisper-ers at Walmart, Hal declares to himself, *Let them point. I've made my mistakes, but I'm not a monster as I've been portrayed.*

At one point he sat down with his kids and told them how sorry he was for the way he'd let them down and embarrassed them in front of their friends. As he knew it would, the anger of years came pouring out. It felt hot upon his ears and he had to take it like a coach's locker-room harangue. But it was a beginning, a down pay-ment of reconciliation. Though both his kids are hanging out with him now (which wasn't the case for a while), his relationship with them is not yet as close as he would like it to be. As more years of freedom from drug dependency, of responsible citizenship add up, and as they all grow older, they may begin to trust him more. This is his hope.

"I look forward to waking up in the morning now," Hal says.

"For the last seventeen or eighteen years, that was the last thing I wanted."

He has a way of looking off into the distance when he says, "I know there's something better for me."

Hal also has a mission: to help others avoid the problems that drugs brought to him. In his spare time, Hal speaks to young people in church and school groups about the dangers of drugs. The kids listen to him because he's been to the end of the road that some of these kids are just starting down—and he's come back to tell the tale. Hal has joined me in speaking before large medical groups to help the audiences understand why people in pain get into trouble with drugs and how he was able to emerge as a productive and proud person.

Hal says, "My sister tells me maybe all this was meant to be. I don't know. All I know is that I'm at a point in my life where I'm happy again. My friends see it. My family sees it. I can do everyday, normal things. I don't have to worry about my medications. I wanted that all along, but I didn't know how to do it. I was afraid to do it. I was scared of the withdrawals. Scared of the pain.

"I thank God every day I'm where I am. Maybe it *was* meant to be. Maybe it was so I could tell others."

What to Know About Addiction

There are four simple guidelines to follow if you want to avoid the risk of becoming addicted to opioids:

1. Never use an opioid if there are alternative therapies that would work for your pain.
2. Never use an opioid to treat a mental health disorder, such as attention deficit hyperactivity disorder, depression, anxiety, or post-traumatic stress disorder.
3. If you do begin taking opioids for pain, discontinue them as soon as possible.
4. Know your risk factors for developing addiction-type behaviors.

One widely used tool for determining addiction vulnerability is the Opioid Risk Tool. If you would like to quickly calculate your opioid addiction risk level, go to LynnWebsterMD.com and click on the "Opioid Risk Tool" link.

If you've already developed an opioid addiction, do not give up hope! It is possible to back away from opioid use while successfully treating your pain at the same time. Hal Garner's story proves that. See a medical professional, preferably one with addiction treatment training.

CHAPTER 6

Soul Mates

You may need only one person in your life to experience the joy of living again.

I'VE KNOWN PEOPLE WHO have walked alone in their journey with pain. The outcome has never been good. Companionship, by contrast, has a way of catalyzing the healing process. Following a drug regimen, recovering from a surgical procedure, going to physical therapy appointments, processing negative emotions, keeping engaged in one's own health care—all the things that people in pain must do to find healing are easier, less scary, and more effective if they can do it with someone by their side.

The kind of companionship I'm talking about is not primarily professional medical attention, although certainly that's important too. I'm talking about someone who is already naturally close to a person in pain (spouse, parent, sibling, child, friend) seeking to understand what's going on and being available to help. Every relationship is unique, but regardless of how this kind of relationship develops over time, it is beautifully open to giving and receiving. *Love* is as suitable a name for it as anything.

Providing loving companionship to someone in pain is not easy. Just as a person in pain experiences loss, so the people closest to him or her have to make unwelcome adjustments. And I know not everyone is great at being a companion, just as not everyone is great at seeking out companionship. I believe, however, that all of us can grow in the ability to accept someone who is in pain and be there for him or her through the rough patches, the fogs of confusion, the disappointing setbacks and the exciting advances. We'll be getting more specifically to the topic of caregiving in Chapter 8. Here, though, we'll be looking at the importance of people with pain finding someone who is going to be with them simply as a friend or lover.

Two of my greatest instructors in the power of love to people in pain are named John and Marsha.

The Slide

John Kay has lived all his life in the Ashley Valley of northeastern Utah, an area rich in petroleum, natural gas, phosphate, and a unique form of natural asphalt known as Gilsonite. Much of the economy of John's hometown of Vernal is based on the extraction and exploitation of these natural resources. The year after John was born in 1963, his father, Lawrence Kay, founded Uintah Engineering and Land Surveying, which has since grown to become the region's largest provider of these services for the oil and gas industries. It was here that John grew up as a son of one of the leading citizens in Vernal, looking forward to a prosperous career of his own within the company his father had built.

He certainly had the drive to be successful at whatever he attempted. At the age of twelve John began working for his father, and he became one of the youngest licensed land surveyors in the state shortly thereafter. He was leading surveying teams before he was old enough to drive. By age sixteen, he was working on jobs in several states that kept him away from home for weeks at a time during the summer. He was a published professional photographer at eighteen. He married at age twenty and earned his pilot's license the next year. For recreation, John loved hunting and fishing. He satisfied his sense of civic responsibility by joining both the Uintah County search and rescue team and the volunteer fire department in Naples (near Vernal). He was gregarious and outgoing, enjoying a life crowded with challenges and friendly relationships. This was a man who lived in the sunshine of life.

Ambitious most of all at work, John had a habit of begging for the hard jobs that would set him apart and earn him recognition. In October 1984, at the age of twenty-one, John was part of a Uintah Engineering team flown in by helicopter to survey a remote well site in the Book Cliffs near the Colorado border. So rugged was the site, and so crowded with trees, that the helicopter pilot couldn't set the craft down. The plan was for the pilot to descend as closely as possible to a rock ledge and let John hop out, then pick him up later. In preparation for the maneuver, John opened the cabin door, slid his body into the roaring downwash of the rotor, and took up his stance on the landing skid. When the moment seemed right, he jumped the six feet or so to the ledge. He grabbed on to the rock face...

...and at once felt his handholds and footholds breaking loose.

With a shock, John realized he was sliding down the face of the ledge and couldn't do a thing to stop his descent. After twenty feet of a jolting slide, he came to a sudden stop on his backside when his fall deposited him on a sandy slope. The drop was over, but the pressure on his body, especially on the stack of vertebrae in his back, had been tremendous. He lay in the sand, rolling and writhing in pain.

Like Carolyn Tuft going to the mall at the worst possible time, or like Jason Bing stepping in a hole during a pre-dawn workout, John Kay discovered that pain can enter a life instantly and unexpectedly.

Delivered home by his coworkers, John knew he was hurting, but the initial medical advice he received in his hometown led him to believe that his injury might not be so bad. He hoped that chiropractic treatments would enable him to avoid back surgery. That self-delusion quickly came to an end one morning when he got out of bed, went into the bathroom, and while brushing his teeth, suffered a stab of pain in his back so severe that he collapsed on the floor in agony. The physician he saw in Salt Lake City later that day, Dr. Glenn Momberger, realized the severity of his injury and recommended a radical discectomy and fusion of three vertebrae.

The goal in this emergency operation was to reduce the movement in that section of the spine to prevent him from being paralyzed and to hopefully reduce his pain.

A disc fusion actually occurs in the post-operative period and not during the operation. The surgeon harvests small bits of bone from other areas of the skeletal structure and places them in the unstable section of the spinal column so that the bone will grow together and fuse that section of the spine. This process of fusion typically occurs over three to six months. John, accordingly, was sent home with instructions to take off work for six months and rest his back. Unfortunately, the limitations of John's disability insurance would not permit him to stay off the job that long, and he went back earlier.

Throughout my career, I would see firsthand how disability insurance companies would keep their eyes on cost containment more than on healing outcomes, denying claims, refusing to cover certain treatments, or limiting the scope of therapy. This kind of adversarial conduct would inevitably pile more stress on people who were already stressed by their pain situation. Sometimes this added stress from the insurance companies, I believe, was enough to tip the scales so that someone who had been prescribed opioids for pain would begin abusing the drugs in order to feel better emotionally. Other times, insurance payout limitations would directly lead to a worsening health situation through preventing people from obtaining the therapies they needed. In John Kay's case, his insurance company's policy forced him to go back to work too soon, and his pain grew worse instead of better.

John was referred to me in 1988 after a second disc fusion operation one vertebra above the previous one failed to resolve his pain any better than had the earlier operation. (He would have a third and final fusion operation in 1990.) He began making the 180-mile trip from Vernal to Salt Lake City to meet with me at least once per quarter year. I gave him epidural steroid injections, muscle relaxants, and a small amount of opioids and monitored his progress.

Medically, John was now gradually improving, although he

remained plagued with pain. Socially, he was struggling. He wasn't as active or as engaged in life as he once had been. Friends and family would ask what was wrong with him and he would try to explain. He found what so many other patients of mine have also found: that no one can really understand chronic pain unless they've gone through it themselves. His coworkers wondered why he wasn't getting back fully to being his old self on the job—they thought he was shirking. His parents confidentially shared their doubts about his taking narcotics long term. Like Jason Bing, John was experiencing the loneliness of a socially enforced separation from the healthy population. Worst of all, the sense of isolation and misunderstanding followed John all the way into his home.

As with everything in his life during his younger years, John had been impatient to start a family and had married "way too early," as he would express it to me. So now there were two young people dealing with this life-altering injury. His wife wanted the happy, normal life she had enjoyed with John before the accident. This was just like many other situations I have observed over the years where the companion has expected the person in pain to shrug off the effects of an injury and return to his or her normal lifestyle, including going to work to restore their income. As a person who hated anything medical and would never go to a doctor herself, John's wife resented it when he started seeing physicians. Eventually she even stopped taking him to Salt Lake City for his medical appointments, forcing him to spend the three hours each way in the car by himself.

It was the lowest point for John Kay.

So far.

Rescuer in Need of Rescue

In response to the fusion operations and the treatments I was trying with John, his back pain subsided to a manageable level. He was able to do some less-demanding work for his father's engineering and surveying business. He was even promoted to the position of chief of the volunteer fire department in Naples.

All of the department volunteers, and particularly John, were ready night and day to put out house and grass fires and provide the usual range of paramedic services in emergencies. Knowing that highway accidents accounted for some of the greatest emergency needs in Uintah County and the areas beyond served by the fire department, John led fundraisers that brought in $160,000 to buy a rescue truck, jaws of life, and other lifesaving equipment, along with training, to turn the department into a real rescue unit. Over a period of years, John responded to hundreds of calls to provide rescues at accident sites in town and country. He never could have foreseen the way one of these accidents would turn rescuer into victim.

On Saturday afternoon, April 18, 1992, John got a call from Utah 911 emergency services about an automobile accident and then sped with his team to a spot twenty miles to the northeast of Vernal on the Browns Park–Brush Creek Road, inside the boundary of Ashley National Forest. John had seen a lot of auto accidents, but this was one of the worst. A drunk driver in a three-quarter-ton pickup truck had plowed head-on into a small sedan with such force that the sedan's engine block had been pushed up against the legs of the fifty-eight-year-old female driver of the car. The brake pedal had been driven all the way through the woman's lower left leg, while simultaneously her seat had slid forward, locking her against the mangled dashboard and steering wheel. She was conscious but disoriented from shock. John's own adrenaline was causing his heart to beat abnormally fast, producing a choking feeling in his throat from the intense pounding.

The first job was to release the stuck driver's seat so that the team could begin removing the woman. Jaws-of-life cutting shears in hand, John went in through the broken rear window as the other men on his team held him upside down. In a cramped spot behind the driver's seat, he positioned the shears and activated the hydraulic pump. At that point, something went wrong with the usually reliable tool. It rotated, pinning John's wrist and forearm to the floorboard of the car, continuing to torque for many excruciating seconds until his team was finally able to turn it off. John had experienced pain before, a lot of pain, but not like this—this was beyond words. He knew his arm was severely injured.

The other men pulled him out of the car and, at his instruction, set him to the side as they proceeded to remove the driver from the automobile wreckage using hand tools. After she was transported to Salt Lake City (where doctors saved her life), the rescue workers made sure their own chief was transported by ambulance to the Pleasant Valley Medical Center in Salt Lake City. There Dr. Douglas Burrows performed surgery to put the broken bones in John's wrist and arm back together in a semblance of what they had originally been. He would wear a cast for eighteen months. But that was not all or even the worst of it. At the site of this injury, John soon developed complex regional pain syndrome, a chronic condition in which nerve damage leads to pain that's more intense and long-lasting than the original injury would normally be expected to create. Without early intervention, the syndrome can lead to permanent and ever-worsening pain and loss of use of the extremity.

When John came to see me, I knew his new injury could progress to contractures and total loss of the use of his arm. This meant I had to be aggressive with his treatment to help avert the worst. For the new injury and its attendant disease, I performed many stellate ganglion blocks, depositing a local anesthetic near John's spine to block the small nerve fibers contributing to sustaining the pain in the hand. When this approach became inadequate for him, I tried radio frequency lesioning, passing an electric current through the stellate ganglion complex of nerves next to the spine in an attempt to extend the pain-relief effect to several months at a time. In addition, I was regularly prescribing anticonvulsants, sleep aids, and opioids. John was now a person in serious chronic pain.

Fighting against all my efforts at this time was a new source of trouble in John's life: stress derived from a legal battle. Because John and the other fire department volunteers were not employees of Naples, the city had never taken out workers' compensation insurance on them. John needed those insurance payments now because he was out of work again due to the new injury. He filed a lawsuit against Naples so the town could in turn seek damages from the State of Utah. This lawsuit cast John in the unwelcome role of antagonist toward the town he had so selflessly served as fire chief, and this action significantly compromised his reputation in town. As his stress level rose, so did his pain. After five years, John finally won his lawsuit, being awarded reimbursement for his medical expenses and lost wages. His reputation within the community never fully recovered.

John's pain was proportional to his stress. I have seen that pattern often. Many of my patients would have to resort to litigation to get the benefits they deserved. In the workers' compensation system, medical concern for a person can be less important than deciding who is going to be responsible for paying the bill. I quickly concluded that workers' compensation does not exist to protect individuals but to protect an employer. More immediately for my concerns, I saw that it was nearly impossible for people who were in litigation to heal. Stress alone would prevent improvement from occurring. This is what John Kay had to go through. Litigation, however, was not the only source of stress in his life.

With John's chronic pain worsened and his ability to work affected, his relationships deteriorated further. John's days of working for the engineering company were over, causing some of his colleagues to stop speaking to him. Even worse, John felt that his father was disappointed in him. As an authority figure, John's father loomed large in his life. At one time the elder Kay was not just John's father but also his boss in the engineering firm, the mayor of the city where John served as fire chief, and the bishop of his church. Lawrence Kay always supported his son, even when he didn't fully understand, but this didn't stop John from feeling as if he had let his father down.

John's unemployment led to financial stress, which further led to depression severe enough to require counseling. He tried applying for jobs that he thought he could handle in his fragile health state, but each time interviewers would ask him about medicine use because word had spread throughout the town that he was a drug user. When he admitted that he was taking opioids, he wouldn't get the job.

More than once, friends or acquaintances, including some of the best-thought-of members of the community, offered to pay him for his drugs. He might be approached anywhere with a question like this: "I've got a headache. Could I buy some of your pills from you?" On one occasion, a stranger who observed him picking up painkillers followed him home from the pharmacy to pinpoint where he lived. John's home was never actually broken into for prescription drugs, but other homes in town, even in John's own neighborhood, *were* broken into. Vernal was even the site of one bizarre but well-publicized incident where police officers barged into a hospice just minutes after a woman died and demanded that her grieving husband help them collect her medicines.[1] It seems that America's prescription drug abuse problem was alive and well in small-town Utah. John already knew that people were suspicious about him, and now he was suspicious about them as well.

At home, John explained to me, his wife was becoming even more disgusted with his medical needs. She thought he was a drug addict and a malingerer, just as many others in the community believed. Their children, aged six years, three years, and two months at the time of John's jaws-of-life injury, saw only a part of the way that his pain affected him as the years continued to go by. The children derived their opinions about him, especially about his opioid use, largely from their mother. John began feeling alone in his own home among his family.

John told me a story about the complications his pain inserted into his marriage. "One day I was in worse pain than usual," he said, "and I was at home lying in a recliner with a heating pad under my back. I needed to use the bathroom but couldn't get out of the chair on my own because of the pain. I called out to my wife, but she didn't answer. I called out again. She at last came into the room. 'Would you help me upstairs?' I asked."

In his face, I could see the hurt of the remembered slight as he continued with the story. He said, "She came over and grudgingly helped me out of the chair and up the stairs to the bathroom. After she helped me back down the stairs and into my chair, she stood and faced me and said, 'Are you going to have another operation so you can stay on the pain pills even longer?'

"She knew what the injury had done to me, yet she could say this to me," he told me. "I couldn't believe it."

John's wife didn't understand him, and now he didn't understand her either. They would go on maintaining their marriage and family life for a while yet, but from this point on, it was barely working.

Unable to get a job in someone else's company, John decided to go to work for himself. Thinking it would be something he could handle despite his pain, he started a photography business called Western Exposure. Two years later he sold it and started a small surveying company called JK Land Surveying, carrying out property surveys. But this, too, got to be too much for him with his pain problem. He sold the surveying company and from then on lived primarily on Social Security disability payments. His life consisted largely of trying to prop up a collapsing marriage and traveling back and forth to Salt Lake City all by himself so that I could help him keep his pain problem under control.

It was a long way from the original hopes and dreams of one of Vernal's fortunate sons.

Meanwhile, at about this same time, another resident of Vernal was introduced to chronic pain.

Need for Resilience

It was a weekday in October 1995. Marsha Miller, a forty-one-year-old secretary with light-brown hair, worked at the Ashley Valley Education Center, an alternative high school in Vernal, Utah. While printing a lengthy document, she heard the sound made by the printer sitting on the floor shift from the regular rustle and settle of collation to a sharper striking noise with slither as pages struck the wall. She knew the exit tray was overloaded again.

Marsha bent sideways in her swivel chair and reached down to pull the printer away from the wall and reach the fallen papers. As she yanked on the heavy printer in her awkward twisted position, she felt a *pop* low in her back and let out an "Ouch." At once she straightened and stood rubbing her back. The pain seemed to be easing. Maybe she hadn't hurt herself too badly.

But she had. The pain didn't go away.

Marsha kept trying to ignore it. She thought it prudent to back off from some of her usual physical activities, but she avoided seeing a doctor. After all, she was busy taking care of not only her job but also her family. (One of her three children was still at home with Marsha and her husband.) Then she got the news that her son's wife had gone into labor and delivered a premature baby.

Over the Thanksgiving holiday, Marsha traveled to Salt Lake City to visit her son, Jamie, and his now family of three. While she was walking with Jamie in a department store, her right leg suddenly collapsed under her and she fell to the floor. Stumbling back to her feet with Jamie's help, she discovered that she couldn't feel her right leg. It was completely numb. Her back, though—she could feel *that* for sure. It was hurting worse than ever, "like an ice pick stuck in my back," she said.

Upon returning to Vernal that afternoon, she contacted her primary care physician, who ordered an MRI to be performed on her lower spine. It would show that the disc separating the vertebrae lumbar (L5) and sacral (S1), in the area that had been injured in the printer incident, had herniated again. A large piece of the disc was protruding beyond its normal boundaries, squishing and pushing her L5 nerve out of its normal position. This protrusion was likely already in the process of killing a part of her nerve by preventing blood and oxygen from feeding it.

Spinal surgery performed in early December restored partial feeling to Marsha's leg, but she was disappointed to find that the back pain didn't go away as her body healed from the operation. Adding further discouragement, her surgeon in a follow-up appointment delivered the news that, because she had scarring around the nerve, she would likely need pain management for the rest of her life. So in 1996 Marsha showed up in my office at Lifetree for the first time, seeking help for her pain.

I'd heard her story of backache in a thousand permutations from other patients already by this time, injuries to the spine producing more cases of chronic pain than any other cause. In her case, the painkillers that her other doctors had prescribed—Percocet and Lortab—were not adequately dealing with the pain. They may have blunted the sensation of the ice pick in her back, but it was still there, jabbing away. Marsha never enjoyed an uninterrupted night's sleep anymore; she would be up and down in the early hours, wandering the dark house whenever the pain got worse. She had trouble getting comfortable in any chair or seat. Making it through a workday was a test of will. Life was miserable because of her pain.

She needed a reprieve from the daily punishment she was forced to endure. Physical therapy, non-steroidal anti-inflammatories, and anticonvulsants were among the many therapies that we tried but that failed to provide the relief she needed to enjoy life. From there, we moved on to opioids.

In the late 1990s, and early in the twenty-first century, opioids were the recommended treatment for moderate to severe pain, particularly if other therapies had failed. OxyContin was the darling of the opioids because it supposedly was less likely to be abused and would work for longer periods of time, obviating the need to use as many Percocets or Lortabs. So, consistent with the standard of care at the time, Marsha was started on OxyContin. This finally gave her substantial relief.

After being away from her job for a few weeks with surgery and recovery, Marsha went back to work. She also applied for workers' compensation to help with paying for time off to recover as well as her medical and travel expenses—a process that took about three months before she started receiving the benefits. This exercise of her legal right as an employee disgusted one supervisor, who later had Marsha transferred, first to a new job at Uintah High School and then to another at Vernal Middle School as records clerk. Her coworkers in this last office were more understanding and tried to accommodate her with a better chair, a cushion, and a footrest. She ended up being glad for the job transfer. Still, it wasn't easy putting in a full workday while in pain.

Then, in 1997, her surgeon recommended a procedure recently approved by the FDA—the insertion of a small titanium cage in the disc space between two vertebrae to create fusion of the bones. It was similar to the operation John Kay had already undergone. Believing it might give her permanent improvement and eliminate her need for pain medications, Marsha decided to proceed with the operation. This second operation did improve her back pain somewhat, but it didn't entirely fulfill her hopes, leaving her with a disabling level of back and leg pain and numbness. It was at this point that, in her own mind, she truly accepted her surgeon's word that pain was going to be her destiny for life. This was the sort of turning point that every person in chronic pain reaches sooner or later if she is going to move ahead to a better existence. *This is my life from now on,* Marsha told herself. *I've got to either deal with it or crack up.* She decided to deal with it.

Experts who study these things say there are two kinds of acceptance of a severe problem such as chronic pain: *acceptance with resignation* and *acceptance with resilience.*[2] Acceptance with resignation steals hope more thoroughly than pain itself can do. Acceptance with resilience makes it possible for a person to reinvent himself or herself on the other side of a problem's onset. Marsha was resilient. Like all of the people I know who have experienced substantial healing from pain, she acknowledged that pain had become a permanent presence in her life and then set about trying to make the best of her new situation.

I stepped in with a procedure of my own to recommend: the implantation of a spinal cord stimulator. This device—which Jessy Klain and many other of my patients have tried—consists of a battery-operated electrical generator about the size and shape of a pacemaker that is placed under the skin in the abdomen or lower back, with wires running to electrodes placed in the spine near the point of injury. By pressing a button on a remote control, the patient can activate the generator and send a small charge of electricity into the spine, suppressing the sensation of pain in the lower body. I've had female patients tell me that, when the stimulator is activated, the tingling sensation makes it feel like they're wearing vibrating pantyhose. Some patients don't want to use it all the time due to this tingling, especially when they sleep. When they do choose to use it, however, it often provides significant help with pain. That's what Marsha discovered.

Still, I was only managing Marsha's pain. I wasn't fixing her injury—something that, regrettably, nobody could do. The enduring fact was that Marsha's life could no longer be what it had been. Before her injury, Marsha had participated in skiing at Park City. She had also enjoyed biking with her kids, joining a friend at the high school track for an early morning jog, and going for long motorcycle rides in the Ashley Valley with her arms wrapped around her husband. None of this was possible for her anymore, and she became a bystander to the prior joys in her life.

One day a young grandchild asked her to give him a piggyback ride.

"I'm sorry, honey. I just can't," she apologized.

"Why not, Grandma? You used to give piggyback rides."

This was one of many times Marsha was put in the position of having to explain to family members why she could no longer do what she used to.

There was one more issue. She described it to me like this: "For women, chronic pain takes away femininity. It makes it hard to feel attractive when you're wearing a bathing suit, tight leggings, or lingerie. Sometimes even the way you look because of your pain makes you feel unattractive." Marsha was acutely aware of the scars from her surgeries and the lump under her skin where I had implanted her spinal cord stimulator.

The pain had taken away so much from her. From her children, grandchildren, and husband too.

At first her husband drove Marsha to her appointments at Lifetree Clinic from faraway Vernal. He seemed supportive but kept asking when she was going to be "fixed"—a sign that he didn't understand the nature of chronic pain very well. As a migraine sufferer, he might have been more sympathetic to what Marsha was going through. Yet intermittent migraines of the type he had were different from the feeling of an ice pick stuck in your back all the time. The sympathy he initially felt devolved into resentment and resistance. Before long, it was Marsha's younger daughter, Caradie, who was driving her to Salt Lake City for her appointments.

Once, the marriage had been a happy one, and it had produced three now-grown children whom both partners loved dearly. But it had been eroding for some time, the process of disintegration accelerating noticeably when pain crept into the marriage like a third-party interloper. Still, Marsha was not expecting it the day in 1998 when her husband came home and announced that he wanted a divorce, packed his bags, and left. Their children, by this time, were all living on their own. Now Marsha's husband was gone too.

She was all alone.

Together

In the summer of 1999, John Kay drove to Salt Lake City, rode the elevator up to the second floor, and signed in at the front desk of Lifetree Clinic for his regularly scheduled appointment with me. Then he glanced to his right down one length of the L-shaped waiting room and saw someone he thought he recognized. He approached her.

"It's Marsha Miller, right? I didn't know you came here."

"I didn't know *you* did," she replied, smiling.

He sat down beside her to explore this coincidence.

These two residents of Vernal had both been coming to my office for years—John since 1988 and Marsha since 1996—and until now neither had known the other was my patient. They weren't close friends, but coming from such a small town, they naturally knew one another and had mutual friends. At one time John had gone goose hunting with Marsha's husband and had stopped in their home briefly. Both now were experiencing the collapse of their marriages and would soon be divorced. Both were struggling with chronic pain.

With so much in common, they decided on the most natural thing in the world. They can't remember who first suggested it, but one of them said, "Why shouldn't we schedule our appointments at the same time and drive together from home?"

The three-hour trip on Highway 40 would never seem so long again.

The friendship that Marsha Miller and John Kay formed during their long car rides to and from Salt Lake City for medical appointments gradually developed into something deeper. Not only were the pair compatible in a lot of the usual ways, but also they shared the reality of living with chronic pain. Both knew the ups and downs of pain treatment. Both had faced misunderstanding and rejection. Both had fought legal and administrative battles to get what they deserved. Both in time had accepted their new lives with resilience. After Marsha had to quit her job because it was causing her back condition to deteriorate, both were adjusting to being unemployed and living on disability.

It's not surprising that their spouses, as well meaning as they may have been, found it hard to understand and adjust to the changes John's and Marsha's pain brought about. I see the same thing happen all the time in close relationships where one partner is in pain and the other is not. Now, however, John and Marsha had found each other, perfect counterparts for a new life that accepts the presence of pain but isn't defined by it.

When Marsha and John talk about their courtship, one incident often comes up in the conversation. It seems that, when it looked as if their relationship might be moving toward something closer than friendship, Marsha thought she needed to make a disclosure to John. "I've got this funny little thing in me," she began hesitantly. "For my back. It's called a spinal cord stimulator, and the electrical generator's right here under my skin—"

John interrupted her. "Feel this," he said, guiding her hand to the generator of his own spinal stimulator underneath the skin of his abdomen.

She looked up into his face and both laughed.

John and Marsha married the week of Valentine's Day in 2005. They still live in Vernal and see some of their eight children and sixteen grandchildren almost every day. They live together modestly in a frame home on what their disability payments bring in. They like taking the grandkids fishing and love photographing Utah scenery. Although they go to church every week, the three-hour block of time sitting on a bench is too much for their backs, so they attend only the first hour of services. They love going to movies and out to dinner with family and friends, but sometimes they beg off because they need to get out and move after sitting for too long. When driving to their doctor visits, they have to allow time to stop and walk around to stretch. If a rare longer trip is in the works, they have to plan ahead and make sure they have medications on hand. After all these years, much in their lives still revolves around their pain problems, yet they have found a new path—a new purposeful existence—and look forward to their future together.

These two are among the happiest people I know. That has everything to do with the fact that they now have each other.

Marsha says, "We wouldn't be where we're at if it weren't for each other. John is my right hand and I am his left. We're seldom on the downhill at the same time, so we can encourage and lift each other up." Whereas she used to try to hide the full extent of her pain from her first husband, fearing that he wouldn't understand or appreciate it, she doesn't even have to tell John when she's having a bad day—he just knows. "When John says he needs to stay in the recliner today, I believe him and understand. He does the same for me. We relate to each other in ways most couples wouldn't understand."

John testifies, "I can honestly say that Marsha is my soul mate and we found each other for a reason and a purpose. During the low points of my life's journey, I rely heavily on Marsha. She battles the same things I do, and together we cope rather well. We basically spend 24/7 together. I love every minute of it."

Willing to Care

The Kays have taught me that having someone close to you is a key to restoring happiness after pain appears. It doesn't always have to be a spouse who provides this love and companionship, but it has to be someone who accepts you and tries to understand and help you. If you're really lucky, you may have more than one person who is willing to come along with you on the journey of pain. People with different kinds of connection to a person in pain can provide different levels of support at the times when it is needed.

To take a small example of what this kind of caring relationship can mean, think about what happened when Marsha and John admitted to each other that they had spinal cord stimulators implanted in their bodies. A funny moment, yes. But there was more going on. Knowing that the other had the same device took away the embarrassment for both of them. In particular for Marsha, it helped her feel better about her appearance as a woman. John and Marsha were beautifully suited to each other in normalizing the abnormal and going on to face the future with lighter hearts.

Several research studies have established that supportive relationships tend to alleviate depression and reduce the perception of pain in those people who are experiencing chronic pain.[3] One study of more than five hundred people with chronic pain examined how they fared, relative to the supportiveness they perceived in their families. The results?

> The patients who reported having non-supportive families tended to have liability and work-related injuries, relied on medication, reported having more pain sites and used more pain descriptors in describing their pain. These patients also tended to show more pain behaviors and more emotional distress compared with pain patients coming from supportive families. On follow-up, patients who described their families as being supportive reported significantly less pain intensity, less reliance on medication and greater activity levels. They tended to be

working and not to have gone elsewhere for treatment of their pain compared with patients who described their family as non-supportive. The results of this study demonstrate that perceived support is an important factor in the rehabilitation of chronic pain patients.[4]

Relationships, even supportive ones, should never undermine a person's motivation to take charge of his or her own pain care (see Chapter 9). I've seen that happen in cases where a loved one hovers over a person in pain like a helicopter, rushing in as soon as the person in pain needs something. This steals the person's initiative to help himself or herself. But this adverse reaction is relatively rare. People who have caring relationships generally do a better job, not a worse one, at the self-management of their pain problem.[5]

Studies have also shown that when a loved one is too solicitous of a person in pain—frequently asking how he or she is feeling, offering to help, bringing the subject of pain—it can make the person feel worse. No doubt this is because it reminds the person in pain about the pain he or she is feeling.[6] So it would seem that developing the skill of being there, but not interfering too much, is a skill that loved ones need to learn. We have to be loving *and* wise.

For people with chronic pain, having good relationships can even save your life. A meta-analysis of 148 independent research studies found that, for people with health conditions (not just chronic pain), supportive relationships increase the odds of survival by 50 percent! A lack of social relationships, on the other hand, constitutes a health risk rivaling the effects of such well-known health risk factors as cigarette smoking, high blood pressure, high levels of blood lipids, obesity, and lack of physical activity.[7]

My hope for everyone who has pain is that they will find one or more people who will love them toward healing.

_____ ⋁⋁⋁⋇ _____

CHAPTER 7

The God Prescription

Believing in something or Someone bigger than yourself invites healing into your life.

I SAID IN CHAPTER 1 that pain is a bio-psycho-social-spiritual condition. Actually, however, it might make more sense to reverse the order and put "spiritual" first, because for many people the spiritual dimension is the most important. More times than I can remember, I've known people in pain to cry out to God for mercy, kneel in silent prayer, cross themselves or finger their rosary, practice yoga or meditation, wear crosses or angel pins or crystals, express a longing for heaven, mention attending religious services, or tell me about their belief in God.

The simple fact is that most people have a tendency to turn to God and faith when they are in need, including when they are in need because of pain. I and most others in my specialty have come to see this as generally a good thing, because relating to God or a perceived spiritual reality beyond oneself can affect one's pain experience positively.

Of course, not everyone who is in pain is also religious or spiritual, or wants to be, and certainly I've known many people with pain who have experienced a substantial increase in their life satisfaction without recourse to spiritual beliefs and practices. I'll be addressing the nonbelievers' situation later in the chapter. But if we're interested in what promotes healing for those enduring long-term pain, we can't ignore the interaction between belief and pain.

One person who has taught me much about this interaction is a former patient of mine named Walter Alexander.

Not in the Business Plan

In March 2001, Walt was a forty-nine-year-old former athlete, former Air Force officer, husband, father of nine (!), and CEO of the commercial real estate development company he had founded several years earlier.[1] He was perhaps the most prominent businessman in Salt Lake City's small but vibrant African American community. He was also a devout Christian and was not only a leader in the ethnically diverse evangelical church his family attended in Salt Lake City but also was occasionally a speaker at Christian events held around the country.

Walt's schedule was always packed, and he loved it that way. After all, he was blessed with boundless energy and it had to go somewhere. He was always gregarious and always smiling, but underneath this genuine friendliness was a steely core. This was a determined man, a man whom seemingly nothing could stop from accomplishing what he intended. But in March 2001 a change was about to enter his life that Walt never saw coming.

That's when he went in to an outpatient clinic for arthroscopic surgery on his left knee. The previous autumn, Walt had been playing football with some of his sons and their friends when he injured his knee, and he'd been feeling stiffness and twinges of pain from the knee ever since. The orthopedic surgeon he consulted assured him that an operation would repair the damage and get him back to life as usual in short order. That sounded good to Walt.

When he woke up from the surgery, however, he noticed burning pain in his left leg that radiated into his foot, along with numbness down the length of his leg. This was worse than the pain for which he'd been operated on in the first place! At first he thought the pain and numbness were normal side effects of the procedure he'd undergone and that they would quickly go away. But when both persisted, he became concerned.

During a follow-up visit, the surgeon offered what was probably the correct explanation for the source of the pain. Before beginning the operation, the surgeon had applied a tourniquet to Walt's thigh and inflated it to 300 PSI. The operation had wound up taking somewhat longer than expected, so the tourniquet was in place for a full two hours. The tourniquet pressure remaining on Walt's leg for that long had damaged the sciatic nerve—a rare but not unheard-of consequence. The surgeon apologized profusely and said he thought the pain would clear up soon. He recommended that Walt go for long walks.

Walt walked. The pain didn't go away.

Constant agony and two hours of sleep a night became the norm for Walt. He lost his appetite, and the weight started dropping from his formerly 210-pound frame. Although he tried to ignore the pain and maintain his usual schedule, he couldn't manage as he had before. His wife and kids and business partners became concerned.

A local neurologist gave Walt my name, and then Walt came in for his first appointment with me five weeks after the surgical mishap.

When I first met Walt in the exam room, I saw a tall, erect man who was impeccably groomed and had faultless manners. Despite the way pain was distorting his personality, I could sense a reservoir of compassion and goodness within the man. With his energy and his obvious intelligence, I could easily understand why he had been so successful in so many areas.

Over time, though, as we began to work on his pain problem, I observed something that was troubling to me: Walt was treating his pain like it was an obstacle in his business life. It was a problem to be solved and dispensed with. He had heard from the neurologist that nerves could regrow (true in some situations), so he thought that he just had to survive until the problem would resolve on its own or until he found the right treatment that would fix him. Walt believed there must be a simple solution somewhere that would put his pain behind him.

Walt was nothing if not persistent. "Give me something to do and I'll do it" summed up his attitude. One time, for example, I asked him to do one hundred repetitions of a certain exercise for his feet before he came back to me. When I saw him next, he reported that he had done not one hundred but *twenty thousand* repetitions! On another occasion he brought in a graph he had created, on one axis showing the amounts of the medications he had taken at certain times of the day and on the other axis showing his corresponding levels of activity. I had never seen anything like this before.

But by this time I knew that neither graphs nor foot exercises, nor anything else, was going to erase Walter Anderson's pain. I had to break the truth to him.

One day we were in my office when he said, "Lynn, tell me what I need to do."

I let out an audible sigh. Then I removed my glasses and leaned toward him. I said, "Walt, your recovery may take longer than you think it is going to."

Silence.

At length Walt said, "I know this is going to get better." He still wasn't convinced of the truth.

Some time passed. We were making progress in treating his pain, but only little by little, so at another office visit I became more direct with him. I asked Walt's wife to leave the room and then said to him, "You may be living with this pain for the rest of your life."

He dipped his eyes and finally nodded his head. At last he believed me.

I didn't want him to give up hope. Certainly I hadn't given up hope that we could help him get better, and I wanted his active participation in his own healing. But I wanted us both to have a realistic hope. It was Walt's expectation of a cure, or at least the time frame of a possible cure, that I wanted to change, because it wasn't helping us to make progress in his care. I wanted him to have "acceptance with resilience," just as John and Marsha Kay had.

Meanwhile, Walt was discovering that life with pain as his companion was very different than his life had been before or the life he had expected to live.

A New Walter

Before the pain entered his life, Walt had been a highly capable man at the height of his powers and influence. His real estate firm was responsible for some of the most innovative new retail and office developments from Provo to Ogden. The Salt Lake City Council tapped him to provide volunteer leadership for civic building projects. He was increasingly featured in business, Christian, and African American–oriented magazines. He somehow kept up with many of his kids' activities. He worked out before dawn almost daily at the Sports Mall athletic club.

The knee surgery was supposed to be a temporary interruption in his schedule. Instead, the pain it produced caused the humming works of Walt's life to come grinding nearly to a halt.

The first months were the worst, before the treatments we were trying began to provide some relief. Although many people display few outward signs of their inner suffering, Walt noticeably changed in a short period of time. When his son Cameron came home from college that summer of 2001, seeing his father for the first time since the operation, he was astonished to discover how gaunt Walt had become. By then, Walt had lost fifty pounds. Cameron realized how fragile his father had become one Sunday when the Alexander family was leaving church. The walk to their van in the parking lot was a short one, and the day was only slightly cool, but by the time they got into the van, Walt had broken out in convulsive shivering. He was so thin and weak that he couldn't resist even a minor chill.

Walt was able to maintain little in the way of normal relationships. The pain was so bad that he was rarely able to carry on a conversation that lasted more than thirty seconds. Sometimes he was withdrawn and uncommunicative, dealing internally with the pain. Other times, he became almost manic, speaking rapidly and going from issue to issue, excessively enthusiastic about whatever he was talking about. Although he was always polite to me, I heard from others that he could be antagonistic and rude to the people he lived and worked with daily, and he wasn't even aware of it. This was completely unlike him.

His relationship with his wife changed, too, as her role evolved into that of a caregiver instead of a lover. As much as Louise wanted to be close to him in what he was going through, he was incapable of being emotionally intimate with her. He said to me later, "Intimacy has a stillness and a quietness about it. But pain comes roaring in when you're quiet." For Walt, trying to have an intimate relationship with Louise was like trying to carry on a conversation next to a freight train hurtling down the tracks.

One strategy he relied upon to cope with the ongoing pain in the midst of all this was something he learned at the Pain Rehabilitation Center at Mayo Clinic: he distracted himself. He kept in his pocket a list of things he could do to take his mind off the pain when it got really bad—things such as going to a movie, taking a drive, and calling someone he hadn't talked to in years. He used these activities like channels to redirect the flow of his thoughts. He wanted to keep the pain pressed down in his mind by refusing to think about it.

This part of Walt's pain management strategy was hard on his family. They couldn't talk to him about what he was going through— that was against the rules. As his oldest son, Jayden, said, "If you had one good conversation about his pain with him in a year, it was twelve months of repressed emotion." This may not have been quite what the Mayo pain clinic had in mind, and it may not have been the best choice, but cutting off discussion of his pain was one way Walt chose to ignore the pain.

Distraction worked, to an extent. But his attention had to go somewhere, and the obvious choice was his job.

Walt worked. And worked. And worked some more. This wasn't business for the love of the game. It wasn't even ordinary workaholism. It was work as salvation, work so that he could keep his mind engaged in something other than his pain. Sometimes he stayed awake for as long as forty-eight hours at a stretch, working nonstop. When he finally reached the point of utter exhaustion, he would fall asleep. But then, after an hour or two, the pain would wake him up again. So he'd go back to work and it would all begin again.

At times when the pain got to its worst—when no distraction strategy he could try, no business matter he could attend to, and no pill he could swallow would help—he would focus on survival in its barest form. He would slip off his watch and declare, "I'm going to stay alive for the next minute," then sit there staring at the watch face. Once the second hand had swung all the way around, he would repeat, "I'm going to stay alive for the next minute."

He would keep this up *for hours.*

Is this what his life had been reduced to? Not living but surviving? Relationships on lockdown? His work no longer fun but turned into emergency therapy? He couldn't help feeling discouragement over how he had changed.

Walt believed in a God who was all powerful and all knowing. So he struggled to imagine what meaning his pain could have in God's larger plan. Answers would eventually come that were better than he could have imagined.

Listening to Pain

Walt did not like talking about his pain problem with others, but when he did mention it to his fellow Christians, he generally found that they were sympathetic and wanted to support him. He appreciated that. He wasn't so sure he appreciated what they had to say about it to him.

He found that their responses tended to fall into certain biblically inspired categories. Some would mention Job, the Old Testament character who underwent a period of severe testing because of a contest between God and Satan that Job was not privy to. Their point for Walt was that we don't know the whole cosmic significance of the pain we are subject to in life and so we have to trust God. Others described Walt's pain as a possible "thorn in his side," alluding to a comment made by the New Testament's apostle Paul when he was afflicted with a chronic condition. In other words, Walt's pain, they were suggesting, was a trial sent by God to keep him humble in his work. Still others would say something like "Do you have sin in your life?" This was the trip-to-the-woodshed response implying that Walt might be to blame for his pain, sent as discipline from God.

Walt had to ask himself if these responses were applicable to him. He concluded they were not. He didn't think that God primarily intended his pain experience to grow his faith, keep him humble, or cause him to get clean about sin, though the experience did have those effects to varying degrees. He concluded, instead, that his pain was meant to teach him things: things about himself, about others, and about living life. This became a focus of his spiritual life.

Walt's family and many friends prayed for God to heal his affliction or miraculously take away Walt's pain. These were the fervent prayers of people who loved him, not casual acquaintances. Yet, while Walt would have more than welcomed relief from his pain, he had a sense that asking for healing was not the path he was on. Instead, he prayed that he would learn the lessons God had for him. And in time he did.

For one thing, Walt came to understand better than ever before that he is not in control of the big picture; God is. While failure and hardship had come to him in different sizes from time to time over the years, nothing compared to the pain and loss that followed his medical injury. The hardships he had experienced before were temporary, and he had accepted them as a risk of living an engaged life. But this kind of pain, and its accompanying losses, were an imposition that came upon him from outside himself and rested deep within. For one who believed in a God who was intentional, this could only mean that the pain was not random. It seemed that God had chosen to allow the pain in his life for divine purposes Walt could not fully understand. The pain was happening to him, but it wasn't really about him. God was in the process of bringing out of it something that was godly. Indeed, his years of severe pain were "littered," he would say, with paradoxes, unexplained and unwarranted successes, and numerous opportunities to use his unique pain and loss experience to benefit others. Walt viewed all these as "God sightings."

In addition to settling the matter of who was ultimately in control, Walt learned some things about compassion through his pain experience. He had always been a caring man who tried to help others, but previously his wealth, achievements, and good health had shielded him personally from much of life's suffering. Now he didn't just *know* about suffering as an observer; he *understood* it, felt it deep inside. He was no longer an outsider to hardship but one intimately familiar with it. It taught him what it was like to need help, and it caused him to grow and mature in his understanding of compassionate giving.

Insights like these didn't get rid of Walt's physical pain, but they did help him mentally deal with it by removing the sense that his pain was pointless. He was on a journey of discovery.

A "Miracle"

After those first few months, Walt and I were able to adjust his treatments to a point where his pain was bearable. But only just. The pain in his leg remained severe for nine years.

He finally turned the corner in 2010. As we had done more than once before, one weekend we had him go off his pain medications so that we could recalibrate them at a lower level. Each time we had tried this before, he had gone through a period of intense pain and withdrawal from the drugs. This time, though, the pain dropped 80 percent and he had no adverse symptoms of withdrawal. Walt attributed this startling improvement to supernatural causes. To him, it was a miracle. I think his medications (as sometimes will happen) had gotten to the point where they were causing pain more than they were relieving it, and so going off the pain medications paradoxically helped his pain level. Maybe the nerve injury had healed some too. In any case, after nine years of pain, Walt was at last much better. And he has remained that way ever since, with careful observation and close management of his drug regimen to keep him there. His friends and family report that the Walt they used to know has come back from long exile.

This was a wonderful outcome, however you choose to interpret it. Yet I found one aspect of Walt's response to it to be most interesting.

One day I was talking with him about the improvement we were seeing in his pain condition. Walt was clearly pleased, but I sensed some reservation in his enthusiasm about the drop in his pain level and asked him about it.

"I'm worried, Lynn."

"Worried about what?"

His answer went back to the lesson that pain had taught him about compassion. "What I discovered when I was hurting so badly," said Walt, "is that pain has a dialect. It has a way of revealing itself that other people in pain can recognize and respond to, like you both come from the same region. You have credibility with each other and almost an instant relationship.

"Before my injury, I was reasonably sympathetic to someone in a wheelchair, for example. But when something like this happens in your life, you become aware of other people's pain on a whole different level."

He was saying that his severe pain had attuned him to other people with severe pain, not just physical pain but also mental, emotional, and spiritual suffering. When he came across someone who was deeply hurting, he would notice the signs of pain in that person's words and tones, gestures and body language, the subtle giveaways that others who are made near-sighted by their own good health might overlook. It gave him empathy for others, rights of membership in the fraternity of suffering. It fueled his drive to do works of compassion.

He went on, "Now that I'm getting better and I'm caught up in other things, I'm worried about losing my fluency in that dialect."

One can only respect a desire not to lose brotherhood with humanity's most hurting people. Yet I know that today Walt is actively trying to make a difference for others. He still speaks at Christian gatherings around the country, but he no longer talks about how to be a success, as he used to. Instead, he talks about being faithful to God and being loving to others. Although they don't talk about it much, with some of their wealth, Walt and Louise have started a nonprofit foundation with the mission to create quality low-cost housing in Haiti. Many lives in this poor country are going to be different because of them. When people praise Walt, though, he's quick to say, "It's not about me. It's about God."

Pain has permanently changed Walt. And if he's right, that was God's plan all along.

The Medicinal Properties of Belief

Medical researchers have looked into the effects of religion and spirituality on chronic health conditions, including chronic pain, for many years. It turns out that Walter Alexander is far from alone in finding his faith to be important to him in his struggle with pain. In one major survey conducted among people who have chronic pain, half of the respondents said they used prayer to deal with their pain.[2] Another study concluded, "Prayer is the most used complementary therapy; religious coping is among the most common strategies used to deal with pain."[3] Even religious skeptics, when in pain, often show an interest in praying for themselves, having others pray for them, and attending a religious service.[4]

In many ways, pain and addiction are intertwined subjects. So maybe it's not surprising that, just as twelve-step programs start out with acknowledging a higher power, so people in pain often find themselves turning to God. There's something about the seeming helplessness of being in pain that makes many people look for a source of strength on high.

I've seen the importance of spirituality over and over in people who are enduring pain. I've worked with evangelicals like Walt, many Mormons, Native Americans who practice traditional rituals, and other types of believers. Some are *religious*, by which I mean they express their faith in God within a particular religious system. Others are *spiritual*, a more general term that includes religious faith but also encompasses any belief in a higher power and spiritual practices that are unconnected to organized religion.

Researchers are especially interested in how effective religion and spirituality are in helping people deal with their pain. Studies have shown a connection between having a religious or spiritual orientation and experiencing an improvement in pain. One report summarizes, "The best available evidence supports a positive association between religiousness and positive affect, and a negative association with depressive and anxiety symptoms."[5] In other words, people in pain who are religious or spiritual tend to feel better than those who are without belief. They are "more likely to have better psychological well-being and use positive coping strategies."[6]

Karl Marx called religion "the opium of the people." In a more literal way than Marx intended, religion and spirituality are similar to opioid analgesics for people in pain. They actually help to alleviate pain.

Prayer, meditation, religious rituals, attendance at a religious service, forgiveness—these are the kinds of religious activities that help. For example, Roman Catholics who were shown an image of the Virgin Mary reported a drop in their pain perception.[7] Zen Buddhists who practiced mindfulness meditation likewise felt less pain.[8]

Not all actions inspired by a belief in a higher power, however, are helpful in reducing pain. Some can actually make the situation worse. For example, people who believe in God but are angry at God over an extended period of time can feel worse. Or if people think "it's all in God's hands" and neglect to pursue treatment for chronic pain, they are setting themselves up for trouble.[9] As one report concluded, "Lack of forgiveness and negative religious coping may serve as an impediment to healthy emotional functioning."[10]

Still, overall there is a strong positive correlation between religion or spirituality and healing from chronic pain. There are at least three ways in which the benefit comes:

1. inner peace
2. connectedness
3. meaning making

For believers, praying, meditating, reading holy scriptures, and the like can have a calming, soothing effect that reduces the sensation of pain. These practices take people's attention off their symptoms of pain and set it on a higher plane, reminding them of God's power and love and reinforcing their hope. The prospect of heaven gives them a better life to look forward to, one without pain. All this helps to provide a sense of peace that pours healing oil on the internal agitation caused by their pain.

In addition to the personal experience of peace, the communal sense of connectedness to others improves pain. As we have seen often in *The Painful Truth,* relationships heal. Religion is helpful to a person in pain by providing an instant connection to a community—a church, synagogue, or temple congregation. Sometimes fellow members of a faith community can be insensitive and unhelpful, even if well intentioned, as Walter Alexander found at times among his fellow evangelicals. But religious participation does provide a built-in body of like-minded individuals who (at least in theory) can provide companionship and compassion, crossing the divide that pain creates. Rachel Hutchins took comfort from her Catholic congregation. The Kays worship regularly at their Mormon church. Many others seek and find help in a faith grouping of some kind.

Last, there is what the medical researchers term "meaning making." People who are hurting often ask the "Why?" questions. Why me? Why now? Why this? What's it all for? We seem to be so constituted as humans as to resist the notion that our most deeply felt emotions could have no ultimate meaning. Consequently, we look for purpose that will set our pain in a context that will somehow make it worthwhile, or at least understandable, and therefore more bearable. Religion and spirituality can help people to identify some meaning for their pain. Maybe religion and spirituality can also help to draw some good out of their pain and pass it on to others—a further healing benefit. This is what Walt was doing when he found lessons from God in his pain and became a more sensitive, giving person than before.

As one of the medical research analyses puts it, if we want to know why people of faith tend to handle pain better, "perhaps the answer can be found in the seeking of understanding, meaning, strength, and transcendence, the desire to go beyond."[11]

Believing in Belief

I have learned a great deal about the importance of spirituality from people of faith such as Walter Alexander. Walt believes to his core that life is a gift from God and that our paths are determined for a reason. He uses faith to guide his choices, not only to deal with pain, but also to help him in every area of his life. He has helped me to see that faith can be healing.

The scientist in me knows that belief can motivate, inspire, provide the foundation and inspiration for existence and survival. It is an energy for life. It can be the spiritual spine to resilience. It provides an understanding. It can be righteous and good. It provides a reason and explanation and can lead to acceptance.

Excluding science, it is a metaphysical connection that is "real" and natural. It provides a reason for hope. A power greater than human beings can provide the explanation for why a person has seemingly been chosen, like Job in the Old Testament, to experience pain. Pain is not punishment; it is a part of life. How we choose to experience it is left to the individual. Spirituality shows the way for many.

Yet what about those who don't believe in God? Are they left out of the potential healing effects of belief? Sally Quinn, an author and journalist at *The Washington Post*, asked these questions. Here is her advice to nonbelievers:

They should look for meaning.
    Happiness is love. Full stop.
    My life has been full of happiness and full of sorrow.
    But it has always been full of love.
    You have to be as loving as you wish to be loved.
    To me, it's about generosity of spirit.[12]

Love, compassion, giving, and relationships are within the reach of all of us, whether we're believers or doubters when it comes to God. These are the ingredients in the elixir for pain. And therefore my advice on this topic boils down to the following simple guidelines.

If you're a spiritual or religious person who is enduring pain, explore how practicing your beliefs can aid you in your journey through pain. Let your faith reduce your pain, and let your pain increase your faith. Draw on the presence of your fellow believers to give you strength and comfort. Surround yourself with medical professionals and others who will support your spiritual approach to dealing with your pain.

If you're neither spiritual nor religious, you can still cultivate the attitude that all the great religions of the world promote:

Love.

___ ⋇ ___

CHAPTER 8

Everyday Saints and Unsung Heroes

A caregiver accompanies another in the journey of pain and recovery.

WHEN SOMEONE SUFFERS A major injury, undergoes a serious operation, or learns about the onset of a debilitating disease, friends and family cluster around and express their sympathy. There are visits, cards, phone calls, flowers, sweets, encouragement, and promises. This is normal and helpful.

But what happens when the medical condition extends beyond the acute phase and into chronic territory, weeks and months after the start? Many lose interest. They might even begin to resent ongoing reminders of ill health or to blame the very one they were sympathizing with earlier. They drift away. The flow of encouragement slows to a trickle. Promises come to naught. This, too, is normal, but it leaves the person with a chronic health condition feeling alone in facing challenges he or she can't escape.

But if the person with the chronic condition is lucky, there are one or two or perhaps a few left standing nearby when the rest of the crowd has dispersed. These, by elimination and by choice, are the caregivers, the ones who will take up the challenge of providing the continuing support that's needed. They might include a parent, a spouse, a sibling, a grown-up child, a friend.

Caregivers for those in pain face innumerable challenges. They deprive themselves of a normal schedule. They forgo pleasures and other responsibilities to be there for the one in need, out of duty, love, or both.

People who have chronic pain may live for years, and so goes the role of the caregiver. The responsibilities are never ending. They may include nursing, banking, cooking, housecleaning, bill paying, and all the other practical activities required for a person to exist in society. They include, in addition, advocating and interceding, listening to complaints, bearing with ill humor, providing comfort, sometimes exhibiting tough love, and always nurturing hope.

Just as I have been privileged to meet many people who have faced a future of pain with bravery and faith, so I have been fortunate to know many loved ones who have voluntarily taken on a caregiving role that they never sought. They are the companions on the journey toward healing. I think of them as the everyday saints and unsung heroes in the world of pain.

One who exemplifies for me the finest qualities of caregiving is a woman named Ann who cared for a husband in pain for three decades. Although her experience ended up being more tragic than that of most caregivers, it shows that caregivers—just like the people they help—are deeply affected by the experience of pain.

Helpmate

A slim, dark-haired girl, Ann Nuttall grew up in a happy family in Sandy, Utah, south of Salt Lake City. The model of love she observed in her parents and grandparents would have a lot to do with her compassionate caregiving later in life. When she met the funny and good-looking Michael Petersen in high school, started dating him, and then married him while both were still teenagers, she expected to enjoy a happy family life with him similar to the one she'd grown up with. And in fact there *would* be much happiness, much laughter and pleasure to remember from the thirty-two years of marriage that lay ahead for them. But a specter entered their mutual life early on: pain.

Michael was prone to intestinal blockages. He had his first surgery to relieve blockage at age four, with two more following at age ten. The growth of scar tissue would continue to cause him pain periodically for the rest of his life. At the time of his marriage to Ann, however, he was largely in good health.

That changed two and a half years into the marriage. By this time, Michael was working for the Church of Jesus Christ of Latter-day Saints in the family records department. Ann had also worked for the church for a while but was now at home taking care of their first child, Rachel, a toddler. One day in November 1975, Michael was walking with two coworkers down a hallway when a third coworker came running up from behind, accidentally tripped, and butted—hard—into Michael's lower back with his head. This simple accident set off the chain of problems for Michael and his wife.

The evening of the accident, Michael came home and told Ann what had happened at work. His back was hurting badly and he needed crutches to walk, so they scheduled an appointment with their doctor. Ann went along to the appointment with Michael and heard the news that a bone fragment from his spine had moved and was impinging on a nerve.

Some weeks later, Michael had surgery to remove the bone chip, and the pain afterward gradually improved. He and Ann were hopeful it would recede entirely over time. Like most people in a situation like theirs, they thought the pain was a temporary problem. But they were destined to be disappointed—the tide of pain rose again.

When Michael was told that he needed a second back surgery, Ann began to get her first inkling that his back debilitation, with its associated pain, might become a permanent presence in their lives. Michael would, in fact, undergo a total of four back surgeries. Each one helped for a while, but none gave sustained benefit. As I've seen verified many times, the chance of significant improvement from back surgeries dramatically declines with each successive operation. After two operations, many patients will be no better or worse than if they had not been operated on in the first place. For the rest of his life, Michael would have severe pain and areas of numbness in his back, legs, and feet. The nerves exiting his spine were irreparably injured. Sometimes the pain would get better; sometimes it would get worse. It would never go away, except briefly near the end.

Meanwhile, Michael's childhood intestinal problems returned, leading to two more surgeries to remove scar tissue and damaged sections of his intestines. He ended up with a bowel only forty-two inches long, or about 15 percent of the usual length. His abdomen and back were often in agony at the same time for two separate reasons. Over the years, he went to doctors who put him on opioids such as OxyContin, muscle relaxants such as Soma, antidepressants such as Lexapro, and sleep aids such as Halcion. He tried traction, chiropractic therapy, acupuncture, heat and ice treatment, biofeedback, relaxation training, counseling, physical therapy, and occupational therapy. Most of it helped some. None of it cured the pain.

For many years, he continued to work in the family history records department of the LDS Church. As with most people in pain, his job helped him maintain a sense of normality in his life. In this way, it was good for his pain situation. This benefit is why I always encourage people in pain to continue working if they are physically up to it. Like everyone else, they need the social context and psychological diversion that comes with being active. But whenever stress flared up at Michael's work, it could make his pain worse. That, too, is common. It affected his wife as well as himself.

From the date of the accident in the hallway, Michael was in pain for the rest of his marriage to Ann. Life would not be what she had expected when she married him. But she never considered not being his caregiver. Of course she didn't call it that to herself, at least not at first. It was just the role life had given her, a variation on the daily demands of wifehood. But a caregiver she was.

Not all spouses or other loved ones are willing or able to accept this responsibility. Some, like Jason Bing's wife, hang in there. Others, such as John Kay's and Marsha Miller's first spouses, feel that they have to bail.

Until very near the end, Ann never seriously considered abandoning her husband, regardless of how much easier that might have made her life. In part, her commitment was due to the example she'd been given in her birth family of offering unconditional love and support to those in need. But in addition, she and Michael had held their wedding at the central Mormon temple in Salt Lake City, and a temple wedding, in Mormon belief, involves a special sealing and an eternal bonding. Theirs was a "celestial marriage," they believed, and so any thought that they would not remain together was alien to their mindset.

Ann would give Michael massages to relieve his pain and stiffness. She would bring him food and entertain him by playing movies on the television. She would sing songs and pray for him. She listened to his complaints. She shouldered most of the responsibility for raising the kids. Eventually she bought a hospital bed and turned the living room into a bedroom for him. Whenever he needed something, it was usually Ann who came to him and supplied the need.

She can recall one time when she broke down and cried because of all that she was having to do for Michael. She felt sorry for herself. The endlessness of it all was getting to her. Another operation was coming up, and she kept thinking, *Oh, man, we have to go through this again!* After her crying spell, though, she felt better, and she got up and did what she had to do next for Michael. She felt guilty over her moment of weakness, but the truth is, she was a more faithful helpmate to Michael than many other spouses would be in the same position.

Family life went on, as normal as they could make it. In addition to Rachel, the couple would have three more children: Ben, Camille, and Laura. Their youngest, Laura, a preemie, had cerebral palsy and deafness. And thus Ann became caregiver to two—her daughter as well as her husband. As she came to see it, this was a task she had consciously accepted.

One of the lesser-known planks in the Mormon theological platform is a belief in premortal covenants. The LDS Church teaches that humans have a spiritual existence before being conceived on earth and that in their pre-existence they can make covenants, or vows, to accept challenges on earth that result in personal spiritual growth. This doctrine helped Ann make sense of her role in taking care of her husband and daughter. She believed that, in her existence before this one, she had willingly accepted these challenges and adventures.

"I know that I agreed to be Laura's mother," she said to me, "and I think I also agreed to be married to Michael and to go through these things and help each other."

Most caregivers for people in pain will not settle on this explanation, but they do all need to get to a point of accepting their new role. (Or if they don't, then they choose a different path in life.) Just as people who have pain need to work through stages of grief to arrive at a place of acceptance for their new condition if they are going to begin to heal, so their caregivers also have grief for a loss and also have to accept and adjust to their role.

Caregiving was so much in Ann's blood that she took a job at Jordan Valley School, a public school for children of all ages who have severe and multiple disabilities. This is the school Laura attended. Ann has worked in the preschool, providing early intervention for children with disabilities, for more than a quarter century now.

The Costs of Christlikeness

Being there for Michael was not easy for Ann, especially as the years rolled on and his medical condition worsened.

Michael's natural tendency was to be upbeat and amusing—that was one thing that drew her to him in the first place. His sense of humor could be downright silly, and his wife and children loved this about him. But the constant pressure of pain from his back and abdomen distorted his temperament. Combined with some of the medications he was taking, his pain changed his personality. He could go through mood swings that made him appear to Ann as if he were bipolar.

One day Ann was watching television in the family room with Camille. Michael was in another room trying to get through to someone on the phone, and the television seemed too loud to him.

He yelled at them to turn it down. They turned it down a bit, but not enough to satisfy him. The next thing they knew, he came into the family room, shouting at them, and grabbed a pair of scissors, which he proceeded to use to cut the power cord to the TV.

Camille made a move to confront him, and he threw a bowl of cereal at her. The milk splashed on the ceiling. They would later try to scrub the milk stain off the ceiling, but it wouldn't fully wash off. "I think God left that stain on the ceiling as a reminder to me," Michael said.

Apart from these family dramas, Ann was also present and shared with him the humiliations that cropped up occasionally with his pain treatment.

From the time of his back injury, he was on opioids prescribed by his surgeons and other doctors who treated him before he came to me at Lifetree Clinic. The amount of opioids had to be increased gradually as his condition worsened and his body built up a tolerance to the medications. Eventually he was taking large doses.

At one point, a new physician's assistant looked at Michael's records and said, "I do not believe that you can be on that much OxyContin and be alive. I want you drug-tested. I think you are selling it."

Ann and Michael both took offense at this. Michael would never dream of selling drugs. He was taking large doses, but that was only because smaller ones didn't work for him anymore. The drug testing verified that Michael was taking what he had been instructed to take, no more and no less, and the physician's assistant apologized.

Another time, though, Michael informed a gastroenterologist that he was taking OxyContin for pain, and this doctor got angry and blurted out, "Are you going to blow your head off?"

Ann and Michael were shocked and confused. Probing, they discovered that this physician had had a friend who had shot himself in the head while on OxyContin. Ann and Michael considered it highly unprofessional for this doctor to make the statement he had. They separated from this doctor by mutual agreement.

But it wasn't so much these occasional run-ins with insensitive people that made life hard for Michael and Ann. It was the way Michael's pain conditions wore him and Ann down. Over time, Ann saw Michael's personality bend toward melancholy. He became de-pressed—another medical condition that needed treatment.

One day Michael was lying in bed and he started crying. From across the room, Ann asked him what was wrong.

"I'm just so tired," he said.

She went over to the side of the bed, knelt down, and hugged him and kissed his forehead and his cheek. She was trying to com-fort him the best way she knew how.

After a little while, he said to Ann, "I am so sorry you have to go through this with me. I wanted to take you on vacations. I wanted to buy a boat and teach you to water-ski and—"

She interrupted. "I did not come to earth to learn to water-ski. I came to earth to learn what our heavenly Father wants me to learn, and I *am* learning a lot with you, and that is okay."

"You are so Christlike," he told her, the tears still in his eyes.

Later she would remember that comment and take comfort in knowing that he thought of her that way, as an unselfish, sacrificial-ly loving presence in his life.

It's impossible to say when thoughts of suicide first entered Michael's mind. He was naturally reticent about talking about this, even more so than many other people would be, since Mormon doc-trine regarded suicide a sin (though that position has softened in recent years). But if he was like many people with severe chronic pain, then early on he began feeling some longing for release from his life of suffering.

The first inkling Ann got of his suicidal ideation occurred in 2002 when the family was looking forward to the happy event of their daughter Laura being married. Out of the blue Michael said to Ann, "Let's go on a trip after Laura and Shane get married."

She replied, "Okay. Where do you want to go?"

He said, "Let's go back home."

"What do you mean?"

He spoke more plainly. "Let's go to heaven."

She looked at him and said, "I'm not ready to leave. It's not my time."

"But I'm so tired," he said.

She reassured him, "You'll be okay."

At the time, she didn't explore his ideas and intentions any more deeply than that. She was shocked. She didn't know for sure if he had suicide in mind and was planning to include her in it or not, and she didn't want to know. So she tried to put a stop to that talk and put it out of her mind. But suicide was an issue that wouldn't go away.

OD

On a Monday morning in October 2002, the bedside alarm went off at 5:00 a.m. Ann heard Michael groan, fumble with the clock to switch off the alarm, and then shuffle into the bathroom to start getting ready for work. Ann closed her eyes to try to get a little more sleep.

In an instant she was wide awake. She'd heard strange sounds, and now there were something like kicking and scratching noises coming from the bathroom. She ran to check on Michael.

He was sitting on the toilet, his eyes closed, his face grimacing, his whole body seizing.

"Michael!"

Ann stood beside him. As she watched, he grew rigid and stopped breathing. "Michael!" she called out again.

She began performing chest compressions the best she could because he was sitting up, and prayed aloud at the same time: "Please do not let it end this way!"

Finally Michael took a breath, then another.

Ann called 911 and Michael's parents. The paramedics arrived soon after and took Michael to Alta View Hospital. Michael's parents followed.

Ann wanted to go with him in the ambulance, but twenty-one-year-old Laura, their daughter, was asleep in another room. Laura had hearing loss as a consequence of her cerebral palsy, and she had slept through the entire incident. Ann didn't feel she could leave Laura alone. So she called Laura's fiancé and paced the room like a caged animal until he came to be with Laura. As she paced, she wondered how Michael was doing at the hospital. Would he live to attend Laura's wedding, scheduled for the next month?

When Ann finally arrived at the hospital, she learned that Michael had overdosed on amitriptyline. This drug is usually given as an antidepressant, but his primary care physician had prescribed it to him to help him sleep despite his pain. "He should be dead," the doctor at the hospital told Ann. The level of amitriptyline in Michael's blood was six times the amount usually considered lethal.

Michael spent several days in the hospital before going home. While recovering, he assured Ann that he had not overdosed on purpose. He didn't remember taking the medicine, he said, but the overdose must have been an accident. "I am so glad I did not die, because I don't want people to think I tried to kill myself," he said.

Ann believed him—or thought she did. He had been complaining a lot about stress at work recently, and he had been sleeping worse than usual. Probably he had just been careless with his medications, as he claimed. Again, she wasn't sure how suicidal he was and she didn't really want to know.

In any case, from this point on Michael was never the same. He complained of not being able to focus his mind. When speaking, he would jump from one topic to another. Ann attributed the changes to brain damage incurred during the seizure. In retrospect, it was the beginning of his final slide.

Michael was fully aware that his mind wasn't working as well as it used to, and it bothered him. Here was another hardship to bear. How much more could he take?

One day not long after coming home from the hospital after the overdose, Michael was feeling depressed and frustrated by his condition. While sitting in a recliner, Michael held his breath. Somehow he had learned that holding his breath could induce a seizure, which could become fatal for him. His breath holding was a kind of suicide attempt.

Ann ran over to him and said, "Stop that! What are you doing?"

Michael started breathing again. "I just can't take it anymore," he said.

They had an argument about the incident, but then both let it pass.

Ann was upset about the troubling trend Michael had taken toward a loss of interest in living, but she didn't do anything about it. This is common for family members in her situation. They tend to play down the seriousness when their loved ones in pain talk about or attempt suicide. They just want their loved ones to be normal. It's too hard to face the fact that someone close to them no longer wants to live and in fact may be nearing the final scene of life. They try to shut the possibility of suicide out of their mind, and when they do think about it, they may feel impotent and fatalistic.

Psychological counseling and better pain management (if it's available) may help a person in pain regain an interest in living. Caregivers can benefit from counseling, too, and their faith in God may help them come to terms with their loved one's mortality.

After the overdose and the breath-holding incident, Ann took charge of Michael's medications, giving him what he was prescribed at the times and in the amounts indicated. This was another responsibility that she accepted as his caregiver. Because his pain would be so severe, or because his mind was in a fog and he couldn't remember that he had already taken his pills, he would sometimes ask for more medication than he had been prescribed, and she would refuse to give it. This led to more arguments. She hated being in charge of the medications, but she knew she had to if she were going to keep Michael safe.

About this time, Ann read the book *Some Miracles Take Time* by paraplegic motivational speaker Art E. Berg, who lived in Utah. The book impressed Ann, and she looked up the author's number in the phone book and called him. His wife, Dallas, picked up the phone and informed her that Art had recently died. On the phone, the two women talked about their experiences as caregivers.

Ann asked Dallas what she had gone through. Dallas said that

Art wanted to be in control and deal with his needs by himself. This made it hard to help him. "They get frustrated because they are men," Dallas commented. This helped Ann understand Michael's reaction and realize she was not alone.

In his more clear-headed moments, Michael realized that his desire for opioids was getting out of hand. In past years Michael and Ann had gone through two pain clinics at the LDS hospital. On another occasion, he enrolled at The Bridge Health Recovery Center, in southern Utah, for the same purpose of bringing his craving for opioids under control.

Ann accompanied him to The Bridge program where they talked with the counselor about what Ann did for Michael. By this time, he could not work and was on disability, and so he was home nearly all the time. She would get him breakfast before going off to work herself. Later, she would serve him dinner in bed, where he would watch TV while eating. She would do almost everything for him.

At hearing this, the counselor accused her of being an enabler. The issue wasn't that she was dispensing medications to him. In fact, if anything, she was standing as a barrier between Michael and overconsumption of opioids. The issue was that she was doing too much for him in his daily living, thus making his situation worse and not better. Michael needed to take care of himself as much as possible if he were going to live a more normal life. As important as caregiving was, Michael needed to exercise maximum self-reliance in order to heal.

That word "enabler" stung Ann. Her first impulse was to deny it. Then she began to think, *Could it be possible that I am enabling Michael? Maybe he's begun asking for things like dinner in bed just because he likes it, not because he needs it.* She found herself saying to the counselor, "There's a fine line between enabling and trying to be Christlike. How do I know whether he really needs the help or not?" This is much like the dilemma that physicians sometimes must navigate between doing too much and doing too little.

The counselor told Ann to make Michael get up, walk, and do the things for himself that he was capable of. She was not his mother;

she was his spouse. It was a hard lesson to learn, but it was one she needed. In her case, caregiving *had* graded over to enabling. For Michael's good as well as her own, Ann had to maintain a margin of independence.

Set Free

After Michael's amitriptyline overdose, his primary care physician said he would not see Michael anymore. He was afraid Michael would die under his care and he would be held responsible. He referred the Petersons to me and washed his hands of them.

So often it was the case that I (like other pain specialists) would receive the toughest-to-treat, most at-risk patients—individuals whom no other physicians wanted to deal with. People in pain often have other chronic illnesses, such as diabetes, heart disease, and cancer, making their cases complicated and life threatening. Many of them are the sickest of the sick. Of course I would be nervous about treating them, but if I didn't, who would? If pain specialists are looked at askance because they prescribe more opioids than other kinds of physicians, or because some of our patients die while under our care, a big part of the explanation lies here: the people we treat are often in great need and at considerable risk by the nature of their health condition. Yet compassion goads us to promote their healing the best way we know how. In a sense, then, I was like many caregivers—when others vanished, I felt I had to be there for Michael and provide the best medical care I could, even if it presented a professional risk. That's what I was trained to do.

I was Michael's pain physician during his last, and worst, three years of life. One of the first strategies I tried for him was implanting an intrathecal pump under the skin of his abdomen to automatically deliver a small dose of opioids directly to his spine. This enabled Ann to stop dispensing oral opioids to him and reduced the amount of the medications he was receiving.

Michael did better for a while with the pain, but I was in a familiar race against a deteriorating health condition. By the fall of

2005, Michael's disc degeneration had worsened to a point where his surgeon said he needed a fifth back operation. Michael and Ann's hearts sunk at the news. The previous operations had been traumatic for him, with long recovery periods following each one, and now Michael's overall health and strength were worse than ever. They weren't sure that he would even survive the new operation.

Death was, in fact, looking more and more enticing to Michael. He kept saying to Ann, "I don't want to leave you alone, but enough is enough."

By this point, she understood that he had good reason for saying this. She wasn't thinking that he would kill himself but instead that he would die of natural causes, the result of his health problems. She told him, "You know I love you, and I will be okay if you need to go home." She meant home to heaven.

He seemed relieved by her words.

Several times Michael said things like this: "People have cancer and they get to die. I just have to stay here and suffer. We put our animals to sleep, but no one will help me. I am so tired. I do not want to keep doing this forever." He had reached a point that researchers call "mental defeat"—a risk factor for suicide in people enduring chronic pain.[1]

They were in limbo because workers' compensation insisted on a second opinion before approving payment for the operation, and the designated second-opinion doctor would not be available for an appointment with Michael for six weeks. Ann and Michael didn't know if he could wait that long. He was hobbling around on two canes or in a wheelchair and in awful pain all the time.

Ann called me one day and said, "Michael's been in the bathroom crying. I don't know what to do."

I heard the desperation in her voice. I knew how bad Michael's condition was, and I knew I had to try something new.

Beginning a few years earlier, I had used intravenous ketamine with patients who had neurologic pain disorders. Ketamine is perhaps best known as a drug used by veterinarians to put animals to sleep before an operation. It is also sold illegally on the street as

"Special K" and unfortunately is used as a date-rape drug. But doctors have also found that it can be useful as an analgesic. Because it can have temporary psychotic effects, doctors usually give it only to patients who are admitted to the hospital. But I felt that ketamine, like other strong analgesics, could be delivered in small amounts with manageable side effects. Further, I felt that for the treatment to work, a patient's pain receptors would have to be exposed to ketamine for days to weeks. I may have been the first physician who would start a continuous infusion of ketamine in patients and then send them home with it to lead their everyday lives until the course of treatment was over. I tried this treatment with Michael to deal with his back and internal pain.

The ketamine had a profound effect on Michael's pain. In fact, for the first time in three decades he was pain free. He explained it to Ann like this: "When you're in pain, you're like a hot air balloon tethered to the earth. No matter how hard you try, you cannot get loose and be free. You're always tied to the pain. But the ketamine cut the ropes and set me free."

Ann, of course, was thrilled that Michael was at last free of pain. But what he said next worried her. Still thinking of himself as a hot air balloon floating free, he said, "It's like I can see the other side really clearly." As he interpreted it, the medication had not only set him free from pain in this world but had also lifted him within sight of the next world. It was ominous.

On the same day that I had started Michael on the ketamine infusion, his family set apart the whole day for fasting and prayer. In the past they had prayed many times for God to help Michael get better and give him the strength to go through what he faced. But this time Ann and the others felt that God wanted them to pray differently. They asked for the Lord to take Michael home to heaven. Ann didn't think for a moment that this would mean that Michael would kill himself; she thought he would die in surgery because his body just couldn't take the trauma anymore. And later, when she heard him say that he could "see the other side," it confirmed her opinion of what might be coming.

Meanwhile, his behavior became disturbing. He was acting "loony," as Ann termed it. He would sometimes disappear for hours and Ann wouldn't know where he was. When he finally returned home, he would say he had been out walking. Sometimes he would sit in the rain with no umbrella or raincoat. Ann would try to talk him into coming into the house, but he would refuse—there was no reasoning with him. Sometimes his eyes would shake or his legs would suddenly give out. One time he said that he was Jesus Christ and she needed to get on her knees and ask for forgiveness and pray. Ann is still haunted by the memories of the creepy laugh he would randomly emit.

One day when he was doing a little better, he called his parents and asked them to come over. He said to his mom and dad, "Thank you for loving me. Thank you for caring for me all these years." He also said thank you to Ben, his son. Then he said to Ann, "Thanks for putting up with all of my shit all these years." This was the Michael she knew resurfacing. Reasonable. Thinking of others. But soon he was back to his odd behavior again.

There's no way of knowing how much of a role the ketamine may have played in his behavior in the last weeks of his life. Pain itself can change brain function and affect behavior, and Michael had been in severe pain for a long time. I took him off the ketamine after the scheduled five weeks of treatment, which should have lifted any psychotic effects the drug may have caused, but the strange behavior continued. Michael was in an end stage of a progressive and decades-long battle with pain. His pain was as malignant as any cancer.

The most concerning new feature in his behavior was his growing interest in weapons. He already had guns, but he wanted to buy more. He told Ann, "I cannot protect you anymore because of my health. We need more weapons." So he asked her to drive him to the outfitter Cabela's to purchase more weapons. At first she refused, but when he said he would drive himself if she wouldn't, she agreed to take him. He bought a rifle, a handgun, and a knife with a serrated edge.

For years, Ann had tried to downplay the seriousness of

Michael's suicidalism. Now she couldn't help but confront it. Could he be seriously preparing to kill himself? She kept remembering the time he had suggested that they both "go home" to heaven. Could he become violent not only toward himself but also toward her? And then there was their daughter Laura, who was living in a duplex across the street after having been divorced from her husband. Could Michael want to kill her, releasing her from her own suffering from cerebral palsy before killing himself?

Finally the turning point came. One day in early November, Michael loaded one of his guns and fired it out the back of the house. Still holding the gun, he said, "The heavenly Father is sending Jesus tomorrow." Ann felt the hairs on the back of her neck stand up. A mother's protectiveness finally overrode a wife's loyalty. She grabbed Laura, who was visiting, and left the house. "I knew something was going to happen if I did not leave or if something did not change," she explained to me.

At first she moved in with Laura across the street. But that was still close to home—what if Michael came after her and Laura? So after a couple days, Ann arranged for Laura to go and stay with her oldest daughter, Rachel, who was living in Idaho. Then Ann went to live with her brother Jim in Tooele without telling Michael where she was. Every night while she stayed with him, Jim slept on the living room couch with a loaded gun beside him in case Michael showed up.

An uneasy stalemate had settled in that lasted a couple of weeks.

On Saturday, November 19, 2005, Michael went to LaVell Edwards Stadium with his father, his brothers, and Ben to watch the Utah football team defeat BYU in overtime. While he was gone, Ann—who was still living with her brother—took the opportunity to clean their home. That evening she called Michael from her daughter Camille's home in the Tooele area. She told him that Rachel was going to be sending Laura back from Idaho. Michael insisted that he take care of Laura, but Ann would not agree. Then Michael's tone became more plaintive and he begged Ann to come back home.

"I will, Michael, but only if you give up the guns. All of them."

He hesitated but finally agreed to get rid of the weapons. She promised him that, in that case, she would come home. Then he replied with something that evaporated the brief hope that a truce had been reached: "You'd better learn to clean the house better and give me more compliments."

Ann started crying. Camille, listening to her mother's side of the conversation, said to her, "Tell Dad to stop it!" At this, Ann became concerned because she understood that Michael had heard Camille's voice and would know where she was. She quickly hung up.

Ann began pacing, just as she had that time when she couldn't get to the hospital right away after Michael's overdose, only this time she was trying to decide what to do about their relationship. Finally she made up her mind. She called Michael back and said she wanted a divorce. That was all. She hung up. Temple wedding or no temple wedding, the situation had become too dangerous to let the marriage continue. Inwardly, she hoped that her pronouncement would help Michael turn things around. She still didn't really want a divorce.

She and Camille and Camille's family left to spend the night at a relative's house in case Michael would come after them. That's where they were when Ann's mobile phone rang at eleven p.m. It was Michael saying he had written a suicide note. He read it to her over the phone, then said goodbye. Camille and her husband were worried. Ann reassured them, "He won't do anything." But the truth was, she wasn't so sure about that.

The next morning, Ann anxiously called the police to do a well check. The police checked on Michael. He called Ann and said he was all right. With this, Ann relaxed somewhat about what was going on with Michael.

Two days later, though, Michael's brother Steve called Ann. Steve said he had called Michael and had gone over to the Petersens' house in Sandy, a ranch-style home with white siding and brick facing. He had knocked on the door and looked in windows but had seen no sign of Michael. Both knew what this might mean.

They agreed to meet at the parking lot of a natural foods store near the Petersens' home. From there, they called the police. They waited until a squad car pulled up, and then Ann gave the officers a key to the house. Several minutes later, one officer returned and gave them the news they were expecting and yet couldn't truly comprehend: Michael was dead.

Steve made calls to Ann's children and other relatives while Ann departed in the squad car for the house because the police wanted a statement from her. Flashing cruiser lights were bouncing off the neighborhood homes. Yellow crime scene tape was out at the Petersens'. It all seemed surreal to Ann, like she was watching it on TV. *This didn't happen, this didn't happen,* she kept repeating to herself.

Ann stayed outside. She walked around the corner so that she wouldn't see the body bag come out. She found out from the police that Michael had shot himself through the heart with a rifle while sitting in a recliner. It had probably happened the previous day. The suicide note was near his body. Ann didn't need to see it (she'd already heard it over the phone), so she told the police to throw it away.

The family delayed Michael's funeral until the next Monday because this was Thanksgiving week and some friends and family were out of town. He had planned his funeral years ago, so the scriptural text preached on and the hymns sung were all the ones Michael wanted. Ann recited the words to one of the church songs she had often sung to comfort him when he had been especially hurting and despondent. After the service, the family proceeded to Elysian Burial Gardens for the interment.

Years earlier, Ann, Michael, and Laura had been talking about the next life. Laura said she looked forward to it because then she would be whole. She wouldn't have cerebral palsy anymore.

Michael said, "I'm looking forward to it too. I am in pain all the time here." Then he got in one of his silly moods. "When I die—you know what?—I am going to spit on your head from heaven!"

Laura laughed.

Soon they all forgot about the incident.

Then came the day of the funeral, and it had been snowing, so the burial grounds staff had set up a canopy to cover the family. But the canopy had holes and the melting snow was dripping through it. Laura said, "Ha! Dad is spitting on our heads."

Ann thought, *Yeah, he probably is.*

In the end, none of the therapies that other doctors and I tried provided enough relief for Michael to want to continue living. He had Ann's love and the love of his family, but even this wasn't enough to prevent his hand from pulling the trigger. When he finally forced the rest of his family away by his behavior and was left all alone, he took his life.

Suicide is an unpleasant but inescapable subject when we talk about severe chronic pain. Estimates of the number of people with chronic pain who think seriously about taking their lives range from 20 to 50 percent. Between 5 and 14 percent of individuals with chronic pain actually attempt suicide. It is believed that, out of the approximately thirty-six thousand completed suicides every year in the United States, at least 10 to 15 percent are people who have chronic pain. Conservatively, the risk of suicide is more than double for people who have chronic pain than it is for the general population. Experts investigating this topic say that risk factors for suicide by people with pain include high pain intensity, long duration of the pain, a family history of suicide, a personal history of suicide attempts, the presence of co-occurring depression and insomnia, a pre-pain history of depression, a family history of depression, unemployment, pain-related helplessness, the use of illicit drugs, social withdrawal, and a history of sexual or physical abuse.[2]

Because of the prevalence of these factors, I draw three conclusions:

1. Physicians should screen for depression and suicide ideation routinely, especially when prescribing potentially lethal medications, such as opioids, benzodiazepines, and sleep medications.

2. If a patient screens positive for suicide ideation, has risk

factors for suicide ideation, or has poorly controlled depression, a behavioral health specialist should be consulted.

3. Since high pain intensity is a known risk factor for suicide ideation, we need to treat pain with all the tools we have, possibly including opioids if other therapies are ineffective.

We may not always be able to prevent people who have terrible pain, as Michael did, from killing themselves. But until medical science can better control pain, the three steps I cited above are some intermediate means we can use to save lives. The people who are in the best situation to see a developing suicide problem are the family caregivers. They are the linchpins in the support system for those who have pain, although ultimately it is the person with the pain who is responsible for his or her own actions.

Caregiving That Works

Today, Ann Peterson is remarried. She and her new husband, between them, have seven children and twenty-two grandchildren, and they love seeing every one of them as often as possible. Ann has moved on from the tragedy of Michael's death. Her life is easier today without the challenge of caring for Michael.

Ann marvels that Michael lived as long as he did, considering the physical debilitation and pain he experienced, the major operations he went through, and the heavy doses of multiple medications he had to take. Why did he live so long? I think a big part of the answer is Ann herself.

Her love, and their children's love, gave him something to live for. Although she could not save him in the end, she eased his load and helped him survive longer than anyone could reasonably expect. She's an example of what steadfast love and self-sacrifice can accomplish for someone whose body has been invaded by pain. But it was far from an easy road for her to take.

If you're a caregiver for someone with pain, your loved one has the condition, but you're both living with it. Pain exacts a toll from you just as it does your loved one. You may feel overwhelmed with all you have to do. You may regret the loss of personal time and freedom. You may be stressed and exhausted. You may go through periods of sadness at watching someone you love struggle. You may feel a sense of loss as you see your relationship with the person in pain begin to change to something more like nurse and patient than husband and wife (or other close relationship). You may feel isolated. You may resent it when other family members aren't helping, or you may get angry when the medical-social support system fails you. You may dread the possible deterioration of your loved one's condition and eventual death. Your loved one probably won't kill himself or herself, but then again, it may be a possibility. You, yourself, if you're like some caregivers, may have a reduced life expectancy simply due to the increased pressure of caring for someone so needy.

Suzanne Geffen Mintz, a wife taking care of her husband with multiple sclerosis, offers these practical tips to fellow family caregivers:[3]

- Take time for yourself. Seek respite help when necessary.
- Keep yourself healthy.
- Give yourself permission to say no sometimes.
- Decide what is worth getting upset over and what isn't.
- Acknowledge your grief.
- Express your anger but don't get stuck in it.
- Keep a positive attitude.
- Research your loved one's condition.
- Figure out how the healthcare system works and how to get the most out of it.
- Be a strong advocate, demanding good service and fighting for what you believe is right.
- Plan ahead. Think about how your loved one's condition may develop and what you'll need to do about it over time, including planning for death.
- Develop your skills in caregiving, such as communicating more effectively with healthcare professionals.

Looking back, Ann Rose realizes she didn't do a perfect job in taking care of Michael, any more than he handled his pain condition as well as he possibly could have. But both did their best. And it was enough. Their love stretched to the very end.

"The main key is unconditional love," she reflected to me. "If we can learn to love everyone, that's really what it's all about. Everybody needs to be loved."

Recently, Ann was cleaning out the family home in Sandy, readying it for sale. She came across a Christmas card she wrote to Michael the month after he died as a kind of catharsis. In it, she apologized for the way it had all ended and said she loved him and looked forward to seeing him in the next life.

Tears formed in her eyes as Ann read that rediscovered card, and she let herself remember some of the old days with Michael. Curiously, she didn't remember the hard times so much. Instead, mostly she remembered the laughter that bounced off the walls of the house, the bright hopes and dreams they'd talked about when young, the tender moments they'd shared, the joy of raising children, the prayers and the faith building. In her memories, Michael wasn't sick or hurting at all.

Then she put the card away and got on with the rest of her life.

CHAPTER 9

---·illlı.·---

Coming of Age

The best advocate for a person in pain is the person in pain.

IN 2010, MOST OF the Salt Lake City theatergoers who watched twenty-two-year-old Alison (called Ali) Goldsmith performing in a production of *Grey Gardens* had no idea what an achievement it was simply for her to be on her feet for an entire act of the musical. They didn't know what hidden emotion might have lain behind some of the lines she belted out:

Mother darling, let a daughter have her day!

It's a day for me and all of us to shine.[1]

This musical, based on the eccentric relationship between a real-life mother and daughter, is about dreams deferred, the need for love, and the fear of loneliness. Ali has had to struggle with all of these issues and many more in her young life as she has seen chronic pain tear apart and re-form her image of what her future can be. Up on the stage, she deserved a day to shine.

Ali came of age with a chronic pain problem. Her pain experience played a part in molding her into the woman she has become. But she has asserted her independence by taking control of her pain management, and she has experienced substantial healing in doing so. This is the way it often is for people in pain. Although they need medical advisers and family caregivers, they do best if they are proactive, positive, and involved in advocating for their own care.

For Ali, it's been a process that she and her family could at one time never have imagined.

Runaway Pain

Ali Goldsmith is the younger of two daughters born to a Salt Lake City couple: Steve Goldsmith, formerly a pharmaceutical salesman (now a property manager), and Tina Goldsmith, a women's health nurse practitioner. Ali began developing bunions, a painful deformity of her feet, when she was in junior high school. The pain escalated to the point where it was interfering with her favorite activities, things like taking dance classes and participating in school musicals. She began taking Lortab, an opioid combined with acetaminophen, to treat the pain. When that wasn't enough, her parents decided she should have surgery to correct the deformity. So in early April of 2003, when Ali was fourteen, pediatric orthopedic surgeon Peter Stevens restructured the bony tissue beside her big toes and temporarily placed five metal pins in her feet to hold his work in place.

Bunion surgery is typically quite painful. In Ali's case, the pain during recovery seemed even worse than it should have been. She had casts up to her knees on both legs for six weeks, and she spent most of that time in bed, receiving homeschooling to complete the ninth grade. She only periodically was able to go in for classes at her school, and then she had to be in a wheelchair. Ali was a popular girl, a student body officer with lots of friends, but this period of recovery from the operation gave her a first taste of loneliness, because although her friends would occasionally drop in to visit her at home, she couldn't do much with them. Soon her friends would say goodbye and head out the door, leaving Ali alone.

When the casts came off in June, Dr. Stevens went to remove the pins projecting from Ali's feet. Three of them in one foot came out easily. For some reason, though, when Peter moved to the other foot, one of the pins wouldn't budge no matter how hard he tugged on it. He asked several of his colleagues to come into the room and try their hand at yanking out the pin, until finally someone managed the feat. Everyone was as careful as they could be and apologized for how they were hurting Ali, but it didn't change the fact that this experience was extremely painful for her. The slight teenager was slumped, weeping and exhausted, in her mother's arms by the end of it.

Except that this wasn't really the end of it. From the knees down, her legs, instead of gradually feeling better, became *more* sensitive and painful over time. She could hardly sleep at night because of the agony created by the bed sheet rubbing against her legs. Even a light breeze against her legs would be painful for her. She found herself having to go through the same self-protective motions she had used while in the casts—propping her feet up, remaining in bed or her wheelchair so as not to have to put weight on her feet, and never wearing shoes. This didn't make sense. Ali kept telling herself that she couldn't be feeling as much pain as she seemed to be. But she was.

Less understanding parents might have thought their daughter was imagining things. Tina and Steve Goldsmith, however, took Ali seriously and brought her back to see the surgeon a week after the pin removal to find out what was happening to Ali. Dr. Stevens listened to them and made a test by pulling a facial tissue from a box and brushing it across Ali's foot. This light touch on her skin, Ali reported to me later, was one of the most painful things she had ever experienced. It was like her foot had been lit on fire. Dr. Stevens guessed at once what had gone wrong. The trauma from either the bunion surgery itself or the pin-pulling episode had triggered complex regional pain syndrome. He knew how serious this condition could be for a young woman starting out in life. Grim faced, he gave the family the news.

Dr. Stevens initially referred the Goldsmiths to the University of Utah Pain Management Center and told them to go there right away, since early intervention can sometimes lead to a better outcome with CRPS. They did as he said, and the university docs, in their turn, did all they could for Ali. Three times, they had her come in to the clinic every other day for a week to inject the local anesthetic bupivacaine into her spine through an epidural. For Ali, it was a strange experience telling her friends that she was getting an epidural, since they associated this procedure only with childbirth. Several times the doctors also tried performing intravenous injections in the feet. It was a safe if disconcerting and extremely painful procedure that started with squeezing the blood out of Ali's legs using a tourniquet. The worst of it was when they placed the IV in her highly sensitive foot—every time, she thought she wouldn't be able to bear it. Each procedure left her wrung out, in tears, desperately hoping that the temporary relief it would give would be worth it. Additionally, she tried acupuncture, heat and ice applications, biofeedback, hypnosis, relaxation training, ultrasound, Reiki therapy, physical therapy, and counseling. By the time she was referred to me, she was on three analgesics as well as pills to help her sleep and more pills to relieve the depression she'd developed since having her young life hijacked by pain.

Trying all these procedures and taking all these medications would not have been a bad thing if they had worked. But, after everything she'd tried, Ali was still in great pain when she came to me. The agony would be set off even by the movement of air across her feet created by people walking past her bed, even by the vibrations of music emanating from a car stereo. In the middle of winter, she was wearing flip-flops because she couldn't bear any other shoes on her feet. She was managing to show up for classes at Cottonwood High School that fall, but she had to navigate from room to room in a wheelchair because she couldn't walk. She would have to elevate her legs and rest for hours after going to school. At an age when kids want to fit in, Ali was immediately set off as different in her new school.

The doctors Ali was seeing told her that CRPS can sometimes go away completely, a fact that is true in a small number of cases. But for Ali this turned out to be a false hope that led to additional discouragement. Ali herself intuitively sensed early on that something had come into her life that was never going to entirely leave her. By contrast, her parents were convinced at first that Ali's pain problem would resolve. Only gradually and grudgingly did they come to admit that they were looking at a long-term, possibly permanent, condition in their daughter's life.

I first saw Ali a week before Christmas in 2003, when she was a fifteen-year-old high school sophomore. Peter Stevens, a friend of mine since we were medical residents together, referred her to me. When Ali came to my office, I saw before me a beautiful girl with an oval face, blue eyes, and long, dark hair who was walking in sandals with the wary steps of one whose legs were hurting her. Chronic pain is always cruel. Somehow, though, it seems more cruel when the victim is a young person with a great deal of life in front of him or her.

Most people think of pain as something that grown-ups, especially the elderly, must face. But even though it's true that the older you are, the more likely you are to be in pain, the young are not immune. They can experience pain from injuries, from some common childhood illnesses, and from chronic diseases (such as sickle cell anemia and cystic fibrosis) that develop during childhood. They may, in fact, be more sensitive to pain than adults and may experience longer-term effects from the pain.[2] With her CRPS, Ali Goldsmith had one of the worst pain diagnoses you can get. I decided that I had to try to help her.

A Beginning of Relief

Ali and her parents came to me as most of my patients come—having tried just about everything and yet still wanting the pain problem to be fixed. They had a very good reason for this motivation: complex regional pain syndrome was stalling out Ali's young life. Since my colleagues at the University of Utah had tried all the usual treatments with Ali, I knew I had to go to an approach that was *unusual*.

Beginning a few years earlier, I had tried intravenous ketamine in patients with neurologic pain disorders. It is the same drug I used with Michael Peterson as he neared the end of his life. It proved to be useful, without side effects, to Ali Goldsmith.

Ketamine is given to people with CRPS because it can sometimes reverse sensitization, lowering overall pain and occasionally even eliminating the condition. I explained the ketamine infusion to the Goldsmiths, and Steve and Tina were eager for Ali to try it even though insurance would not cover the procedure. With their consent, I gave Ali several of these ketamine infusions. She had to keep the peripherally inserted central catheter (PICC line) in her arm day and night for up to a month at a time before we discontinued the catheter. And since she had this line in her arm, leading to a small pump and a bag of ketamine she kept in her purse, it affected her activities and indicated to her friends at school what was going on. But it worked far better than anything else had in treating her pain. Many of her previous treatments had provided no relief at all, or at most had helped for a few hours, and some of these procedures themselves caused pain. But we found that each infusion of ketamine would give Ali instantaneous and substantial relief that would sometimes last for months. When the benefit wore off, we would repeat the procedure.

Simultaneously with the ketamine treatment, we would try other approaches to give relief. For one thing, we tried lumbar sympathetic blocks, which involved taking Ali to the operating room and using x-rays to guide me in placing needles along her spine in the lumbar area, then depositing ten to twenty cc's of a local anesthetic. Sometimes the treatment would have a dramatic effect that could last for weeks, though it always wore off sooner or later. We also tried peripheral nerve stimulation, which consisted of placing a surface electrode that emitted electricity. But we did this only once because it did not help Ali. I prescribed anticonvulsants, antidepressants, and prescription topical medications, all to make Ali more comfortable and better able to function in life as a teenage girl should.

Ali's pain was more bearable now, primarily due to the ketamine. But there was no doubt about it: she was fairly launched on a lifetime regimen of pain treatment. Much as we wished differently, there was no going back to what her life had been like before the bunions showed up on her feet.

Adolescence is ordinarily a difficult enough river to navigate. Add in the turbulence of a chronic pain condition and it becomes exponentially harder. Her family witnessed it all.

Benevolent Liars

Ali has a sensitive heart and an intuitive sense for what people around her are feeling. After she was diagnosed with complex regional pain syndrome, she would watch her parents watching her. Every sign of pain she exhibited was immediately reflected in their faces as in a mirror. She knew her hurt was causing them to hurt inside, and this was the worst thing of all to her. And so she started to lie. Because she didn't want her parents to feel badly, she downplayed how much she was hurting. When she talked to her older sister, Cameron, away at college in Georgia, she minimized her suffering to the point that Cameron had no idea what Ali was really going through until she came home on break and saw for herself. Ali didn't share the burden of her pain any more than she had to but rather kept it inside her, where it lay like a boulder on her spirit.

At one point Ali spent a week in the pediatric hospital receiving an epidural treatment that doctors from the university hoped would reset her pain at a lower level. It was a long week for the whole family, especially Ali. Few of her friends came to visit. Her loneliness was reinforced when she called to ask a boy to a dance, was turned down by him, and later learned that he had accepted another girl's invitation to the dance—all while she was still stuck in the hospital. But there was more disappointment to come.

When the doctors removed the epidural, that was the test to see if the treatment had changed anything. The pain quickly returned, and Ali knew the procedure hadn't provided any lasting palliative effect.

Both parents had come to the hospital for the removal of the epidural. Tina asked her daughter, "Are you feeling all right, Ali?"

"Yeah, we're good," Ali said. "Let's go home."

Ali, a daddy's girl at heart, couldn't bear to break the news to Steve, at least not yet. Since Tina and Steve had arrived at the hospital in separate cars, Ali chose to ride home with her mother. When they got in the car, Ali started to cry and through her tears said, "Mom, I was lying. My feet are hurting the same as they were before."

Tina, in tears now herself, reassured her daughter, and the two of them decided to go ahead with the family camping trip that was planned to celebrate a victory over pain. A dismal celebration it was.

Scenes like this one were repeated many times. And it wasn't just the physical pain itself that Ali tried to hide from her parents. She also started to worry that her personality was changing. She could tell that she wasn't laughing and enjoying life as much as before. She was afraid that she was becoming someone different and that she would stay that way forever. This was another worry she hid from her parents. It's one that haunts her to this day.

The truth is, though, that it wasn't only Ali who dissembled about her pain. All of the Goldsmiths tried to keep each other from seeing how bad it was for them. They were lying to one another out of love. This was understandable, but it wasn't healthy.

Tina, in particular, was alert to the fact that the whole family unit was being affected by Ali's pain. She repeatedly sought psycho-social evaluation for her family, but she couldn't find anyone to help with this, so in her own amateur way she took on the mental health of her family as a project. She pushed everyone in the family to talk more about what they were going through. At the same time, a hypnotherapist whom Ali started seeing helped her to understand that her pain wasn't her fault as well as to see what was driving her parents' reactions. Gradually, she and the others in her family became more comfortable with disclosing how they were really feeling.

Not that they all didn't still need some release now and then. It even became comical. They laugh now about how Tina and Steve started drinking martinis every night while Ali lay drugged beside them on the couch. They were all high together.

There were also changes that the family had to make in the way they conducted their lives together. Skiing, for example. Tina and Steve had both originally moved to Utah from out of state because of the world-class ski slopes in Utah. Skiing had been the family's passion, Ali participating as much as the others. But now she couldn't go to the slopes. The rest of them stopped going too because they didn't want to leave Ali behind.

As time passed, both Ali and her parents began to gain some perspective. What Ali was going through was terrible, but it could have been worse.

Before Ali saw me, she was admitted to Primary Children's Medical Center and met kids with cancer and other catastrophic conditions who didn't have long to live. *At least I have a life ahead of me,* she thought. *At least there are drugs that can give me some relief.*

Ali has an exceptional family. The support she received was a rarity. Many of my patients, when they find themselves dealing with a debilitating pain problem, rather than receiving understanding and support within the home, find themselves standing on the brink of an emotional void within their family. This is particularly a problem when the person in pain has been the primary emotional well for the family. Less sensitive or caring families than Ali's drain the well, leaving every family member and friend parched.

As the Goldsmiths look back, they realize that dealing with Ali's pain problem actually deepened their family's bonds. It was not easy adjusting to the reality of what she was going through, but fighting a common enemy drew their little platoon together. And a good thing, too, because Ali would need the support.

A Schoolgirl in Pain

Today, Ali suppresses memories of high school. It was a time when she was out of control. She doesn't even like to look at photos from those years, because they remind her of clothes that hurt her to wear, of weight fluctuations she had no control over because of the medications she was taking, of friends whom she once thought would be there for her but who drifted away one by one. In those years Ali should have been a popular figure at school, a top student, a good actress and athlete and dancer. But her pain problem changed all that. Notwithstanding some bright spots, high school became an ordeal she preferred to forget.

Public schools are legally required to provide accommodations for students with special needs, of whom Ali was certainly one. When she was in a wheelchair, she needed to leave class a couple of minutes before the bell sounded to avoid getting caught in the crush of hallway traffic. When she was out of school for medical procedures, she needed makeup quizzes and more time for homework. With her mind affected by the medications, she needed as much as twice the normal time for taking tests. But just as some of my adult patients have trouble getting accommodations in their workplaces, so Ali found that not all of her teachers were as cooperative as they should have been.

When Ali graduated from high school, one female teacher apologized to her for being a "bitch," as she herself put it. This woman had finally realized that she should have been better at accommodating Ali's needs, such as by letting her make up quizzes. She came to her understanding rather too late to do Ali much good.

Ali's biggest problems in school, though, had to do with the effects of being on powerful medications.

Before the pain problem, she had been an A student. Now she felt "zoned out" and incapable of performing well in her academics. Most days, due to the drugs, she would spend her time in class staring at the wall as if paid to do so. Topamax—a nonopioid anti-seizure drug that can reduce pain by decreasing abnormal excitement in the brain—was particularly a problem. In the Goldsmith family they called it the "skinny, dumb drug" because it caused Ali to lose weight and forget things.

With her short-term memory affected, Ali had trouble comprehending lectures and passing tests. There was one paper on *The Scarlet Letter* that she just couldn't complete. The obvious symbolism in the book was somehow more than her mind could get around. When she got a C in physics, that was particularly hard for this previously high-performing student to take, but she realized there was nothing she could do about it. Fair or not fair, the school year kept rolling on and the grades she received were the grades that went on her record.

Meanwhile, she had to deal with the insensitivity of the people she knew at school.

One day when Ali was feeling more alert than usual and was talking a lot in class, a teacher said to her, "You should take more medication." The teacher meant it as a joke.

Ali didn't find it funny.

This same teacher, when Ali came to class with ketamine, took to calling her "Special K"—the street nickname for the drug.

Another unappreciated joke.

Kids her own age became interested in the medications Ali was taking for a different reason. More than once, she got an offer to buy some of the opioids she was taking.

One day she met a school friend and the friend's boyfriend at Mount Olympus, a popular hiking spot southeast of the city. She had never met the young man before. He started asking her about the ketamine she was on at the time. She had an IV bag full of it in her purse. "If I get a syringe, would you give me some?" he asked.

She gave him various reasons for saying no—*I need it, it's expensive, you might have a bad reaction to it*—and only later chided herself for not just saying, "Piss off."

Many people like this teenager wanted her drugs to get high, but Ali was acutely aware of the way that the drugs impaired her. She wanted to use fewer and fewer drugs that would affect her in this way. All she wanted was to *not* get high. All she wanted was to be normal.

Cinderella's Return

In the fall of her senior year in high school, Ali wanted to attend the homecoming football game and "stomp" (dance) to follow. Her parents encouraged her to go.

On the day of the dance, she spent a couple of hours with girl-friends getting decked out in school pride with black, white, and gold clothes and face paint. She was nervous about the game because she knew that everyone in the student section of the stands would be up on their feet for the entire contest. At the time, she was still struggling with being on her feet longer than ten minutes. Two hours seemed like an eternity of hurt to endure. Would her friends understand if she had to sit down or leave? Would they even care about what attending this event would cost her? As it turned out, she managed to get through the game by taking breaks to sit down and just sticking it out with her brave face on under all that paint. When the play got exciting, there she was, up on her feet and shouting with the rest. It felt good to be a part of this scene; she had missed so much else.

Next came the stomp. With feet like hers, the very word *stomp* made her wince. She hoped, though, that if she were on enough medication she could dance safely for one entire song before resting her feet to dance again later. And at first her plan worked. But then suddenly, while she was out on the dance floor, one of the other students accidentally stepped on her foot. The clumsy boy spun away, not knowing what he had done, while Ali was left standing in excruciating pain. Her eyes burned with tears. She hobbled out of the gymnasium as fast as she could, like a wounded Cinderella at midnight, heading for home.

Her parents were surprised to hear Ali come in the door so early, but when they heard her howling in pain, they looked at each other and knew something had gone wrong with her feet.

In a few words she told them what had happened. "It isn't fair! What did I do to deserve this?" she wailed before heading up the stairs and down the hall to her bedroom.

Assuring Tina that he would handle this, Steve took a couple of minutes to collect his thoughts about what he should say to Ali. The competing fatherly instincts to baby his daughter and to toughen her up warred within him. Finally he followed her to her room at the end of the hall.

Sitting down on the bed next to her, he said to his curled-up daughter, "Ali, you've got every right to feel badly for yourself. What you've been thrown in your life so far is a bitch. It's horrible. But you've got to figure out how you're going to live your life as normally as possible. You can't let your feet interfere with the fun you want to have in life.

"So listen to me, here's what you're going to do. You're going to cry a little longer, then you're going to pull yourself together. And you're going to go back to the dance."

When Steve left Ali's room, he didn't know whether she was going to take his advice or not. Would she rise to the challenge it had secretly been so hard for him to give his hurting daughter? He waited.

Ten minutes later, the sobbing from the end of the hallway subsided. Steve and Tina heard the water running in the bathroom as Ali washed the tear stains from her face. They heard a drawer open and a bottle rattle as she moved to down an extra tablet of morphine. And a minute later they heard the front door close behind Ali as she stepped back out into the world.

Finding Herself

When asked what it is like to be a child with a chronic pain problem, Ali responds, "Lost. Lost with lots of questions."

Her whole experience was altered by the intrusion of pain into her life. She didn't know what was going on, how to get better, or what she could expect in the future. She felt helpless, dependent on grown-ups to cope with the day's challenges and to plan her next step.

At first she totally relied on parents. And she was luckier than most children with chronic pain because she had parents who were motivated and had the means to get her all the help that was available. With their medical knowledge and contacts, they were quick to research and seek out treatment. But their activism on her behalf had an unanticipated downside—it made her passive in her own medical care.

Gradually, she and they saw the need for her to take more responsibility for her own care. But negotiating this transition was no easy maneuver. Her pain problem created new battlegrounds to fight out the usual skirmishes between an adolescent and her parents over taking responsibility.

One time, at the university, a nervous medical student tried to draw blood from Ali. His hands shaking, he hurt Ali by repeatedly poking the needle in her arm, failing to get the flow he needed, and trying again. Ali grimaced each time. Tina, meanwhile, knew that Ali wouldn't want her to interfere in the flubbed phlebotomy. She was sitting in a chair nearby, apparently taking no notice of what was going on, her upset showing itself only in the way she kept violently flipping over the pages of her *Newsweek*.

"It's okay, Mom," said Ali. "I'm used to it."

Another needle poke. More noisy page flipping.

Finally Tina could take it no more. "Look," she said to the inexpert med student, "why don't you go get someone else to do this?"

Ali hadn't wanted to stand up for herself. She hardly understood that she could. At that point she would have done better if she'd let her mother intervene sooner.

By the time she was nearing the end of high school, she was more prepared to take a stand for her own independence. Once when she was transitioning off a certain drug and onto another, her father took her obsolete medication away, not wanting her to accidentally take what she shouldn't. This infuriated her. She considered herself to be very organized, and it seemed like he was intruding on her space. Didn't he trust her? I've known other families where this kind of situation could lead to arguments, swearing, even violence. But the Goldsmiths handled it by having a sit-down family meeting that resolved the situation and took them one step closer to a handoff of responsibility to Ali.

After graduating from high school, Ali expressed her ownership of her own health in a dramatic way. She joined a team with the British NGO Azafady going to the other side of the world to provide volunteer social services to rural poor in Madagascar. For four months she lived in a tent, helping to build schools and desks, digging wells and latrines, teaching English and sustainable gardening methods, and planting endangered species of trees in deforested areas. Going to Madagascar was a bold decision for Ali, bolder than for the other young people with her, because for those four months Ali was as far away as she could possibly be from her parents and from the medical network that had been taking care of her. She had medications with her, but otherwise she was on her own in looking after her health.

She was not only declaring her emancipation to others; she was also testing herself. For example, when the rest of the team were going to take a day off to climb a mountain, Ali was faced with a choice: would she stay behind and protect her feet, or would she seize the opportunity to take part in this group adventure at whatever cost in pain? She seized it.

When Ali finally came back to Utah, she was in charge of her own health care, driving herself to doctor's appointments, picking up prescriptions, and accepting the responsibility to take her medications as directed. She had graduated from being a child in pain to being an adult in pain. And there's something about being in charge of managing one's pain that gives a sense of mastery, that gives dignity.

Self-Advocate

Regardless of the age of a person who contracts a long-lasting pain condition, it is important to reach a point where the person takes as much responsibility as possible for getting care and making wise choices for healing.

I'm concerned when I see a person who has become passive or, worse, fatalistic about his pain. I love it when I see someone who is proactive in seeking help for her condition, because then I know this is a person who is taking charge of her pain rather than letting pain take charge of her.

Certainly those who are in pain need loving, caring people

surrounding them. These others can provide invaluable support. But ideally, the one who is most engaged in the pursuit of health is the person with the pain.

One educational video defined self-advocacy as "the ability [of a person in pain] to communicate, convey, negotiate, or assert his or her interests, desires, needs, and rights."[3] It involves making informed decisions and taking responsibility for them. When working with medical professionals, it includes describing your problem clearly, being a good listener to feedback, asking questions, and working with the team to develop and understand treatment. In addition, it involves making wise choices in nonmedical areas that can help to improve pain, such as eating well, exercising, showing up for therapy appointments, maintaining good personal relationships, and coordinating effectively with caregivers.

Self-advocacy not only helps a person make the most of opportunities to feel better; it also enhances confidence and self-esteem. It can be healing in itself.

Of course, the debilitating effects of health problems, a lack of education, language barriers, poverty, the stigma associated with taking opioids, and other limitations can make it harder for some to effectively advocate for themselves. But with determination, even those with severe pain and other handicaps can often be effective managers of their own healing process.

Standing on Her Own Two Feet

Ali Goldsmith has completed her undergraduate degree in community health promotion at the University of Utah. She gets major roles in community theater and has an active social life. She still lives with her parents for the convenience of it. She plans to get a job in which she helps other people maintain a healthy lifestyle, move into her own apartment, do more overseas volunteer work, take part in more plays, and eventually get married.

Through a combination of medical treatments and the consistent support of her family, and through her own determination to take charge, her pain is much better now. The area that hurts has shrunk from the whole area south of her knees to just her feet and ankles. The twenty-something woman is a much different person from the fifteen-year-old who hobbled into my exam room all those years ago. Still, she has her worse days and her better days.

Not long ago, Ali went skiing for the first time since before her complex regional pain syndrome set in. When they were skiing, Ali and her whole family were crying, and laughing at each other for crying, because it felt so good to be there on the slopes together again. That day in the snow-dazzled sunshine of the Utah high country was glorious for them. What a victory it was for her to be able to put those troublesome feet of hers into ski boots and take the pressure of carving a run! But a few weeks later, when they were hoping to repeat the miracle, Ali had to tell her family she wasn't up to it.

Some days shine. Others are dimmer. But none are so dark as they were. Ali isn't cured, but she's experiencing healing.

In the midst of it all, Ali has learned something about herself. She says, "My pain is a *part* of who I am; it's not *who* I am." Although pain may have joined her identity, it hasn't become her identity. When she shows up for medical appointments, she's always ready with questions and comments to help the process along.

Ali has seen some friends wander out of her life when they haven't been able to understand how to deal with her pain problem. But at the same time she's formed a few close friendships that are all the stronger because these friends know how to talk to her about how she's feeling—and how not to make too big a deal out of the pain. Ali worries that she won't find a husband who will commit to her with this problem. But this seems a most unlikely outcome to me. I think everyone who takes the time to really know her must be attracted to the strength she's developed, the insight she's honed, and the rare and precious appreciation for life she's developed.

As for her parents, they're just thrilled when they see her pass through the doorway on her own two feet—to work, to play practice, to a date—and say breezily, "Bye, Mom and Dad."

Everybody's Problem

CHAPTER 10

———— ⁀⁀ͷͷᵙ̧ ————

The Chilling Effect

Doctors have second thoughts about prescribing opioids when they know authorities are looking over their shoulders.

IN PART 1 OF this book we saw how people who have chronic pain can heal. Let's briefly review some of the things people can do for themselves: First, by accepting the new reality of pain in their lives and being prepared to live with an attitude of resolve that life will not be deterred (what we called "acceptance with resilience"), they are able to take steps that will result in a better quality of life for themselves over the long term. They understand that quality medical care requires becoming knowledgeable about their condition and forming relationships of mutual trust and honesty with their doctors and nurses. Through an integrative approach that may include not only surgical procedures and drug treatments but also such things as physical therapy, psychological counseling, exercise, diet changes, and mindfulness, they can bring all available forces to bear on reducing their pain. Meanwhile, they can seek to cultivate helpful relationships, staying away from others who have ill-informed prejudices against people in pain and drawing near to those who are caring, supportive, and encouraging. If they are spiritual or religious, people in pain may take comfort from their beliefs and their spiritual practices. By taking responsibility for their own care, maintaining a positive attitude, and staying engaged, they can get themselves onto—and then remain on—a course toward less pain and more enjoyment in life, even if it doesn't include a total cure for their pain.

I have seen many people emerge from the sere and colorless desert of pain and enter a place where life is greener, more peaceful, more productive. So I never want someone in pain to give up hope. It is possible to experience healing, sometimes a great deal of healing.

I am an optimist and always hopeful.

But I am a realist too. And the painful truth is that, as I survey the landscape of pain and pain treatment in America, I see some individuals who are being well served and making progress—but I also see many others who are suffering needlessly. So whereas in Part 1 we looked at the lives of a handful of representative people who have pain, in Part 2 we'll take the discussion to the level of society, looking at the large-scale problems that must be solved if we're going to make more progress against pain.

In the next chapter we'll look at how society needs to take the problem of chronic pain more seriously in order to make real progress toward curing pain. But before that, we need to look at a special problem area that always seems to crop up when people talk about pain: opioids. These strong analgesics are both a curse and a blessing. People who have pain and their caregivers need to understand the pressures that doctors, physician assistants, and nurse practitioners feel whenever they consider writing prescriptions for opioids.

Show of Force

It was business as usual at Lifetree Clinic on the morning of Friday, August 27, 2010, when suddenly nine men and women—some with guns in their holsters and all wearing black jackets emblazoned with either "DEA" or "POLICE"—trooped in and started fanning out to take up positions in offices and at the clinic's exits.

Receptionist Kathy Lowe, who was at the front podium when the uninvited visitors showed up, immediately phoned me in the research area on the other side of the building, where I was rounding on research subjects. When I arrived at the clinic suite, I could see the frightened expressions on Kathy's face and those of other staff who were standing around, waiting to see what was going to happen next. The patients in the waiting room were whispering together.

Just then, a woman in her thirties with a bob of light-brown hair and an all-business attitude marched up to me and said, "I'm with the Drug Enforcement Administration Diversion Unit. I have a subpoena signed by a judge empowering me to collect records from your computers." She handed me some papers.

I looked at the list of patients the DEA was interested in. Some of the men and women on the list were receiving unusually high doses of opioids because of their severe pain. Others had exhibited behaviors suggesting they were abusing medications and had already been discharged from the clinic for this reason. Most seriously, in a few cases patients who had a history of substance abuse had died through taking excessive amounts of their medication despite our warnings. In investigating these cases, the DEA presumably wanted to find out if our clinic was reckless, negligent, or unlawfully contributing to the public supply of drugs.

Pat Budge, the clinic administrator, came up to my side. She asked the agent the question that was on all of our minds: "Why did you come here in such a show of force?"

The agent replied, "We never know what we're going into."

I suppose that was true in the most literal sense. But a clinic full of doctors, nurses, and patients is not likely to pose much danger to law enforcement agents. It was obvious to me that the show of force was more to intimidate us than it was to protect the agents.

Although I wasn't intimidated, I was disturbed. I had heard of these types of events occurring elsewhere in the country and had long wondered if I would become a target myself. Now, without warning, it had come. I worried about what the investigation would do to my reputation and to my clinic's ability to help patients.

Within an hour, I was fielding phone calls from colleagues on both coasts asking if they could help. I later learned that pharmaceutical reps who were in the clinic at the time the DEA arrived had immediately called their colleagues in other parts of the country, who in turn had told of the incident to physicians they were visiting. News of the investigation spread throughout the pain medicine fraternity like a wildfire. My fellow pain physicians were just as concerned as I was about the trend toward increased DEA scrutiny.

Just as I was not the first doctor practicing pain medicine who was targeted by authorities, so I was not to be the last. Far from it. To this day, many physicians practicing in my field continue to be investigated, threatened, restricted, and in some cases arrested and prosecuted for trying to help patients the best way they know how. Some of them have stopped treating people in pain, at least with opioids, simply to avoid the possibility of a conflict with authorities.

It is certainly true that the DEA and other government agencies have a role in protecting the public from an inappropriate distribution of drugs, and in some cases they have been effective in preventing medical professionals from misusing the power of the prescription pad for personal gain. But it is also true that the authorities often do harm, not only to innocent doctors in many cases, but also indirectly to vast numbers of people who are in pain. The regulators' actions can have the effect of pinching off the supply of opioids to those who need them and who would use them responsibly if they could obtain them.

Regulators attempting to curb opioid abuse don't need to outlaw medicinal opioids; if they want to reduce the number of opioid prescriptions, they just need to throw a scare into the prescribers. Whether we pain medicine practitioners say it in so many words to ourselves or not, we fear that we can be punished for mistaking a drug abuser for a pain patient and prescribing pain medications. Meanwhile, we realize that no doctor is punished for mistaking a pain patient for a drug abuser and refusing to prescribe pain medications. It's easier to err on the side of safety.

Easier for the doctor, that is. Of course, for the person whose pain goes untreated as a consequence of a doctor's fear, the situation is much harder. Let us remember, these are often people with terrible pain—people like the shooting victim Carolyn Tuft, the injured vet Jason Bing, and so many others. People who really need help but are less likely to get it when doctors go to prison, lose their licenses, or voluntarily withdraw from treating pain because of the risk of repercussions. It's changing the way some physicians practice medicine and what treatments they recommend. It's introducing suspicion and misunderstanding into the patient-physician relationship. It's making it more difficult for people holding opioid prescriptions to get those prescriptions filled.

This is called the "chilling effect." In recent years, pain medicine has felt downright frigid. In this sense, the intimidation tactics by legal and regulatory authorities are working. So this isn't just a matter for physicians to be concerned about. People who are in pain need to understand what misguided enforcement of prescription drug laws is doing *to them*. It's all too often slowing down or standing in the way of proper pain treatment.

I never heard from the DEA investigators after they barged into my clinic in August 2010. I suspect that the agency hired doctors to review the seized clinic records and that these doctors told them that neither I nor anyone else on my staff had done anything to justify legal action against us. So the agency let the investigation languish. For four years. And in the absence of public exoneration during that period, a cloud hung over my reputation. It was a painful episode that weighed heavily, not only on me, but also on my family throughout those four years.

My own travails with the authorities, though, are not the point; they are just an illustration of what is going on in my field. The point is that people in pain are unwittingly stepping into controversy whenever they have an appointment with a physician and opioid prescription becomes a possibility. In the war against opioids, people in pain are often the casualties.

But before I get into any more details about what people in pain and their caregivers need to know about the opioid controversy, I want to briefly remind us of one simple truth that often gets overlooked in the discussion:

Pain treatment is about so much more than opioids.

Perspective

The range of treatments for pain is immense, including not only many types of opioids but also non-opioid medications, surgical procedures, and much more. New treatments are coming online all the time. So opioid treatment should not be looked at as the gold standard of pain care, much less as the only type of care available.

Opioids happen to be the focus of controversy because of the dangers connected with their misuse, including addiction, diversion, and overdose. Furthermore, I believe, they have been singled out for excessive criticism in some cases because of the cultural prejudices associated with addiction and pain. There are legitimate concerns with opioids, to be sure. We need a wider and better-informed national conversation about the proper medical uses of these analgesics. But as we're waiting for a more mature consensus to emerge, let's not allow criticism of this one treatment modality for pain—opioids—to taint the whole universe of pain medicine. And certainly let's not further burden people with our suspicion because of an association with prescription painkillers they may or may not be taking.

So, should opioids be a part of a physician's arsenal against pain, or should they not? I find it is helpful in understanding the duality of opinions to look at the issue of opioid use in historical context.

The Sky's the Limit

The pendulum has been swinging for decades, oscillating between openness toward opioid use and resistance to opioid use. Shortly, I will argue that being pro-opioid or anti-opioid is actually not the most helpful way to look at the issue—there's another duality that better describes the situation we find ourselves in as a society. But undeniably, opinions have moved back and forth on the use of opioids in pain treatment.

The analgesic effects of opioids have been recognized for millennia. But for a long time in the modern period, the use of opioids was restricted to short-term use in treatment of post-operative pain and cancer pain, because these drugs were considered highly addictive and not of much use for chronic pain. In fact, in 1941, Lyndon E. Lee Jr., M.D., wrote an article in the *Journal of the American Medical Association* in which he discouraged the use of narcotics even for terminally ill cancer patients because it would "[condemn] the patient to a life of dependence on narcotics."[1] Out of fear of addiction, he was prepared to condemn the dying to spending their last days in great pain! Fortunately, most physicians were not that callous, at least in regard to end-of-life palliation with opioids. Still, these analgesics were left out of most physicians' arsenals when it came to fighting chronic pain.

Then the pendulum began swinging in the opposite direction in 1986 when Russell Portenoy and Kathleen Foley published an article in the medical journal *Pain* reviewing thirty-eight cases in which noncancer patients received opioids. "We conclude," they said, "that opioid maintenance therapy can be a safe, salutary and more humane alternative to the options of surgery or no treatment in those patients with intractable non-malignant pain and no history of drug abuse."[2] It seemed that opioids were effective for chronic pain after all. If prescribing opioids for chronic pain was justified in the professional literature and was becoming the standard of care, then doctors were able to prescribe these drugs for chronic pain with less concern about losing their licenses.

Thus began what I call the "sky's the limit" era in opioid prescribing. Not only did many physicians start prescribing opioids for chronic pain, but also we believed there was no upper limit to the amount we could prescribe. Unlike with a drug such as acetaminophen (which will lead to liver damage if used in large amounts), we thought we could keep prescribing higher and higher amounts of opioids until we reached a point where a person's pain was adequately relieved. If in time someone developed a tolerance for the medication and was no longer getting the same relief, we would just increase the dose some more. It seemed safe and effective in many cases. For doctors like me who wanted to help people in agony because of pain, the opioids seemed like the closest thing to a cure that we had available to us.

But a new trend was emerging that would lead to a reverse swing of the pendulum. It was a trend that was reaching even to my own State of Utah.

Zeroing In on Unintentional Deaths

In January 2005 I read a local newspaper article quoting Utah's chief medical examiner, Todd Grey, as saying that prescribed pain relievers had become increasingly responsible for Utahans' deaths from drug poisoning. "A whole lot of [people] who died shouldn't have died," he said.[3] I immediately thought, *My God, could this be true? If true, could we doctors be contributing to the problem?* At the time, I was president of the Utah Academy of Pain Medicine and felt I had a responsibility to look into it.

I immediately called Dr. Grey and said I wanted to talk about the opioid-related deaths he was seeing. He said, "I'll be at your office in an hour." We talked, and what Grey told me convinced me that there was indeed a major upswing in opioid-related deaths in Utah. A lot of the deaths were due to drug diversion (one person taking medicines prescribed to another person) or a patient's failure to take medicines as prescribed, whether intentionally or accidentally. In addition, though, it seemed likely that some doctors were giving at-risk people too many opioids and that some doctors were not properly managing titration (slowly increasing doses as people develop a tolerance to the drug) or conversion (switching from one opioid to another without allowing too much of the two drugs to build up in the body). These were dangerous mistakes.

Several thoughts went through my mind: For one thing, members of the medical profession, and pain specialists in particular, had a moral and ethical responsibility to do something to address the growing problem of overdoses and unintentional deaths involving opioids. For another, if we didn't deal with the problem quickly and effectively, there was a good chance the authorities would reflexively regulate opioid prescription, causing harm to some people who benefit from the drugs.

In the preceding four years, I had already been working to develop the Opioid Risk Tool, an assessment that examines family and personal history of substance abuse as well as age and other factors to sort patients into three risk categories for the potential of misusing opioids. The goal was to help doctors assess the risk of people developing abnormal drug-taking behaviors if prescribed opioids. Now I felt a greater sense of urgency than ever for getting the tool into the hands of my fellow physicians. Later in 2005, after testing of the tool was complete, I was able to publish a partial validation article to let my peers know about it and begin using it.[4]

The following year I launched a campaign called Zero Unintentional Deaths with the belief that education on the safe use of opioids is more beneficial than efforts to limit or regulate its use. The message spread well beyond Utah, with several national news outlets presenting stories that highlighted the risks of respiratory suppression in those taking too much opioids. With the collaboration and support of a couple of friends, I created the foundation LifeSource to promote the Zero Unintentional Deaths campaign.[5]

Between 2007 and 2013, the number of opioid-related deaths in the State of Utah dropped 35.3 percent—the first documented drop of its type in the nation.[6] I like to think that LifeSource contributed to some of the improvement, although of course there is no way to quantify our impact. The Utah Department of Health and the Utah legislature deserve much of the credit for aggressively addressing this problem.

Unfortunately, nationwide the picture is not as hopeful as it is in Utah. In the country as a whole, the number of people suffering opioid overdose incidents, and in many cases dying from them, continues to increase. According to U.S. government statistics, in 2011 opioids were involved in 16,917 deaths in the United States, continuing the steady rise in drug overdose death rates that began in 1992.[7] For comparison, that's equal to a Boeing 747 crashing with a full passenger load every nine days. If those airplanes actually crashed, imagine the magnitude of the response the country would take! The growth in opioids deaths is truly a national emergency.

Public health officials began to become aware of the growth in opioid-related fatalities, and through news reports the public became aware too. In particular, news stories about rising rates of OxyContin abuse, and about celebrities addicted to or overdosed on prescription painkillers, captured the attention of the nation. The problems became major subjects of regulator and medical scrutiny. The White House Office of National Drug Control Policy announced a commitment to reducing deaths from prescription drugs through more aggressive law enforcement efforts.[8] And thus the pendulum began to swing back in the direction of limiting opioid use for chronic pain.

In the "sky's the limit" period, the pain community *had* gone too far with opioid treatment for chronic pain. Most of us had underestimated the risks of diversion, addiction, and overdose. As early as 2007, in a book I wrote for my fellow physicians on safe opioid prescribing, I referred to a *New England Journal of Medicine* article suggesting that it would be a good idea to create a ceiling for opioid prescriptions. It was not a hard-and-fast, one-size-fits-all rule the article's authors had in mind, but instead a flexible upper limit that could be adapted for individual cases at the discretion of physicians. Doctors could still gradually raise their patients' dosing to try to reach a point where the pain was under control, but if they were having trouble doing it, the authors said, then maybe it was a sign that opioids just wouldn't work in this case and should be backed down.[9] In other words, what the authors of the article were suggesting wasn't the kind of imposed limitations that authorities would use to rein in doctors, but it *was* the end of "the sky's the limit."

Right now, the momentum continues in the direction of restricting opioid prescribing through external pressure. The wind is blowing distinctly cold. If people in pain are having trouble finding a doctor who will prescribe the opioids they need, most likely the reason is that pressure is being placed on the medical community to limit opioid use.

But the solution to the treatment gap is not to get the pendulum to reverse its direction, nor even to find a balance in the middle. It's to look at the situation in a whole different set of terms. For if we focus on the duality of being pro-opioid or anti-opioid, we're missing the point.

Pro-Patient

Some might label me as pro-opioid because I believe that some people with chronic pain need opioid prescription, even high doses of opioids. But how can one truly be pro-opioid when these drugs are associated with so much harm? I despise the fact that we don't have safer alternatives that will help more people and that it is still necessary to prescribe opioids if we're going to control some cases of pain. So I'm not pro-opioid. Nor am I anti-opioid.

I'm pro-patient.

Mindlessly shutting down the use of opioids, despite the fact that this will leave people in pain, is not in the interests of patients. Likewise, mindlessly prescribing opioids in higher and higher doses, despite the risks that those drugs could fall into the wrong hands or cause people to go into a sleep from which they'll never wake up, is reckless toward patients. We need to focus on what's best for each individual who is struggling with pain, and this may or may not involve opioids. It's a judgment call made case by case.

I am guided in my thinking on opioid use by a perspective known as *double effect*. Going back at least to the thirteenth-century Roman Catholic theologian Thomas Aquinas, this line of ethical analysis suggests that it's acceptable to do something risky if the intent is to do good and if the evil effect that may accompany the good one is merely an unfortunate and unavoidable consequence. Double-effect analysis also includes a principle of proportionality such that the good achieved sufficiently outweighs the harm caused.

When we physicians are looking into the eyes of someone who is in terrible pain and who has nowhere else to turn, we have to make a decision. We have to weigh the double effect, running a risk-benefit calculation in our mind. Sometimes we conclude that people would find benefit from the medication and have no other real options for treatment. The probable beneficence of the treatment outweighs its possible maleficence in their case. We want what is best—and achievable—in the current situation.

In the debate over appropriate treatments for chronic pain, I say, let compassion lead us forward, and let science light the way. It's all about what's best for the person who has pain.

Left with One Alternative

As we seek to apply the double effect, we need to keep in mind what's at stake if people in severe pain don't get the treatment they need.

A man in his fifties named Jack, a former manual laborer who was on disability because of his pain problem, came to me for help several years ago.[10] He had brown hair, the weathered skin of one who has worked outdoors all his life, and a serious expression—he never smiled. He told me about his three back operations and the pain that wouldn't go away.

I treated Jack for about four years, struggling all the while to get his insurance company to cover his therapies. Sometimes I was successful; sometimes, not so successful. For example, I tried to get him to see a psychological therapist to help him learn to mentally cope with his pain, but his insurance company would not pay for the service. He was left to deal with the stress of his pain on his own.

Jack was on what most physicians today would term a high dose of opioids and other medications, prescribed by other medical professionals before he came to me. That wasn't necessarily a problem. He was clearly taking his meds as prescribed. But in his case I wasn't convinced that a high dose was any more effective than a lower dose would be. He was mostly inactive and reported little improvement in pain or function while on his medication, so I decided that we needed to reduce or eliminate his oral dose of opioids.

As we began the taper, however, Jack claimed that his pain was too severe. "I can't handle it, Doctor Webster," he said.

I insisted that we had to reduce his oral dose, that the medication being delivered to his spine through a pump should allow us to provide pain control equal to or better in effectiveness than the pills he had been taking. He just needed to be patient and he would see better results.

At the time, I truly believed that. But the truth is, I was also concerned that if he continued on such a high dose something terrible could happen to him and I might be held liable. If I had continued to prescribe a high dose of opioids and Jack had died, even from a natural cause, the medical examiner might have said the death was an unintentional overdose from the opioids. Or Jack might even have intentionally overdosed and, in the absence of a note, no one would have known he had committed suicide. Again, I might be blamed. So I wanted to give his lower dosing every possible chance of success.

Jack left my office with disappointment written all over his face.

Three days later I got a call from his daughter, Samantha, saying that Jack had died from a self-inflicted gunshot wound. He left a note saying he couldn't live with the pain anymore. "I've got no future," the note read. "I've got no hope. I've got no life. I love you, Sammy, but I'm not of value anymore to you or anybody."

This news threw me into an agony of moral self-examination. I had to ask myself if my concern for my freedom and licensure had led to this tragedy. Which had held more weight in my judgment—my medical calculation about his treatment or my desire for self-protection? I didn't know. And I would never know what might have become of Jack if I had not tried the medication taper. I was left with the torment of not knowing whether I could have prevented Jack's death.

Here's one thing I'm sure of: Jack is far from alone in paying the ultimate price for not getting adequate treatment for life-destroying pain. To the extent that the current regulatory and enforcement environment puts opioids out of reach of those who have no viable alternative, it increases the death toll of suicides.

There are fatal consequences to being both too permissive and too restrictive about opioids. And this raises a question for us as a society. Why is it that people who die from opioid overdoses receive great sympathy (and their doctors receive great blame), but people who kill themselves because they are not receiving pain treatment, including opioids, are largely ignored? I think it's because of the widespread prejudice against people in pain. As we've seen before, they are considered malingerers, lowlifes, drug seekers. They're not tough enough. They aren't willing to help themselves. If they take their own lives, that's a shame, we think, but it was their choice.

Where's the compassion and understanding for people who are in great pain and just want whatever treatment will make life bearable?

Whether it means using opioids or not, we cannot abandon our moral obligation to bring the best compassionate care available to people in pain. Their lives may depend on it.

Prosecution and Persecution

Here's an irony of practicing pain medicine today using opioids.

Internists know that approximately 7,000 people die every year in the United States from taking too much nonsteroidal anti-inflammatories, such as ibuprofen.[11] Psychiatrists know that about 10,000 people die annually from an overdose of antidepressants or benzodiazepines.[12] Cardiologists are aware that the leading risk of adverse drug events, including thousands of fatalities, comes from taking anticoagulants.[13] All told, an estimated 2 million cases of serious injury, including about 128,000 deaths, occur annually from errors in prescribing various medications.[14] These numbers are unbelievable and tragic, but none of the physicians associated with deaths related to medical prescriptions are threatened with incarceration or revocation of licensure. *Except for those who prescribe opioids.*

Yes, patients do sometimes die from the opioids physicians prescribe to treat pain. And yes, it's tragic. Absolutely. It's terrible every single time. Yet why the disparity in the way opioid prescribers are treated vis-à-vis other medical professionals? Despite our attempt to help the largest and most hurting patient population, with the intention to do good and not harm, we have to accept suspicion and scrutiny if we are going to prescribe the most powerful analgesics in our arsenal.

The biggest influence producing physicians' fear is the Drug Enforcement Administration, the lead agency for enforcement of the Controlled Substances Act. Their investigations into physicians' prescribing patterns have expanded rapidly in the last two decades. This is likely a response to the growth in the number of addictions and deaths from prescription painkillers.

Speaking about this recent expansion of the DEA's reach into the U.S. medical community, journalist Radley Balko says,

> From 2001 to 2004,... the DEA on its own launched 400 investigations with its "OxyContin Action Plan," leading to 600 arrests. Medical professionals made up 60 percent of those arrests. The agency also set up hundreds of local task forces across the country, which carried out 9,000 investigations in 1999 alone. In 2001, the DEA also trained more than 64,000 state and local law enforcement personnel in how to fight prescription drug diversion.[15]

This new reality has changed the experience of pain medicine for both doctors and patients. Balko continues,

> Those efforts, which continue today, have cast a chill over the treatment of pain. Candor in the doctor-patient relationship, a critical component of any medical treatment, is especially important in treating pain. Doctors need to develop a feel for each patient's tolerance for pain, as well as for how they're reacting to the drugs and dosages they're taking. The high-profile investigations and prosecutions of doctors have undermined that relationship. Law enforcement agencies send undercover agents and informants into doctors' offices to lure suspected physicians into writing bad prescriptions. Doctors have then been conditioned to be suspicious of patients, to see them as potential addicts or drug dealers. Patients have

been conditioned to downplay their pain so they don't appear desperate for narcotics, as an addict might.

There it is—the chilling effect brought on by excessive law enforcement interference in medical practice, directly affecting people in pain.

Sometimes, of course, investigation is warranted, given that addiction and overdose deaths are taking a heavy toll in our society. Sometimes it is not warranted. It depends. When we look at what's gone on, the cases against doctors run the gamut from the ridiculous, to the suspect, to the well warranted.

Overreaching Prosecutor

In April 2014, Des Moines pain management specialist Dr. Daniel Baldi was tried for involuntary manslaughter in the deaths of seven of his patients. Prosecutors contended that Baldi caused the deaths of these men and women by prescribing opioids improperly, including to patients who were clearly addicted. They accused him of "reckless, willful, wanton disregard for safety."[16]

I was the expert witness on the standard of care for Dr. Baldi, and in preparation for testifying at his trial, I read all of the medical records of the people for whose deaths Dr. Baldi was being prosecuted. One patient, Brandy Stoutenberg, died of an overdose of amphetamine and Xanax, neither of which Baldi prescribed to her. Paul Gray, leader of a heavy metal band, died of heroin and fentanyl, again neither of which Baldi prescribed. Chad Martin died of pulmonary embolism. Loretta Brown died after taking her partner's medication. The other cases were equally as unrelated to Dr. Baldi's treatment of these people's pain conditions.

The prosecution's case was simply ridiculous. Thankfully, the jury saw this, acquitting Daniel Baldi of every charge. But as a result of the legal proceedings, he had to close his clinic, for two years he endured enormous fear over the possibility of going to jail, and he came out of the proceedings nearly bankrupt because of legal fees and an inability to earn a living. His time every day during the legal process was consumed with trying to build a defense.

Meanwhile, doctors around the country were watching and wondering if it could be them next. Maybe helping people in pain isn't even worth it?

Taken Advantage Of

Dr. Baldi's trial was an obvious overreach by prosecutors. But sometimes the situation is more complicated and more equivocal than that. Sometimes a doctor, with no intention to harm, is naive and sets off adverse consequences that he or she should have avoided.

Journalist Tina Rosenberg wrote a cover story for *The New York Times* about Ronald McIver, a physician from South Carolina.[17] Here was a doctor who kept poor records, was too trusting of some of his patients, and probably underplayed the risks of opioid use. At least one of his patients died, though not necessarily because of opioid overdose (the man suffered from congestive heart disease). Other McIver patients were lying to him about their pain complaints in order to get opioid prescriptions to feed their addictions or to sell. Because of these facts, McIver was sentenced to thirty years in jail.[18]

Other physicians may be in McIver's situation—well meaning but not as careful as they could be. So, is the kind of punishment that was meted out to McIver appropriate for them too?

My opinion is this: Although physicians should be held accountable for their own actions, the kinds of actions should determine the kinds of accountability. Have they prescribed opioids responsibly, using the right drugs in the right amounts for a given situation? Have they made a good-faith effort to identify possible abusers of opioids, taking extra caution if they suspect an individual may take drugs improperly? Have they given sufficient warning about the risks of opioids and done as much monitoring as they reasonably could? If so, then legal accountability doesn't seem to be the answer.

Sometimes the answer is not incarceration. It might be a revoked license, supervision by a more experienced physician, increased education, or some other response that does not treat a well-meaning physician the same as a drug trafficker. A more subtle range of responses seems appropriate in cases where a physician's actions were well intentioned but partially harmful.

Pill Mills

Finally there are the cases where doctors or their staff members and associates are clearly using the power to prescribe controlled substances, not to give relief to others, but to help themselves. There are not as many of these charlatans as many people think, but they are numerous enough to gain notice and to bring discredit to the profession. These are a few examples from recent years:

- A grandfatherly doctor practicing in Muscatine, Iowa, pleaded guilty after being charged with multiple counts of trading opioid prescriptions for sex.[19]
- A forty-something doctor in Orange County, California, eager to save up enough money to open a private practice, sold prescriptions for opioids out of a Starbucks.[20]
- A Manhattan physician and his office manager were arrested in connection with sting operations against two major East Coast drug trafficking networks and were accused of diverting opioids worth $10 million on the black market. Incredibly, they seem to have carried out their illegalities separately—neither was aware that the other was engaged in a medical scam.[21]

For a pill mill in its most undeniable form, look no further than American Pain—the company operated by twin brothers Christopher and Jeffrey George in Florida before being shut down by law enforcement. The twins set up a series of highly profitable no-appointments-necessary pain clinics, employing unscrupulous doctors who would give the same remedy to anybody who came in, namely a month-long supply of opioids sold to the customers before they left the clinic. To get the medications in large enough numbers, the George brothers worked with several drug wholesalers.[22]

The George brothers' operation had the hallmarks of a true pill mill:

- The owners were nonphysicians who retained physicians for the sake of their federally granted registrations to prescribe strong analgesics.
- The appointments were unprofessional because no real medical assessment took place and there was no real patient-physician relationship.
- They offered only one form of "treatment"—pills.
- They dispensed their pills on-site.
- They operated on a cash-only basis, meaning no insurance company was involved.

With the example of American Pain in mind, it's important to note that it would be a mistake to call every clinic that prescribes opioids, even in larger-than-average quantities, a pill mill. Higher-than-typical prescribing and consumption patterns do not always signal illegal activity. Prescription monitoring databases may help make these distinctions clear as long as the databases are used to help inform good medical decisions, not merely chase down "high prescribers."

Physicians who prescribe opioids are charged with thoroughly assessing and monitoring their patients and with keeping clear, complete medical records. Pain relief, not profit, is the motivating force, which is not at true pill mills like the ones operated by the Georges. In the case of pill mills—no sympathy. They deserve what they get from law enforcement.

Pharmacists Practicing Medicine

One outcome of the problem with pill mills in Florida and elsewhere is that the DEA has applied enormous pressure on both wholesale and retail pharmacies for what the DEA sees as a failure to properly control the sale of opioids.[23] And thus the chilling effect has been extended, with people who are in pain and holding a valid prescription for opioids unable to get the medications they need.

In the summer of 2013, Walgreens, the largest drug retailing company in the United States, agreed to pay $80 million to resolve federal charges. Concurrently, Walgreens instituted a "Good Faith Dispensing" policy under which it required its pharmacists to verify prescriptions for controlled substances. "In plain English," writes journalist Judy Foreman, "this means that Walgreens pharmacists are going to call your doctor, or at least your doctor's office, to see if your doctor did the right thing in giving you a prescription for pain relievers and other drugs."[24] The goal is not to protect patients' health. The goal is to protect the pharmacy from having to pay additional massive fines.

As a result of Walgreens's policy and similar ones by other pharmacies around the country, patients have met with delays and even pharmacists' refusals to fill their prescriptions. In one recent survey, 18 percent of patients were unable to fill opioid prescriptions by pharmacists on at least one occasion despite having previously received these medications from the same pharmacy.[25] In some cases, desperate for the pain relief they need, they have tried to fill their prescriptions at more than one pharmacy, causing them to run afoul of their state's prescription monitoring program and appear to be drug seekers, not just people struggling to get their prescriptions filled. Some individuals whose prescriptions have been put on hold or have been rejected have resorted to buying illegal drugs. Some may have even taken their own lives because they couldn't tolerate the pain.

The American Medical Association adopted a resolution condemning the Walgreens policy because, not only does it lead to patients failing to get the medications they need and deserve, but also it essentially puts pharmacists in the role of practicing medicine, even overruling the medical judgment of physicians.[26]

The same could be said for the DEA, which is behind the self-protective policies of Walgreens and other pharmacies. By telling pharmacies how many opioid doses they can distribute in a given area, and how much an individual can receive, the DEA, too, is practicing medicine. It is meddling in the province belonging to trained medical professionals. With its power to indict suspected offenders and to levy multimillion-dollar fines, the DEA is the most significant source of the big chill. But it is not the only one.

Another source of the chilling effect is our legislators.

Unintended Consequences

Legal historians say that the Harrison Narcotic Act of 1914—the first U.S. federal law prohibiting the use of opium products without a doctor's prescription—created all sorts of ill effects. For one thing, it created a flourishing and highly profitable black market in illicit drugs, which in turn created policing nightmares and social prejudices. For another, it was the start of physicians getting in trouble for prescribing opium-based medications to people with addictions.[27]

The problem was not that a law was passed regulating opium. The problem was that opioid use and its related effects are so complicated that, even more so than in most areas, law and law enforcement can lead to harmful unintended consequences. That was true a century ago, and it's true today.

One notable example comes from the State of Washington, where in 2010 the state legislature, reacting to the large number of opioid-related deaths in the state, passed a pain management law that included the following provisions:

- Doctors in the state must carry out detailed patient evaluations, track behavior, and conduct random urine tests for those receiving opioids.
- Doctors are advised against prescribing more than the equivalent of 120 milligrams of morphine as a daily dose to people with chronic noncancer pain unless they get approval by a pain specialist.

The ostensible purpose behind the bill is a good one: to keep people safe. To repeat the obvious, it's tragic when even one person dies unnecessarily. But the unintended consequences of the law have been tragic in themselves.

Large numbers of clinics and doctor's offices across the State of Washington have stopped seeing people with pain because the requirements have become too burdensome and restrictive. The result? People who have severe ongoing pain in many cases have found themselves without a doctor and having to spend weeks or months in finding a new one who will prescribe the opioids they feel they need (if indeed they can find such a doctor at all). In the meantime, their prescriptions have run out and often they suffer pain so severe that is debilitating and dehumanizing.[28]

In the meantime, the new law left untouched one of the biggest drivers behind opioid-related deaths in Washington—overuse of methadone. For a number of years before the 2010 pain management bill was passed, the state had encouraged doctors to switch patients in state-subsidized health care plans (namely, people on Medicaid, injured workers, and state employees) from expensive opioids such as OxyContin to the cheaper drug methadone.[29] Methadone can be an effective analgesic. But because it stays in the body much longer than other opioids, that means that even if taken at low doses (including doses under 120 milligrams), when it is initiated it can accumulate in the body and lead to respiratory suppression. Too often, people taking methadone go to sleep, stop breathing, and never wake up. In Washington, methadone accounts for about 10 percent of the opioids prescribed but nearly *half* of all opioid-related deaths.[30] The state did save millions of dollars per year by pushing the cheaper drug, but it did so at the cost of many unnecessary deaths in the state, especially among the poor on Medicaid.

This highlights real motivation behind the 2010 law in Washington. It is the same as the real motivation behind the pharmacy chains' opioid restriction policies.

Money.

Prior to passage of the 2010 law, I was asked to speak to Washington State's medical directors and leaders of the Department of Labor and Industries (L&I), which oversees medical compensation for injured workers. They said they were trying to understand the reasons why people were dying and what could be done to reverse the problem, and they wanted to know my views as a leader in the field. I told them that they needed to remove methadone from the formulary as a preferred drug. They seemed to ignore my recommendation. And why? I believe it was because (as I found out later) L&I leaders estimated that the new law would save the state around $13 million a year.[31] Preventing people from getting the treatment they need, and forcing them to spend their days in miserable pain, evidently seemed worth it to save the state millions of dollars.

I have seen the same kind of dynamic in play repeatedly around the country.

War over Money

The British and Chinese fought two wars in the nineteenth century, known as the "Opium Wars," over trade disputes. Today we have an "opioid war" over when and how much and what type of opioids ought to be prescribed for chronic pain. But I believe that opioids are really just the pretext for the conflict. At a deeper level, it's really a financial war, just like the ones in China.

Ranged on one side of the conflict are the payers—commercial health insurance companies, government health insurance, and workers' compensation. These are the ones who, along with patients themselves, wind up footing the bills for opioid prescriptions. On the other side of the conflict are the pharmaceutical companies that manufacture opioids and make a profit by their use. An immense amount of money is involved, and believe me, the combatants in this war are fully aware of that fact.

Naturally, the payers want to pay less. How they go about achieving their efficiencies is the problem. In the first place, it's tragic that a large portion of people in pain, just like a large portion of the American population as a whole, have no health insurance at all. And then for those who do have insurance, their plans may cover only a narrow range of pain treatments. Often insurance companies will pay for less expensive opioids but disallow more expensive (and sometimes safer) opioids as well as alternative treatments such as cognitive behavioral therapy and acupuncture. This ties the hands of doctors and forces people to deal with their pain through limited modalities instead of the multidisciplinary approach that most pain experts recognize as best for their healing. Also, by increasing the number of opioid prescriptions, insurers increase the problems of diversion, addiction, and overdose in our society. Ironically, the costs in the long run can actually be higher than if pain problems were dealt with effectively early on.

Big Pharma, for its part, would like to sell more of its drugs. Although pharmaceutical firms are constrained by regulations and standard practices designed to keep them operating in the public's best interest, they are obviously profit-seeking businesses. If they can convince doctors to prescribe more of the medications they make, it's to their advantage. The pressure to overhype their products is ever present. Sometimes they may overstep their bounds, as proved by the nine-figure fines paid by Purdue and Cephalon for false marketing of their opioids.[32]

Doctors who receive payments from pharmaceutical companies for providing education or research on these drugs are seen as being in collusion with the industry in false advertising. Other doctors are considered to be dupes for accepting what Pharma is telling them and prescribing high-cost drugs when safer, cheaper, or more effective alternative treatments are available. These perceptions, in my opinion, are rarely borne out by the reality. The great majority of doctors operate out of personal integrity. Furthermore, medical associations have firewalls and guidelines in place to keep doctors from prescribing certain drugs because it's good for their own profit statement rather than because it's best for their patients.

Insurance company restrictions influence far more treatment plans worked out in exam rooms across the country than Pharma's enticements do. Yet the perception that doctors are in the pockets of the drug makers contributes to opioid-prescribing physicians being cast as the bad guys and subjected to a level of law enforcement scrutiny that other physicians never need to worry about.

I'm not pro-pharma any more than I am pro-opioid. Every case in which a pharmaceutical company and the doctors it has paid have misled people to push drug sales is sad and reprehensible. Patient well-being can suffer as a result. So we need to maintain vigilance to prevent similar abuses in the future. But just as I ask, "Why do the deaths of people who overdose on opioids receive so much more attention than the deaths of those who couldn't stand the pain without their opioid treatment?" so I ask, "Why is the financial motivation of pharmaceutical companies scrutinized while the financial motivations of medical bill payers are overlooked?"

A new trend that highlights the ambiguities in the financial war over opioids is sub-federal governments suing pharmaceutical companies for supposed false marketing of opioids, which has supposedly led to overprescribing of opioids, which in its turn has supposedly led to these governments having to shell out money to pay for the results of drug diversion and addiction. For example, in 2014, Orange and Santa Clara counties in California sued five pharmaceutical companies, alleging that they waged a "campaign of deception" to boost sales of opioids. The counties are hoping to recoup costs related to emergency room visits, overdose deaths, crimes committed by opioid addicts, and other expenses due to opioid misuse.[33]

In this context, remember the example of the pain management bill passed in Washington State. There was a government trying to cut costs on the backs of people with pain. As a payer itself, the state government was forcing its covered individuals to accept the dangerous drug methadone just because it was cheaper. And Washington State is far from alone—most states have methadone on their preferred drug formulary. While criticizing pharmaceutical companies for unfair advertising practices, governments run the risk of hypocrisy by doing harm to people in pain themselves.

Will lawsuits like the one in Orange and Santa Clara counties become more common? Will they be successful? It remains to be seen. What seems obvious, however, is that local governments have peeked at the DEA's playbook and are copying some of its tactics. It's yet another front in the financial war over opioids.

Payers trying to save money. Pharma stretching the truth about their products: None of this is about being pro-patient. It's about being pro-money.

I'm not criticizing a desire for efficiency. Nor am I against the profit motive. But I am saying that what's needed on both sides is an elevation of concern for what's best for people in pain over the question of who wins financially in the short term. What's needed, in other words, is an elevation of compassion over greed. That's a win for all of us over the long run.

I'm optimistic enough to think that the climate surrounding opioid prescribing may eventually warm up. In the meantime, we all need to be realistic about what's going on.

Escape from the Trap

Just as I encourage people in pain to have resilience when enduring pain, so I tried to have resilience when scrutinized by law enforcement for my clinic's opioid prescriptions. As my wife put it, "If you are in the NFL, you have to expect to be hit." I knew that, if I were going to practice pain medicine, the authorities were going to come at me sooner or later. I would just have to keep going, treating people with pain the best way I knew how. But my personal run-in with the DEA—the time those black-jacketed agents barged into my clinic to copy patient records—resurfaced to haunt me three years later, in 2013.

It was a June day and I was in Boston to speak to the Drug Information Association. After making my presentation, I stepped out of the Boston Convention and Exhibition Center and paused to talk to a couple of friends on the way to a media interview. That's when Sanjay Gupta, chief medical correspondent for CNN, approached me, microphone in hand, with a cameraman filming the ambush. My heart sunk. I knew that I was about to be made to look bad on national television.[34]

I was already aware that Gupta had interviewed the husbands of two women who were treated at Lifetree Clinic and died. These women were among the patients that the DEA agents had been interested in three years before. Their husbands had both filed lawsuits against the clinic and practitioners who treated them. I was included in the suits because I was the owner of the clinic. The suits had been settled out of court, but the men still thought I bore responsibility for their wives' deaths and apparently wanted to strike back at me.

Gupta had asked me to agree to an interview on the cases, but I had refused. In fact, I felt that I was ethically obligated *not* to explain my position. To do so would have required me to reveal personal medical information that would not have been appropriate. Furthermore, I didn't want to get into the position of accusing the husbands of making false statements. I understood the grief that the two men were feeling and their natural desire to find someone to blame, and I didn't want to add to their suffering by getting into an on-air tussle over the facts.

That day when I was ambushed, I felt like I was in a cage. I could agree to an interview and expect to look guilty when my statements were edited for television, or I could do what my conscience dictated and look guilty by refusing to even answer Gupta's questions. This is just the sort of nightmare scenario that physicians treating pain fear every day.

I decided to walk away, accepting the fact that I would come across on television as a perp. The truth is, I was very sad about the unfortunate deaths of the two women, yet I was proud of my work with them and with so many others over the years. I could only hope that my life's work to prevent harm from opioids would in time be the salvation of my reputation.

Eventually I was able to walk tall again.

In the spring of 2014, the U.S. Attorney's office in Utah announced that it had "declined" to make a case against me.[35] In the parlance of federal prosecutors, this meant that the DEA's investigation of me, dating back to 2010, had been concluded without allegations being made against me. It was an acknowledgment that there was no merit to the investigation.

That chapter was closed. But because of my personal experience, I will forever feel sympathy with other doctors who fall under suspicion even though they are trying to relieve pain using the best evidence-based and consensus-based medicine available to them at the time. We physicians who are trying to help people in pain are squeezed by the law, ignorance, lack of good therapies, lack of insurance coverage, and a health problem of incalculable intensity. All too often, the drug authorities are overzealous in prosecuting doctors.

Someday, I hope and believe, we will have an improved culture of pain treatment that removes the fear from physicians as well as the stigma placed on the ones they treat. Communities will be far better off when the DEA and regulators work with the medical community to solve the drug problems, rather than seeing physicians as the enemy and perpetuating the current fear-laden system. In the meantime, people who are in pain and their caregivers need to know the risks and pressures their physicians face. Patients lose when physicians, physician assistants, and nurse practitioners are unable to practice medicine without the fear of being prosecuted.

Remember, there are many therapeutic options, but if you are one of those people who may benefit from opioids, understand that your doctor may feel uncomfortable with prescribing them to you. If you sense that your doctor is hesitant to prescribe opioids when they are merited, go ahead and ask your doctor directly whether he or she feels worried about being prosecuted for prescribing the medications. Some doctors will be taken aback by that question, and some might be hesitant to answer honestly, but healing takes place in the context of a healthy relationship, so your doctor needs to be able to trust you and you need to be able to trust your doctor. That kind of trust can develop in time if both sides are honest and share feelings.

If your doctor does admit fears and concerns to you, this may help you understand the reasons behind the decisions being made. In the end, this may help you receive the care you need. It will show your doctor that you are an informed, aware, and self-advocating patient. It may also help you to lessen your doctor's fears, thereby opening the door for more compassionate care.

The answer to opioid risk is to not focus too narrowly on opioid prescribing, to the exclusion of other modalities of treatment. Nor is it to put the big chill of unnecessary and counterproductive restrictions on doctors in an area where too little care is already being given to an immense population of people in pain. The answer instead is to seek a society-wide transformation in the treatment of pain.

CHAPTER 11

———— ⁣⁣⁣⁣⁣⁣⁣𝟄 ————

A Human Right

People in pain deserve respect and access to treatments that make their lives better.

CONSIDER THE FOLLOWING TWO real-life scenarios and judge how successful our society has been in giving relief from pain in these situations.

Scenario 1

In July 2014, Cullen, a thirty-four-year-old fishing guide who lived in Salt Lake City, injured his back while lifting his dog.[1] The pain was disabling, and he quickly sought medical advice. While one surgeon said he could fix the problem with a disc fusion operation, a different surgeon said Cullen should not be operated on, and Cullen had no idea which one was right. Seeking to mitigate the pain while he made up his mind about surgery, he paid hundreds of dollars out of pocket for epidural injections that did him no good. One doctor gave him a week's supply of opioids but refused to give him any more than that. None of the physicians Cullen consulted suggested any alternative treatments, either because Cullen's insurance would not have paid for them or because they simply didn't know there were any other options. Cullen said he felt like a "hot potato" being passed around from clinic to clinic. He felt the doctors he saw didn't care about him. Meanwhile, because of his pain, he was not able to lead fishing trips during the season of the year when he made most of his annual income. The pain left him so restless at night that he took to sleeping in a different bedroom from his wife so as not to disturb her. Their relationship was affected because his back condition made it difficult for him to be intimate with her. He felt dirty and ashamed, and the pain wasn't getting any better.

Scenario 2

Chrystal, a CPA, was in her early forties and living in Florida when she slipped and sprained her ankle, developed complex regional pain syndrome (CRPS), and began seeking help from a University of Miami medical team. She tried numerous medications and surgical interventions, including spinal cord stimulation and cognitive therapy, but unfortunately nothing much helped her. The only treatment that made a significant difference in her pain was opioids. But then in the summer of 2014 it became first hard, then impossible to get the medications she needed to make her leg pain bearable. Because of the DEA's crackdown on pill mills, few doctors would write opioid scripts for Chrystal for fear they would wind up in the catchment area of the DEA. She did finally find a brave doctor who would prescribe the opioids, but then, because of pharmacies' self-protective policies, she couldn't find a single drugstore to fill her prescriptions. She was left to bear the brunt of the pain without medications. Because the pain was so severe, she couldn't sleep, despite the sleep medications she was prescribed. Although Chrystal had never been much of a drinker, the only solution for the pain-induced insomnia she could think of was to deliberately get drunk every few days so that she could pass out and snatch a few hours of sleep. Her husband left her because he didn't want to live with a person who was so altered by pain. She lost her job because of the pain disability and couldn't get another, eventually losing her insurance coverage. She found herself stuck at home, trying to take care of a ten-year-old son while battling the monster of pain alone.

Chrystal and Cullen—and many more like them—have been failed by the system. They should have had their pain treated with the resources available at the time, but it didn't happen. Fear of law enforcement and regulatory guidelines, insurance limitations, and inadequate and uncaring medical care—intertwined factors like these doomed them to being left in their pain.

When I hear about current-day situations like Cullen's and Chrystal's, I feel discouraged. In my worst moments, I ask myself, *Has our society made any progress in relieving pain? Even as our scientific understanding of pain and how to relieve it continues to improve, are we failing to make progress on delivering care to those who need it when they need it?*

Today, people in pain are regularly underserved, but rarely do policy and decision makers acknowledge this. The system works poorly for them, or works too slowly, or not at all. Certain groups within society, notably women and members of ethnic minorities, tend to be disproportionately underserved.[2] Many of those who are receiving medical care for pain are dissatisfied with their treatment and continue to endure moderate to severe pain. The fact that 50 percent of all people with chronic pain consider suicide at some point suggests that their pain is not being treated nearly well enough.[3]

Society's failure of those who are in pain is simply shameful. We can't afford to have an attitude that says, "It's regrettable, but not much can be done about it." We can't settle for people's pain being left untreated or grossly undertreated. We have to see our society's inadequate response to pain for *what it is* but never accept it as *what must be.*

The way to change this is to look upon quality pain treatment, not as a privilege, but as a right.

Many societies have affirmed that human beings deserve such basic protections as a right to free speech, a right to an education, and a right to a fair trial. Pain care ought to be a human right as well. Everyone who has pain should be listened to, believed, and offered the best therapy available. Payers, regulators, and health care providers should facilitate this right, not obstruct it.

At one time, it was revolutionary to think of rights such as the right to free speech as being legitimate. Now we take them for grant-ed. It took transformations in humankind's mindset to establish liberating and life-giving human rights in the past, and it will take another transformation to establish adequate pain care as the new human right. But it's a transformation that I believe we can, and must, accomplish.

Transformation

Although the problem of pain has typically been overlooked or down-played in U.S. society, in 2011 it finally got some of the high-profile attention it deserves. Congress ordered a report on pain, and the Institute of Medicine—the health arm of the National Academy of Sciences—delivered *Relieving Pain in America: A Blueprint for Transforming Prevention, Care, Education, and Research.* It was this report that first definitively established chronic pain as being America's largest invisible epidemic, with some 100 million adults suffering mild to severe chronic pain. More importantly, the report identified what is needed if we are to see progress in the treatment of pain in the future: nothing short of a cultural transformation. As the committee behind the report stated in their summary,

> Pain is a uniquely individual and subjective experience that depends on a variety of biological, psychological, and social factors, and different population groups experience pain differentially. For many patients, treatment of pain is inad-equate not just because of uncertain diagnoses and societal stigma, but also because of shortcomings in the availability of effective treatments and inadequate patient and clinician knowledge about the best ways to manage pain. Some an-swers will come from exciting new research opportunities, but changes in the care system also will be needed in order for patients' pain journeys to be shorter and more successful. In the committee's view, addressing the nation's enormous burden of pain will require a cultural transformation in the way pain is understood, assessed, and treated.[4]

Nearly all of us who have worked closely with the problem of pain in our careers agree with this report: We need more than improvements here and there in the response to pain. We need a complete sea change—new attitudes, new behaviors transforming how we deal with pain.

Such a culture-wide transformation *is* possible.

When nations began rejecting slavery in the nineteenth century, when male electorates began giving women the vote in the early twentieth century, and when Soviet-sphere communism began to collapse in the late 1980s, the world witnessed a cultural transformation around a cause. A new idea appeared. A movement formed. Individuals within that movement advocated a goal to change the existing conditions. The vision for the goal spread widely and took hold. Society was changed.

That's how cultural transformations take place. And that's how a cultural transformation can take place with the goal to see that everyone in chronic pain receives acceptance and effective treatment.

A cultural transformation regarding pain is a movement worth starting. It's a cause worth throwing our weight behind. It's the precursor to establishing good pain care as a human right.

Three Areas That Have to Change

Although there are many ways in which our society could do a better job of taking care of people with pain, three stand out above all the others. We need to…

- ramp up research efforts to discover better therapies for pain
- improve and extend insurance coverage so that people in pain can get the care that's available
- treat all people in pain with dignity and respect

Research

In 2013, the National Institutes of Health spent approximately $475 million on research into pain treatments, most of it funneled to small companies with promising therapies.[5] That amount may sound like a lot, but it's less than 1 percent of the money the NIH spent on research in that year. Or to put it another way, the largest public health problem in the country, affecting around 100 million Americans, receives a tiny fraction of the government's medical research funding expenditures.

I have no desire to take away funding from other important areas of research, but I am convinced that we need more money going to chronic pain research. In medical research, most discoveries prove to be dead ends. Still, a small number of research projects yield therapies that can go to the public and do some good, and no one can know which research endeavor will be productive unless many are tried.

It is important to point out that there is a direct correlation between the amount of money spent on research and the number of new therapies that reach the public. And successful medical research takes *big* money. The average cost of bringing a new chemical entity to market is $2.6 billion.[6] That money has to come from somewhere, or the drugs and devices won't be developed.

The National Institutes of Health are the incubators for much new development of treatments. Without their strong involvement, the financial risks in undertaking research are too great for private companies in the medical industry to bear by themselves. This means that more funding by government spurs more funding by private sources. Private-public partnerships are necessary for advances and cures to emerge. In the United States, about 40 percent of medical research funding comes from governments, while the remaining 60 percent comes from private companies and philanthropic foundations.[7] Government funding becomes seed money for the majority of private funding.

In Hal Garner's story (Chapter 4), we saw how the newly developed medication ziconotide, derived from cone snail venom, changed his life, enabling him to stop using the opioids that had nearly destroyed him. Other new and exciting treatments are currently in the pipeline. The pace of development of pain medications will increase as research increases. Perhaps one day opioids will no longer be needed, as safer and more effective treatments become available. Perhaps one day treatments will emerge that operate by currently unknown mechanisms and that will be able to resolve currently intractable pain.

Today, the approach to chronic pain is largely palliative—helping people feel better through an integrated approach. That's what Part 1 of this book is all about. And of course palliation is a good thing—a *very* good thing—if the only alternative is to let pain run unchecked. But we should not be satisfied with mere palliation. Our end game should be about abolishing pain where possible. In other words, not just healing, but curing. Certain pain types, such as CRPS, post-herpetic neuralgia, post-traumatic neuralgia, migraines, vulvodynia, fibromyalgia, interstitial cystitis, peripheral neuropathy, and arthritis, should eventually be eliminated. We should be able to provide a cure for many pain diseases. This goal is not beyond our reach, but it will require a commitment and more new research. We first have to believe in the purpose and then find the path forward with an Olympian determination.

Insurance

In 2014, around 15 percent of Americans had no health insurance coverage.[8] Of those who did have coverage, few had plans that provided the minimum benefits needed to treat most people who have pain.

The government programs (which about a third of the insured possess), including Medicaid and Medicare, are less likely than private plans to offer adequate services to people in pain. This has been a major contributor to the current opioid crisis, as doctors treating people covered by government health insurance plans have defaulted to prescribing opioids. It's ironic, then, that the growth in the number of adverse events associated with opioid use has in its turn spurred government regulators to try to control opioid prescriptions. This sometimes leaves pain patients without any adequate treatment at all. Government is supposed to protect the public, but in this instance it has created a void and an enormous problem of which it is largely unaware and which it seems unwilling to address.

All people in pain deserve quality medical care, including the ability of doctors to advise a wide range of pharmacological and non-pharmacological therapies. To make this kind of treatment a right in our society, we need to see that the uninsured get health insurance coverage as well as see that every health insurance plan opens the door to adequate treatment of pain.

In 2014 the American Academy of Pain Medicine released a statement on insurance benefits for people with chronic pain, saying:

> In all tiers of the healthcare system, from the uninsured to those on public and private plans, coverage is needed for comprehensive, interdisciplinary modalities of treatment like CBT [cognitive behavioral therapy], physical therapy, stress management, rehabilitation, complementary and integrative therapies (CIM) and alternative therapies and medications that are known to be effective and safer than usual care. At minimum, all payers should provide three months coverage for an interdisciplinary integrative pain evaluation and treatment program for people with pain that is severe enough to warrant ongoing therapy, that has failed or is not expected to respond to first-line therapies, and that is not expected to resolve in the foreseeable future.[9]

The statement goes on to urge coverage for psychological counseling related to pain, monitoring measures to reduce the abuse and diversion of medications, a realignment of incentives toward patient outcomes and away from fee-for-service reimbursement, and a bundling of services in the insurance payment structure.

I realize that the AAPM's statement, which I helped to draft, is just a start. Just as our society has had a conversation around the Affordable Care Act about the best way to extend insurance coverage, so we need to have a conversation about what treatments our insurance plans should cover for people in pain. The bottom line is that, when previously healthy people develop chronic pain, they should not be surprised to find out that the provisions of their insurance plan prevent them from getting the treatment they need.

Insurance is supposed to provide us security and access to appropriate and necessary care when needed. Too often, stingy or poorly planned health insurance policies stand in the way of people getting the help they need for their pain. Arguably, the financial cost to society through such consequences as loss of work time, reliance on emergency medical services, and treatment of substance abuse outweighs whatever savings the insurance companies realize through limiting payments for alternative pain therapies. Worse, the cost in human suffering is incalculable.

A few private insurance companies have already begun adjusting their policies to fit the realities of pain care and to serve their customers better. Good for them. Most, however, still have a long way to go, and they may not make changes until they feel pressure from government or consumers. But leaders of government insurance programs must also look themselves in the mirror, and when they do, they will find that they are in charge of a fragmented system that is inadequate for most people in pain. Providers will also need to participate in the transformation. There will be resistance, but with the right incentives, appropriate change can occur.

Dignity

Our society is failing people in pain because we lack treatment options that would make more of a difference against pain and because inadequate insurance prevents many people from accessing even the treatments that are presently available. But there's a third major component that we have to address if our society is going to undergo a transformation and establish quality pain care as an inalienable right. It's the attitudes that the great majority of people have toward people in pain.

In the stories we've looked at in this book, we've seen many who felt shame or were looked on with suspicion by others. For example, Jason Bing's colonel made him feel small because he was seeking help within the U.S. Army system for opioid dependency. Many of John Kay's friends and coworkers abandoned him when he developed severe pain and had to go on disability. Yet this kind of prejudice against people in pain as being lazy whiners, malingerers, and drug seekers is not only something that individuals must face; it's also woven into our cultural attitude toward pain and is a root cause of the inadequacy of our present pain care system. Cullen the fishing guide felt passed around by doctors at least in part because the doctors he was going to did not take chronic pain seriously enough. Chrystal the out-of-work CPA couldn't get the opioid medications she needed because law enforcement had changed the local culture and threatened the security of prescribers and pharmacists in her state.

The opioid issue looms large in America. With the news of the terrible toll in opioid overdose deaths being disseminated more widely to the public in recent years, leading to knee-jerk reactions by politicians and bureaucrats, opioid treatment has come to color everyone involved or seeming to be involved with it. We're actually at a point where people in pain—whether they personally are taking prescribed opioids or not—are having a harder time getting treated, and even being truly heard, than at any time in my career. It's disheartening. And it highlights the need for vigorous efforts to reverse society's mistaken impression of people struggling with pain. Old beliefs must die to make room for a new set of expectations.

There is no immediate solution to prejudice against people with pain, no easy way to overturn the bias. Yet I am old enough to remember when people with AIDS, mental illness, and cancer bore similar stigmas, and society has largely changed its attitudes in those cases. The same can happen with pain and pain treatment if we educate the public about what is really going on in the world of chronic pain. People with pain themselves can have the greatest impact in this area, as they tell their stories honestly and forthrightly. When enough policy makers and policy implementers get the point on a personal level, they will complete the transformation on a cultural level.

You, Changemaker

If you're not a physician, an executive in the pharmaceutical industry, or an elected official in government, you may not feel there's much you can do to help bring about society-wide change related to pain. That's not true. Grassroots efforts are the ones most likely to change the cultural landscape.

I know that if you are in severe pain, your need for relief may fill your consciousness. You may not have any energy or head space for anything other than your own present needs. You may even be afraid to be seen as an advocate, for fear it will adversely affect your ability to be treated. That's understandable. But if you are a person in pain or a caregiver, your voice is needed. The rest of us should be engaged as well because we will likely fall victim to pain someday and will then ask for the best treatment available.

Carolyn Tuft has told her story to newspapers to spread the news about the barriers some people in pain face in getting access to adequate health care. Hal Garner travels the State of Utah and beyond, telling his story of pain and addiction to young people, no doubt changing the course of many lives. In time, you, too, can take practical steps, large and small, to affect public opinion and public policy about pain.

Let's see what we can do together to highlight the need for more research into pain treatments, show the public that most insurance coverage for pain isn't good enough, and change opinions about people who are dealing with pain. Consider these opportunities that may be easily within your reach:[10]

> *Influence legislation.* When you learn that a bill affecting people in pain is up for debate at either the state or national level, let your elected officials know your viewpoint by sending a letter or email or making a phone

call. Tell your story. Perhaps offer to give testimony at a committee hearing.

Influence the decision makers. If you're disappointed in the comparatively low priority the National Institutes of Health has placed on pain research, write to your congressional representative and speak your mind. If you're concerned about your insurance company's limitations on coverage for pain treatment, write to its customer service department, the company's human resources director, and the CEO and let them know. If you're on Medicaid and have been denied a prescription because it was not on the Preferred Drug List, write to your state's Medicaid prior authorization committee. If you've had trouble getting a prescription filled at a particular pharmacy, contact the corporate headquarters and tell them how their drug dispensing policy has affected you. Copy your letter to your state legislator.

Raise community awareness. Share your story of pain with a journalist, suggesting he or she write an article on the topic. Or write your own op-ed about pain or pain treatment and send it to a news outlet. If you find an article about pain at an online site that allows readers to post comments, give your own view. Join—or create—a community awareness event around pain where you live. Talk with your religious leaders about how your congregation can help people in pain. Use social media, such as Facebook and Twitter, to inform your friends and followers about the realities of living with pain. Push back against the myths, the stigma, and the ignorance.

Combine forces. Join a person in pain support or advocacy group, such as The Pain Community, the National Fibromyalgia & Chronic Pain Association, the National Vulvodynia Association, the U.S. Pain Foundation, or the American Chronic Pain Association.[11] Work with the others in these organizations to promote a cultural transformation in attitudes toward pain.

It feels good to be a part of a movement to transform society's attitude toward pain. It feels good to be fighting back against our primal enemy—pain. Becoming an advocate may in itself be healing.

Two by Four

The painful truth is that society treats people in pain shamefully. We're not doing nearly our best to get them the treatment they need, and we often look at them askance when they try to do their best for themselves within the system as it exists today. May we never become comfortable with this status quo.

When I speak to groups about my medical specialty, I sometimes bring along a small piece of two-by-four wood for each person in the audience. As I begin my presentation, I ask the listeners to take their piece of wood and place it underneath one of their cheeks (not the ones on their faces) and sit on it. Usually they begin the experiment with a good enough humor, but after about ten minutes I begin to see squirming and grimacing, and so I interrupt myself to tell them, "Don't move that piece of wood. Keep it under your cheek." A few minutes later, when most in the audience are in obvious discomfort, I'll repeat the same stern warning. Then at the end of my address I'll say something like this:

"You've been sitting on your piece of wood for half an hour. Uncomfortable, isn't it? I bet after a while you had trouble concentrating on anything else. I bet you couldn't think about anything but getting off that board.

"Now, imagine that the board has dull tacks protruding from it. Imagine you've had that same discomfort not for thirty minutes, not for thirty hours, not for thirty days, but for years and years. And imagine, too, that the medicine you're taking only blunts the pain. Wouldn't you be desperate for some kind of relief that made a real difference? That's what it's like for many people with chronic pain. In fact, for some people, the pain is actually much worse.

"You can remove your board now. But as you do so, tell yourself that the next time you hear someone complaining of pain you'll remember the piece of wood with tacks and then pause to reflect on what it must be like for our patients."

Consider this final chapter a two-by-four piece of wood. I would have liked to have ended this book with Part 1's message of hope for healing, because that is true and good and reassuring. But it's also not the whole story. The controversy over opioid use is making life more difficult for people in pain and their health care providers. Furthermore, many people today are suffering physically and psychologically from pain, and they don't see any relief in sight. All of us need to feel their pain...and act to do something about it.

We have seen that options for healing are available today as people in pain work with their doctors and others for relief, and I urge everyone who is in pain to take advantage of them. But in the long run, we want to move beyond healing to curing. We want to dispel humanity's millennia-long nightmare of pain. That will only happen when quality pain care, and the respect that goes along with it, is a human right. For Walter Alexander and Rachel Hutchins, for Jason Bing and Carolyn Tuft, for Hal Garner and Ali Goldsmith, for John and Marsha Kay, for Cullen and Chrystal, for you and your loved ones, I hope the day will come soon.

Acknowledgments

I owe a deep debt to my wife, Holly, for her critical reviews, insight, and support throughout the writing process. The book has evolved over the years. Holly enthusiastically read the numerous versions many times to provide me with her unique viewpoint and skillful edits. She provided comments as an avid reader, accomplished nurse practitioner, and advocate for those who suffer from any chronic illness.

Thanks also go to our daughter, Rebecca, for her passionate support of my project and work. I have had no greater cheerleader than her. Her skill as a writer and editor was most appreciated in the final version when she was finally allowed to read it. Also, as a coauthor of the paper on the Opioid Risk Tool, she has been a contributor to my success since she was in high school.

I couldn't have accomplished this project without Eric Stanford, who helped me in planning and writing the material throughout its stages of evolution. He peppered me with questions, dug out emotions and thoughts I never knew I could express, and helped to make these thoughts powerful and meaningful. He also educated me about how books are constructed and what readers expect from my type of book. Throughout the process, he has become a dear friend for whom I will always be grateful.

Beth Dove has worked with me on manuscripts, chapters, and op-eds and has counseled me on how to communicate effectively with the media for more than a decade. Many of the stories within the book are ones she originally helped me to shape. Most importantly, she has taught me about the importance of being true and honest in storytelling, whether it is in a scientific publication or a message to the public.

My assistant, Derek Hoffman, made the communications among the rest of us work effortlessly. His organizational skills and multi-tasking capabilities kept me on task and able to finally arrive with a finished product.

Chris Varones and Ron Culp provided input into the themes and concepts of the book so as to help it reach a broad swath of the public. They have been deeply involved in helping me plant a seed for a social movement to find safer and more effective therapies.

Zlatana Alibegovic advised and contributed to my education on my social media campaign around the book's release. Considering my lack of experience in this area, this was not an easy task.

Stacey J. Miller provided the invaluable service of creating public awareness for this book. She helped with the final stages of completing the book, advising on vendors for book cover design, website development, and key processes important to a book release. She distinguishes herself by her personal commitment to me as the author that was obvious with the constant communication between us that started six months before the book was released.

I have been blessed by the above people and many more who have helped bring this book to fruition.

Last, I'm grateful to the people whose lives I have portrayed in this book. They represent the millions of people in the United States and around the world who are struggling to heal from pain and who long for the day when a cure for pain is available.

Notes

Introduction

1. According to the Institute of Medicine, approximately 100 million adults in the United States of America have chronic pain. Institute of Medicine, *Relieving Pain in America: A Blueprint for Transforming Prevention, Care, Education, and Research* (Washington, DC: National Academies Press, 2011), 1–2. The report is available online at http://www.iom.edu/Reports/2011/Relieving-Pain-in-America-A-Blueprint-for-Transforming-Prevention-Care-Education-Research.aspx. Gallup polling came up with a similar number, estimating that 111 million people in America have chronic or recurring pain. This polling also reflected what doctors have long observed—that pain is more common in the older population. Alyssa Brown, "Chronic Pain Rates Shoot Up Until American Reach Late 50s," Gallup, April 27, 2012, http://www.gallup.com/poll/154169/Chronic-Pain-Rates-Shoot-Until-Americans-Reach-Late-50s.aspx.

2. Quoted in Marcia L. Meldrum, "A Capsule History of Pain Management," *Journal of the American Medical Association*, 290, no. 18 (November 12, 2003): 2473.

3. See Perry G. Fine, "Long-Term Consequences of Pain: Mounting Evidence for Pain as a Neurological Disease and Parallels with Other Chronic Disease States," *Pain Medicine* 12, no. 7 (July 2011): 996–1004.

4. Institute of Medicine, *Relieving Pain in America*, 1–2; and Brown, "Chronic Pain Rates Shoot Up."

5. Research!America, "National Poll: Chronic Pain and Drug Addiction," April 2013, http://www.researchamerica.org/uploads/March2013painaddiction.pdf.

6. For more on pain as a global experience, see A. Tsang and others, "Common Chronic Pain Conditions in Developed and Developing Countries: Gender and Age Differences and Comorbidity with Depression-Anxiety Disorders," *Journal of Pain* 9, no. 10 (October 2008): 883-91; Daniel S. Goldberg and Summer J. McGee, "Pain as a Global Public Health

Priority," *BMC Publish Health* 11, no. 10 (October 2011): 770; R. A. Elzahaf and others, "The Prevalence of Chronic Pain with an Analysis of Countries with a Human Development Index Less than 0.9: A Systematic Review Without Meta-analysis," *Current Medical Research and Opinion* 28, no. 7 (July 2012): 1221-9; and Tracy P. Jackson and others, "The Global Burden of Pain," *American Society of Anesthesiologists* 78, no. 6 (June 2014), https://www.asahq.org/For-Members/Publications-and-Research/Newsletter-Articles/2014/June-2014/the-global-burden-of-chronic-pain.aspx.

Chapter 1: It's Personal

1. Demyelination is damage to the myelin sheath around nerves. It causes the nerves to fail to function properly.

2. *Acute pain* is defined as pain resulting from a disease or injury that goes away in a relatively short period of time as the original cause of the pain heals. *Chronic pain* is defined as pain that lasts three months or more.

Chapter 2: More than a Survivor

1. Acute pain will produce grimaces and perspiration, but chronic pain is most often invisible but smoldering and erupting with activity—sometimes spontaneously.

2. "A Car with Four Flat Tires," The American Chronic Pain Association, http://theacpa.org/a-car-with-four-flat-tires.

Chapter 3: Caught in a Web

1. Rachel Hutchins is not her real name. I have altered some of the superficial details of her story, but the gist of it is completely truthful.

2. I will be addressing addiction in more depth in Chapter 5.

Chapter 4: Friendly Fire

1. Erving Goffman, *Stigma: Notes on the Management of a Spoiled Identity* (1963; reprint, New York: Simon & Schuster, 1986), 3.

2. Jason Bing is not his real name.

3. Gregg Zoroya, "General's Story a Warning About Use of Painkillers," USA Today, January 27, 2011, http://usatoday30.usatoday.com/news/military/2011-01-27-1Adruggeneral27_CV_N.htm.

4. Milton Cohen and others, "Stigmatization of Patients with Chronic Pain: The Extinction of Empathy," *Pain Medicine* 12, no. 11 (2011): 1637–43.

Chapter 5: The New Scarlet Letter

1. Eliot L. Gardner, "What We Have Learned About Addictions from Animal Models of Drug Self-Administration," *American Journal on Addictions* 9, no. 4 (fall 2000): 285–313.

2. Lee N. Robins, John E. Helzer, and Darlene H. Davis, "Narcotic Use in Southeast Asia and Afterward, *Archives of General Psychiatry* 32, no. 8 (August 1975): 955–61.

3. To this day, there is no consensus on the definitions of *addiction* and related terms. What aberrant behaviors do you need to find in order to identify a disorder? Likewise, there is no widely accepted figures for the prevalence of addiction among people who are taking opioids for pain. Studies in recent years have indicated addiction rates ranging from 0 percent to 50 percent and higher—an absurd disparity. Simply put, we don't know. S. B. Leavitt, "Opioid Analgesics Less Addictive than Feared?" *Pain Treatment Topics*, November 7, 2012, http://updates.pain-topics. org/2012/11/opioid-analgesics-less-addictive-than.html. My best current guess is that around 20 percent of the population could become addicted to opioids, a figure roughly equal to the number of people who are vulnerable to an alcohol addiction. D. S. Hasin and others, "Prevalence, Correlates, Disability, and Comorbidity of DSM-IV Alcohol Abuse and Dependence in the United States: Results from the National Epidemiologic Survey on Alcohol and Related Conditions, *Archives of General Psychiatry* 64, no. 7 (July 2007): 830–42. The 20 percent of people who could become addicted to opioids would include people who are like the Lewis rats (highly addictable) and the Sprague Dawley rats (addictable if put under stress).

Chapter 6: Soul Mates

1. Brooke Adams, "Vernal Police Sued for Alleged Deathbed Intrusion," *Salt Lake City Tribune*, January 5, 2013, http://archive.sltrib.com/article. php?id=24810712&itype=storyID.

2. Beth Sperber Richie and others, "Resilience in Survivors of Traumatic Limb Loss," *Disability Studies Quarterly* 23, no. 2 (spring 2003): 29–41.

3. Alicia E. López-Martínez, Rosa Esteve-Zarazaga, and Carmen Ramírez-Maestre, "Perceived Social Support and Coping Responses Are Independent Variables Explaining Pain Adjustment Among Chronic Pain Patients," *Journal of Pain* 9, no. 4 (April 2008): 373–9; and J. V. Ginting and others, "Spousal Support Decreases the Negative Impact of Pain on Mental Quality of Life in Women with Interstitial Cystitis/Painful Bladder Syndrome," *BJU International* 108, no. 5 (September 2011): 713–7.

4. Robert N. Jamison and Kitti L. Virts, "The Influence of Family Support on Chronic Pain," *Behaviour Research and Therapy* 28, no. 4 (1990): 283–7.

5. Mary P. Gallant, "The Influence of Social Support on Chronic Illness Self-Management: A Review and Directions for Research," *Health Education & Behavior* 30, no. 2 (April 2003): 170–95.

6. Roger B. Fillingim and others, "Spousal Responses Are Differentially Associated with Clinical Variables in Women and Men with Chronic Pain," *Clinical Journal of Pain* 19, no. 4 (July 2003): 217–24.

7. Julianne Holt-Lunstad, Timothy B. Smith, and J. Bradley Layton, "Social Relationships and Mortality Risk: A Meta-analytic Review," *PLoS Medicine* 7, no. 7 (July 27, 2010), http://www.plosmedicine.org/article/info%3Adoi%2F10.1371%2Fjournal.pmed.1000316.

Chapter 7: The God Prescription

1. Walter Alexander is not his real name.

2. Qiuling Shi and others, "People in Pain: How Do They Seek Relief?" *Journal of Pain* 8, no. 8 (August 2007): 624–36.

3. Alexander Moreira-Almeida and Harold G. Koenig, "Religiousness and Spirituality in Fibromyalgia and Chronic Pain Patients," *Current Pain and Headache Reports* 12, no. 5 (October 2008): 327–32.

4. Arndt Büssing and others, "Spiritual Needs Among Patients with Chronic Pain Diseases and Cancer Living in a Secular Society," *Pain Medicine* 14, no. 9 (September 2013): 1362–73.

5. Moreira-Almeida and Koenig, "Religiousness and Spirituality," 327–32.

6. Marilyn Baetz and Rudy Bowen, "Chronic Pain and Fatigue: Associations with Religion and Spirituality," *Pain Research & Management* 13, no. 5 (September–October 2008): 383–8.

7. Katja Wiech and others, "An fMRI Study Measuring Analgesia Enhanced by Religion as a Belief System," *Pain* 139, no. 2 (October 15, 2008): 467–76.

8. Joshua A. Grant and Pierre Rainville, "Pain Sensitivity and Analgesic Effects of Mindful States in Zen Meditators: A Cross-Sectional Study," *Psychosomatic Medicine* 71, no. 1 (January 2009): 106–14.

9. Amy Wachholtz, "Spirituality and Chronic Pain: The Positives and the Pitfalls," http://vimeo.com/87710714.

10. A. Elizabeth Rippentrop and others, "The Relationship Between Religion/Spirituality and Physical Health, Mental Health, and Pain in a Chronic Pain Population," *Pain* 116, no. 3 (August 2005): 311–21.

11. Carol J. Lysne and Amy B. Wachholtz, "Pain, Spirituality, and Meaning Making: What Can We Learn from the Literature?" *Religions* 2, no. 1 (March 2011): 1–16.

12. Sally Quinn, "How to Be Happy—and the Problem with Advice on Happiness," OnFaith, May 7, 2014, http://www.faithstreet.com/onfaith/2014/05/07/how-to-be-happy-and-the-problem-with-advice-on-happiness/31985.

Chapter 8: Everyday Saints and Unsung Heroes

1. Nicole K. Y. Tang, Paul M. Salkovskis, Magdi H. Hanna, "Mental Defeat in Chronic Pain: Initial Exploration of the Concept," *Clinical Journal of Pain* 23, no. 3 (March–April 2007): 222–32; Nicole K. Y. Tang and others, "Chronic Pain Syndrome Associated with Health Anxiety: A Qualitative Thematic Comparison Between Pain Patients with High and Low Health Anxiety," *British Journal of Clinical Psychology* 48, no. 1 (March 2009): 1-20; Nicole K. Y. Tang and others, "Mental Defeat Is Linked to Interference, Distress and Disability in Chronic Pain," *Pain* 149, no. 3 (June 2010): 547–54; and M. Cheatle, Nicole K. Y. Tang, and Lynn R. Webster, "Pain, Depression and Suicide: Risk Stratification and Mitigation," presentation at the 15th World Congress on Pain, Buenos Aires, Argentina, October 6–11, 2014.

2. Nicole K. Y. Tang and Catherine Crane, "Suicidality in Chronic Pain: A Review of the Prevalence, Risk Factors, and Psychological Links," *Psychological Medicine* 36, no. 5 (May 2006): 575–86.

3. Suzanne Geffen Mintz, *A Family Caregiver Speaks Up: It Doesn't Have to Be This Hard* (Herndon, VA: Capital Books, 2007).

Chapter 9: Coming of Age

1. Doug Wright, *Grey Gardens* (2006).

2. American Medical Association, "Pediatric Pain Management," updated June 2013, http://www.ama-cmeonline.com/pain_mgmt/printversion/ama_painmgmt_m6.pdf.

3. In the Face of Pain, "Self-Advocacy," https://www.youtube.com/watch?v=6kZxpjQ_hGs.

Chapter 10: The Chilling Effect

1. Lyndon E. Lee Jr., "Medication in the Control of Pain in Terminal Cancer," *Journal of the American Medical Association* 116, no. 3 (January 18, 1941): 216–20. Etymologically, the term *narcotics* comes from a Greek

root meaning "to make numb." Historically and popularly, people have used the term *narcotics* when they are talking about morphine, oxycodone, and other opioids. But legally, the term *narcotics* refers to both opioids and some prohibited drugs that are not used medicinally, such as heroin and cocaine. When referring to opioid medicines, then, it's better to use the more precise term *opioids* than the vaguer, albeit better known, term *narcotics*.

2. R. K. Portenoy, and K. M. Foley, "Chronic Use of Opioid Analgesics in Non-Malignant Pain: Report of 38 Cases," *Pain* 25, no. 2 (May 1986): 171–86.

3. Quoted in Lisa Rosetta, "Fatalities Linked to Pain Pills on the Rise," *Salt Lake Tribune*, January 21, 2005, http://archive.sltrib.com/printfriendly. php?id=2531882&itype=NGPSID.

4. L. R. Webster and R. M. Webster, "Predicting Aberrant Behaviors in Opioid-treated Patients: Preliminary Validation of the Opioid Risk Tool," *Pain Medicine* 6, no. 6 (June 2005): 432–42.

5. See LifeSource, http://www.yourlifesource.org/. Through this foundation, I began to study the scientific literature, Utah data, national data, and forensic cases I was consulted on to develop educational material for physicians and patients. I created a lecture for physicians describing six principles that I thought explained some of the deaths. This presentation became the Use Only As Directed physician education material. LifeSource also developed literature, brochures, and posters that were distributed throughout the state. LifeSource organized a group of experts to review the national and Utah data to develop a consensus on the root causes of unintentional overdose deaths. The product of this day-long meeting was a supplement with nine manuscripts describing the Utah experience addressing overdose deaths and what the nation should do to have the same impact.

6. Utah Department of Health, Violence & Injury Prevention Program, "Prescription Opioid Deaths in Utah, 2011," October 2012, http://www. health.utah.gov/vipp/pdf/FactSheets/RxOpioidDeaths.pdf.

7. Centers for Disease Control and Prevention, "Prescription Drug Overdose in the United States: Fact Sheet," updated July 1, 2014, http:// www.cdc.gov/homeandrecreationalsafety/overdose/facts.html.

8. Office of National Drug Control Policy, "Epidemic: Responding to America's Prescription Drug Abuse Crisis," 2011, http://www.white-house.gov/sites/default/files/ondcp/issues-content/prescription-drugs/ rx_abuse_plan.pdf.

9. Lynn R. Webster and Beth Dove, *Avoiding Opioid Abuse While Managing Pain* (North Branch, MN: Sunrise River Press, 2007), 198, citing

J. C. Ballantyne and J. Mao, "Opioid Therapy for Chronic Pain," *New England Journal of Medicine* 349, no. 20 (November 13, 2003): 1943–53.

10. Jack was not his real name. This story was originally told in Lynn Webster, "Pain and Suicide: The Other Side of the Story," *Pain Medicine* 15, no. 3 (March 2014): 345–6.

11. Robyn Tamblyn and others, "Unnecessary Prescribing of NSAIDs and the Management of NSAID-Related Gastropathy in Medical Practice," *Annals of Internal Medicine* 127, no. 6 (September 15, 1997): 429–38.

12. Centers for Disease Control and Prevention, press release, "Opioids Drive Continued Increase in Drug Overdose Deaths," February 20, 2013, http://www.cdc.gov/media/releases/2013/p0220_drug_overdose_deaths.html.

13. Institute for Safe Medication Practices, "Anticoagulants the Leading Reported Drug Risk in 2011," QuarterWatch, May 31, 2012, http://www.ismp.org/quarterwatch/pdfs/2011Q4.pdf.

14. Centers for Disease Control and Prevention, "Opioids Drive Continued Increase."

15. Radley Balko, "The War Over Prescription Painkillers," *Huffington Post*, January 29, 2012, http://www.huffingtonpost.com/radley-balko/prescription-painkillers_b_1240722.html.

16. Tony Leys, "Baldi, Acquitted on All Charges, Wants to Return to Work," *Des Moines Register*, May 2, 2014, http://www.desmoinesregister.com/story/news/crime-and-courts/2014/05/01/baldi--verdict-jury/8576229/.

17. Tina Rosenberg, "When Is a Pain Doctor a Drug Pusher?" *The New York Times*, June 17, 2007, http://www.nytimes.com/2007/06/17/magazine/17pain-t.html?pagewanted=all&_r=0. For another excellent profile of an incarcerated physician with all the ambiguity on display, see Rachel Aviv, "Prescription for Disaster," *The New Yorker*, May 5, 2014, 50.

18. Ronald McIver was released in 2010 after five years due to post-conviction litigation and the report that he was dying of prostate cancer. "SC Doctor Released Early After Cancer Diagnosis," October 17, 2010, WSP, http://www.wspa.com/story/21460784/sc-doctor-released-early-after-cancer-diagnoisis. He died in 2013.

19. Brian Wellner, "8 Years in Prison, $400,000 Fine for Doctor in Drugs-for-Sex Case," *Quad-City Times*, July 18, 2013, http://qctimes.com/news/local/crime-and-courts/years-in-prison-fine-for-doctor-in-drugs-for-sex/article_e3a1f72c-59fe-5c7c-a53a-5042184399f0.html.

20. Anthony Rivas, "Starbucks Doctor Sentenced to 11 Years in Prison for Illegally Prescribing Painkillers, Xanax," *Medical Daily*, November 7, 2013, http://www.medicaldaily.com/starbucks-doctor-sentenced-11-years-prison-illegally-prescribing-painkillers-xanax-262347.

21. Christina Boyle and Shane Dixon Kavanaugh, "Doctor Hector Castro, Champion of Latino Healthcare, Busted for Slinging $10 Million Worth of Oxycodone," *New York Daily News*, March 28, 2013, http://www.nydailynews.com/new-york/manhattan-doc-accused -slingling-10m-oxy-article-1.1301601.

22. Felix Gillette, "American Pain: The Largest U.S. Pill Mill's Rise and Fall," *Bloomberg Businessweek*, June 6, 2012, http://www. businessweek.com/articles/2012-06-06/american-pain-the-largest-u-dot-s-dot-pill-mills-rise-and-fall.

23. Barry Meier, "Walgreen to Pay $80 Million Fine in D.E.A. Inquiry," *The New York Times*, June 11, 2013, http://www.nytimes.com/2013/06/12/ business/walgreen-to-pay-80-million-settlement-over-painkiller-sales.html?_r=0. See also Toni Clarke, "U.S. War on Drugs Moves to Pharmacy from Jungle," June 16, 2012, Reuters, http://www.reuters.com/ article/2012/06/16/us-dea-prescription-drugs-idUSBRE85F09220120616.

24. Judy Foreman, "Backlash Against Walgreen's New Painkiller Crackdown," WBUR's CommonHealth, August 12, 2013, http://common-health.wbur.org/2013/08/walgreens-painkiller-crackdown.

25. Rae Marie Gleason and others, "Current Access to Opioids— Survey of Chronic Pain Patients," *Practical Pain Management* 14, no. 2 (March 2014), http://www.practicalpainmanagement.com/printpdf/12721.

26. American Medical Association, D-35.981, "AMA Response to Pharmacy Intrusion into Medical Practice."

27. Edward M. Brecher and the Editors of Consumer Union Magazine, "The Harrison Narcotic Act (1914)," Schaffer Library of Drug Policy, 1972, http://www.druglibrary.org/schaffer/library/studies/cu/cu8.html.

28. Michael J. Berens and Ken Armstrong, "New State Law Leaves Patients in Pain," *Seattle Times*, December 11, 2011, http://seattletimes. com/html/localnews/2016994769_silent12.html.

29. Not just Washington State but more than half of the states have placed methadone on their preferred drug formulary for state-subsidized health care plans. In other words, they limit access to safer medications, such as abuse-deterrent opioids, by not paying for them or requiring a higher co-payment. By default, methadone becomes one of the few available drugs when opioid use is indicated. A desire for cost savings leads to more methadone prescriptions, and the methadone prescriptions lead to more deaths.

30. Michael J. Berens and Ken Armstrong, "State Pushes Prescription Painkiller Methadone, Saving Millions but Costing Lives," *Seattle Times*, December 10, 2011, http://seattletimes.com/html/localnews/2016987032_ silent11.html.

31. Ibid.

32. Barry Meier, "In Guilty Plea, OxyContin Maker to Pay $600 Million," New York Times, May 10, 2007, http://www.nytimes.com/2007/05/10/business/11drug-web.html?_r=0; and Sarah Rubenstein, "Under Sweeping Settlement, Cephalon Will Disclose Doctor Payments," Wall Street Journal, September 29, 2008, http://blogs.wsj.com/health/2008/09/29/under-sweeping-settlement-cephalon-will-disclose-doctor-payments/.

33. Scott Glover and Lisa Girion, "Counties Sue Narcotics Makers, Alleging 'Campaign of Deception,' " LA Times, May 21, 2014, http://touch.latimes.com/#section/-1/article/p2p-80273903/.

34. Stephanie Smith, "Prominent Pain Doctor Investigated by DEA After Patient Deaths," CNN, December 20, 2013, http://www.cnn.com/2013/12/20/health/pain-pillar.

35. Letter of Robert A. Lund, Assistant United States Attorney, to Peter Stirba, Attorney at Law, June 16, 2014, in the author's possession.

Chapter 11: A Human Right

1. Cullen is not his real name.

2. "Chronic Pain in Women: Neglect, Dismissal, and Discrimination," Campaign to End Chronic Pain in Women, 2011, http://www.endwomenspain.org/Page/14/13; Laurie Edwards, "The Gender Gap in Pain," New York Times, March 16, 2013, http://www.nytimes.com/2013/03/17/opinion/sunday/women-and-the-treatment-of-pain.html?pagewanted=all&_r=0; and Karen O. Anderson, Carmen R. Green, and Richard Payne, "Racial and Ethnic Disparities in Pain: Causes and Consequences of Unequal Care," *Journal of Pain* 10, no. 12 (December 2009): 1187–1204.

3. Laura S. Hitchcock, Betty R. Ferrell, and Margo McCaffery, "The Experience of Chronic Nonmalignant Pain," *Journal of Pain and Symptom Management* 9, no. 5 (July 1994): 312–8.

4. National Academy of Sciences, *Relieving Pain in America: A Blueprint for Transforming Prevention, Care, Education, and Research* (Washington, DC: Institute of Medicine, 2011), http://www.iom.edu/Reports/2011/Relieving-Pain-in-America-A-Blueprint-for-Transforming-Prevention-Care-Education-Research.aspx.

5. "Estimates of Funding for Various Research, Condition, and Disease Categories," National Institutes of Health, March 7, 2014, http://report.nih.gov/categorical_spending.aspx.

6. Tufts Center for the Study of Drug Development, "Cost to Develop and Win Marketing Approval for a New Drug Is $2.6 Billion,"

November 18, 2014, http://csdd.tufts.edu/news/complete_story/pr_tufts_csdd_2014_cost_study.

7. Justin Chakma and others, "Asia's Ascent—Global Trends in Biomedical R&D Expenditures," *New England Journal of Medicine* 370, no. 1 (January 2, 2014): 3–6.

8. Jenna Levy, "U.S. Uninsured Rate Continues to Fall," Gallup Well-Being, March 10, 2014, http://www.gallupcom/poll/167798/uninsured-rate-continues-fall.aspx?utm_source=alert&utm_medium=email&utm_campaign=syndication&utm_content=morelink&utm_term=All%20Gallup%20Headlines.

9. "Minimum Insurance Benefits for Patients with Chronic Pain," American Academy of Pain Medicine, 2014, http://www.painmed.org/files/minimum-insurance-benefits-for-patients-with-chronic-pain.pdf.

10. For more advice on becoming a change agent for people with pain, see In the Face of Pain (http://www.inthefaceofpain.com/advocacy-101/) and U.S. Pain Foundation (http://uspainfoundation.org/advocacy.html).

11. See The Pain Community (http://paincommunity.org/), the National Fibromyalgia & Chronic Pain Association (http://www.fmcpaware.org/), the National Vulvodynia Association (https://www.nva.org/), the U.S. Pain Foundation (http://uspainfoundation.org/support-groups.html), and the American Chronic Pain Association (http://www.theacpa.org/Support-Groups).

About the Author

LYNN R. WEBSTER, M.D., is vice president of scientific affairs for PRA Health Sciences, a leading international medical research organization. He was formerly the founder of Lifetree Clinic and Lifetree Clinical Research, both in Salt Lake City, Utah, and was president of the American Academy of Pain Medicine in 2013–14.

After receiving his doctor of medicine degree from the University of Nebraska in 1976, Webster undertook an internship, fellowship, and residency at the University of Utah. He is board certified in anesthesiology, pain medicine, and addiction medicine. He practiced anesthesiology at Salt Lake City's Holy Cross Hospital, and then pain medicine at Lifetree Clinic, for many years before focusing on medical research and public advocacy for people with pain.

Dr. Webster lives with his wife, Holly, in Salt Lake City. They have two grown children.

- *Facebook*: facebook.com/Dr.LynnWebster
- *Twitter*: @LynnRWebsterMD
- *Website*: LynnWebsterMD.com

For a free reading guide and other resources related to
The Painful Truth, please visit:

www.ThePainfulTruthBook.com

To learn about the full-length documentary on pain from
Webster Media LLC., please visit:

ThePainfulTruthDocumentary.com

CPSIA information can be obtained
at www.ICGtesting.com
Printed in the USA
LVOW04*2003260116
472368LV00006B/42/P